MORALITY, RESPONSIBILITY, AND THE UNIVERSITY
Studies in Academic Ethics

MORALITY, RESPONSIBILITY, AND THE UNIVERSITY

Studies in Academic Ethics

Edited by Steven M. Cahn

Temple University Press
Philadelphia

Temple University Press, Philadelphia 19122
Copyright © 1990 by Temple University, except Chapter 4,
which is © Rudolph Weingartner
All rights reserved
Published 1990
Printed in the United States of America

The paper used in this publication meets the minimum
requirements of American National Standard for Information
Sciences—Permanence of Paper for Printed Library Materials,
ANSI Z39.48-1984 ⊗

Library of Congress Cataloging-in-Publication Data
Morality, responsibility, and the university : studies in academic
    ethics / edited by Steven M. Cahn.
        p.   cm.
    Includes bibliographical references.
    ISBN 0-87722-646-6 (alk. paper)
        1. College teachers—Professional ethics—United States.
    I. Cahn, Steven M.
    LB1779.M69   1990
    174'.9372—dc20   89-28472
                                                               CIP

To Leon Bramson and George F. Farr, Jr.,
in friendship

CONTENTS

Introduction   *Steven M. Cahn*   3

1. Human Rights and Academic Freedom   *Alan Gewirth*   8

2. Free Speech on Campus   *Judith Wagner DeCew*   32

3. Tenure: Academe's Peculiar
   Institution   *Andrew Oldenquist*   56

4. Ethics in Academic Personnel Processes:
   The Tenure Decision   *Rudolph H. Weingartner*   76

5. The Research Demands of Teaching
   in Modern Higher Education   *Theodore M. Benditt*   93

6. The Truth, the Whole Truth, and
   Nothing but the Truth   *Paul D. Eisenberg*   109

7. The Ethics of Graduate Teaching   *Robert Audi*   119

8. Professors, Students, and Friendship   *Peter J. Markie*   134

9. Sexual Harassment in the
   University   *Nancy ("Ann") Davis*   150

10. Beyond *in Loco Parentis?* Parietal
    Rules and Moral Maturity   *David A. Hoekema*   177

11. Business-University Partnerships   *Norman E. Bowie*   195

12. Diversity within University Faculties   *Alan H. Goldman*   218

13. Academic Appointments: Why
    Ignore the Advantage of Being Right?   *David Lewis*   231

14. A Defense of the Neutral University   *Robert L. Simon*   243

About the Authors   271

MORALITY, RESPONSIBILITY, AND THE UNIVERSITY
Studies in Academic Ethics

INTRODUCTION

In recent years philosophers have been examining the standards of conduct appropriate to a variety of professions. The activities of physicians, nurses, lawyers, business managers, journalists, engineers, and government policy makers have all been subjected to critical scrutiny. Serious questions have been raised about the degree of moral sensitivity displayed in medical offices, courts, and boardrooms. Indeed, philosophers have even served as ethical consultants, and today a hospital staff may include not only surgeons, internists, and radiologists but also a specialist in medical ethics.

One feature of the situation, however, is most curious, for the conduct of a particular group of professionals has thus far escaped detailed investigation. No one has carefully examined the examiners: college and university professors. What are the standards of conduct appropriate in classrooms, in departmental and faculty meetings, in grading students, evaluating colleagues, and conducting research? About such important matters we hear mostly silence.

In 1986 I published *Saints and Scamps: Ethics in Academia* (Rowman and Littlefield), a book intended to enumerate, explain, and emphasize the most fundamental professorial obligations. Subsequently, I invited some distinguished colleagues to join me in seeking to shed light on challenging moral issues generated by academic life. This volume incorporates the resultant essays.

The first is Alan Gewirth's exploration of academic freedom and the obligations it entails. His starting point is the apparent conflict between freedom, which is nonrestrictive, and the academic, which restricts by the force of moral and intellectual standards. How are the two concepts to be reconciled?

After developing a justification for academic freedom, Gewirth notes that those who claim this right have the correlative duty to adhere to appropriate methods in their work, such as giving due weight to relevant evidence. He then illustrates this point by considering the case of the creationist, who disregards the findings of paleontology: does such a person forfeit the right to academic

3

freedom, and if so, should the individual, even if tenured, be dismissed?

Judith DeCew examines other difficult cases in which freedom of expression on campus may exceed appropriate bounds. By considering legal history as well as controversial cases of recent vintage, she reveals the tensions inherent in seeking to protect free speech while maintaining the civility appropriate to an environment intended for learning.

Tenure provides professionally qualified persons with the right to discover, teach, and publish the truth as they see it within their fields of competence. But suppose a tenured professor uses the lecture hall to spout bigotry, hatred, or obscenity. Does the university's commitment to tolerance require its permitting such expressions of intolerance?

Tenure itself is the subject of Andrew Oldenquist's essay, which examines arguments for and against what he terms "academe's peculiar institution." Whereas tenure is usually defended as guaranteeing academic freedom, Oldenquist concentrates instead on tenure's role in providing job security and maintaining collegiality. The challenge he poses is how to preserve a sense of community in an institution committed to meritocracy.

Oldenquist also considers who is entitled to vote on a professor's tenure. Such decisions invariably affect students, but does that consideration justify their formal participation in the deliberations?

This issue is also taken up by Rudolph H. Weingartner as part of his discussion of appropriate procedures for making personnel decisions, in particular, the awarding of tenure. As he illustrates, such decisions involve faculty members and administrators in various ethical responsibilities that cannot be escaped by neglect.

Among his recommendations is that those participating in the decision process ought to study carefully all materials in the candidate's dossier. Ignorance amounts to irresponsibility. Perhaps the quality of preparation would be enhanced if participants were expected not only to vote but also to submit detailed statements of evaluation. A related issue is the extent to which confidentiality encourages negligence.

Faculty members are typically evaluated for tenure not only as classroom instructors but also as researchers. Yet it has been claimed that emphasis on publishing can lead to neglect of teaching. Theodore Benditt argues to the contrary that a conscientious teacher ought to engage in scholarship and seek to publish the results.

After sketching the history of the American college and university, Benditt notes that higher education now takes place in institutions devoted to the acquisition of new knowledge. Professors who fail to participate in this advance are in his view evading the challenge of their peers and shortchanging the education of their students. So the issue as he sees it is not whether to choose teaching or research but how to maintain the appropriate balance between them.

Either activity calls for seeking and transmitting truth. But sometimes telling the truth has unsettling consequences. Paul Eisenberg considers a series of such cases. Should a faculty member tell students the truth about a colleague's ineffectiveness? Should a teacher be truthful and give low grades to students doing poor work, knowing that in another section of the same course students doing equally poor work are receiving much higher grades? And what is a faculty member to do when confronted by a student of less than the highest caliber who seeks written support for gaining admission to another institution?

Robert Audi considers these and connected questions as they arise in the teaching of graduate students. He stresses that those who teach on the graduate level face an unusually varied set of responsibilities, including keeping abreast of the most recent scholarly advances, providing students with sound career advice, and encouraging them to think creatively while offering them appropriate criticism and guidance.

Since graduate professors and students work so closely together, is it appropriate that they become friends? Audi warns of ways in which such relationships are problematic. Peter Markie goes even farther, maintaining that professors are obliged to refrain from friendships with any of their students. His argument is that friendship, unlike friendliness or goodwill, implies favoritism and is thus inconsistent with a professor's duty to evaluate students fairly and give equal consideration to all.

An intriguing question Markie raises is whether analogous considerations bar a tenured professor from becoming the friend of an untenured colleague. What if their friendship preceded the untenured professor's initial appointment? Should special precautions then be taken to avoid even the appearance of bias in the tenure process?

Audi and Markie agree that by misusing authority professors can distort their appropriate relationship with students. A particularly egregious case of such abuse is sexual harassment, which Nancy ("Ann") Davis describes as a betrayal of trust.

While female professors as well as male, homosexuals as well as heterosexuals, can be guilty of introducing inappropriate aspects of sexuality into the educational environment, Davis concentrates on the most usual cases, in which female students are forced to deal with a male professor's offensive words or actions. Davis explains how such mistreatment may damage the education of women and harm the welfare of our society.

She calls on universities to prevent sexual misbehavior. But students may be victimized not only by faculty members but also by other students. Should colleges take precautions against such occurrences?

Doing so would reintroduce to the nation's campuses some elements of the now widely abandoned policy of *in loco parentis*. David Hoekema defends such a step, arguing that colleges ought to create environments that support students' capacity for moral action. He points out that schools make efforts to explain and prevent plagiarism. Should they not act likewise regarding sexual misconduct, drug abuse, and alcoholism?

Even those who take issue with Hoekema's conclusion may accept his premise that a school's atmosphere ought to be conducive to producing socially and morally responsible individuals. Indeed, some of those who oppose regulating student activity nevertheless support the regulation of faculty activity that links the university to the corporate world. They argue that such partnerships distort the process of learning by introducing into academia the concerns of the marketplace.

Norman Bowie recognizes possible dangers in the interaction between the corporation and the university, but he also sees important opportunities for both institutions. The university gains financial support and is aided in a variety of ways in achieving its goal of acquiring and disseminating knowledge. The corporation not only obtains access to first-class researchers and research facilities but has the opportunity to gain an appreciation of such traditional academic values as critical thinking, intellectual cooperation, and a sense of community.

Just as campus life has been significantly influenced by developments in the economic sphere, so it has also been strongly affected by social conditions. A chief example is the widespread call for colleges and universities to cease past practices of discrimination and seek diversity not only in student admissions but also in faculty appointments.

Alan Goldman strongly supports the ideal of equal opportunity, but he believes that choosing faculty members to achieve diversity is a misguided policy. If lack of diversity is interpreted as evidence of past discrimination, then the call should be for appropriate compensation to those individuals who were victimized. If the goal is diversity per se rather than recompense, then why should diversity of race, for example, be deemed more important than other sorts of diversity, such as age, nationality, or religion? Decades ago in the United States the ugly policy of segregation was based on considering race the most important criterion for classifying people; surely that idea was fundamentally mistaken.

Apart from using diversity as a criterion in making faculty appointments, might it be appropriate for an individual to be favored for an academic position because the members of the department believe that the person's views on important issues are correct? After considering arguments pro and con, David Lewis maintains that it is to the advantage of all that appointments not be made on the basis of whether the candidate's opinions are thought to be true. The search for knowledge is better served if competence, not creed, is the criterion for personnel decisions.

Yet the ideal of a faculty that evaluates members equitably and seeks truth dispassionately has been attacked on the grounds that colleges and universities are inherently political institutions, which cannot achieve neutrality. Robert L. Simon critically examines this claim, analyzing the concept of neutrality and considering its application to individual faculty members and to the university as a whole. Are professors entitled to teach their personal moral values to students? Is a faculty justified in adopting official positions on moral issues? Are the two cases in essence the same?

Simon's essay fittingly concludes the book by touching on many of the central themes in academic ethics: the scope and limits of academic freedom, the appropriate authority of the faculty, the proper relationship between teacher and student, the responsibilities of a researcher, and the distinctive mission of a university.

These matters are not exotic, but as philosophers have so frequently demonstrated, familiar subjects can often be the most important to study and the most difficult to grasp.

1

HUMAN RIGHTS AND ACADEMIC FREEDOM

Alan Gewirth

Universities stand in a double relation to human rights. On the one hand, all university personnel are the subjects or holders of the rights, including such of their corollaries as the right to academic freedom. On the other hand, university administrators have an especially strategic role as respondents or bearers of the duties that are correlative to the rights in university contexts. These include the duty to protect the academic freedom of their teachers and students and also the duties to provide as adequate educational facilities as they can and to refrain from discriminating against any of their would-be members on grounds of race, religion, nationality, or other irrelevant considerations.

I. CONFLICTS OF MORAL CRITERIA

While many aspects of these rights and duties are now widely accepted by universities and the general public in North America and Western Europe, they raise difficult problems of interpretation and application. Some of the main problems arise from the incorporation in the Western university of two different and potentially conflicting kinds of moral criteria, each of which derives from the general principle of human rights. First, the university embodies the value of freedom, especially intellectual and academic freedom, and the right to freedom is one of the most basic of human rights. But second, the university also embodies the value of education, and thus of moral and intellectual standards of the highest possible sort, and the right to education is also an important human right. But there may be conflicts between the maintenance of moral and intellectual standards and the protection of academic freedom. In the most general terms, these conflicts arise because freedom

8

as such is nonrestrictive, whereas moral and intellectual standards are restrictive. In one of its main concepts, freedom consists in noninterference by other persons, but the maintenance of moral and intellectual standards may require interference by other persons.

We can see the thrust of these conflicts if we consider such questions as the following. Should university researchers, under post–World War II conditions, be free to accept government contracts for developing chemical or nuclear weapons? Should universities employ as professors of history Nazis who deny the reality of the Holocaust or as professors of biology creationists who deny the facts of Darwinian evolution? What if these denials are revealed only after the professors have been previously hired, and even given tenure, on the basis of apparently sound scholarly credentials? In all such cases there appears to be a conflict between the freedom-based rights of professors and the rights of other persons or of the community at large, based on relevant moral and intellectual standards.

These conflicts may already be found implicit in the very idea of *academic* freedom. As we have seen, the concept of freedom involves the absence of external constraints or impediments on conduct, whether physical or mental. But the concept of the academic involves the presence of constraints, for to be an academic requires acceptance of rigorous intellectual standards that serve to constrict what one is entitled to accept as sound, true, or warranted. Thus the idea of academic freedom involves being at once free and not free, bound and not bound by constraints.

It may be possible to avoid a formal contradiction here by appealing to the diverse nature of the constraints from which an academic should respectively be free and not free. Thus we might hold that the academic should be free from nonintellectual constraints, that is, from political and social pressures and other constraints that do not derive from the general requirements or criteria of intellectual teaching and learning. But at the same time the academic should not be free from those intellectual constraints themselves; moreover, the constraints should be self-imposed and thus be matters of rational autonomy. Such a resolution does, I think, have much merit. But carrying it out in practice may raise severe difficulties not only because there may be conflicting interpretations of the relevant intellectual standards or of their applications but also because, even when the standards are agreed upon, their maintenance may lead to significant interference with freedom. Moreover, the resolution still leaves open the question of the relation between academic freedom and moral requirements, especially at the societal level.

II. HUMAN RIGHTS

In order to deal with such questions, I must move back a few steps to consider the nature of human rights and of academic freedom, as well as the relation between them. For it is ultimately from apparent conflicts within the general realm of human rights, both in themselves and in relation to academic freedom, that the difficulties I have mentioned arise. I have elsewhere discussed in considerable detail the objects or contents of human rights and the grounds for holding that they are equally had by all humans; so I shall not repeat these analyses and arguments here.[1] But a few main points must be stressed because of their relevance to what follows.

Human rights are an especially important part of morality because of their bearing on human dignity and fundamental human needs. As their name implies, human rights are rights that are had equally by all human beings; to have them one must simply be human, as against the special rights that persons may have because of some particular status or transaction. In addition to this equality and universality, the moral value and importance of human rights derive from the double fact that their objects, what they are rights to, are the most fundamental goods or interests of human personality and agency, and that in having rights to these objects humans are in a morally justified position to claim them as their personal due, as what they are entitled to for their own sakes and simply in virtue of their being human. On both counts, human rights are normatively necessary or mandatory requirements that set limits to what persons (both in and outside government) may justifiably do and not do to one another.

Like all other rights, human rights serve to secure or protect persons in certain kinds of goods. In the case of human rights, these goods are of special importance because they consist in the generic features and necessary conditions of action and of successful action in general. What makes human rights so crucial for human existence is that without their objects humans either cannot act at all or cannot act with general chances of success in fulfilling their purposes. It is, then, in their capacity of being actual or prospective agents that all persons have human rights. It follows that if these rights are withheld or denied, then either persons are directly deprived of the conditions they need to have in order to be agents and successful agents in general, or else their possession of these conditions is rendered precarious and unstable.

In the most general terms, the necessary conditions of action and successful action are freedom and well-being. Freedom is the *procedural* necessary condition of action: as noted, it consists in noninterference by other persons or, more positively, in controlling one's behavior by one's own unforced choice while having knowledge of relevant circumstances. Well-being as here understood is the *substantive* necessary condition of action: it consists in having the general abilities and conditions needed for achieving one's purposes. The components of such well-being thus fall into a hierarchy of goods, ranging from life and physical integrity (basic goods or well-being) to self-esteem, education, and opportunities for earning wealth and income (additive goods or well-being).

The connection of human rights with action and agency is not antithetical to their belonging to all humans equally. For all humans are actual, prospective, or potential agents. The point of introducing this description is only to call attention to the aspect of being human that most directly generates the rights to freedom and well-being.

III. THE RIGHT TO ACADEMIC FREEDOM: TWO INTERPRETATIONS

Given this brief characterization of human rights, let us now ask how they are related to the university and its members. Like all other persons, academics are actual or prospective agents, and as such they have the human rights. But are there any *special* ways in which academics have these rights, ways in which other persons do not have them? This question may seem self-contradictory, in view of the equality and universality that we have seen to be indispensable to human rights. But there is another possibility: that the general objects of human rights, especially freedom, have a special kind of bearing on the rights of academics. It is this possible bearing that I wish to explore here. Such an exploration should help to clarify both the nature of human rights and their relation to the purposes and methods of colleges and universities.

Let us, then, focus on academic freedom, which is a central right of academics as such. (I shall here confine myself to the academic freedom of college and university teachers or faculty members, although what I shall say will also apply, *mutatis mutandis*, to students.) To begin with, we must distinguish between two meanings of this right—one more general, which I shall call the *freedom of academics*, the other more specific, which is *academic freedom proper*. The freedom of academics is a freedom they share with all other persons. It includes especially the civil liberties of speech, press, and association; in the sense intended here, for persons to have these liberties is for them to be immune from any sanctions or punishment for expressing their opinions on any social, political, religious, or other matters, and thus not to be interfered with in such expression. Academics have, indeed, been punished by dismissal or in other ways for expressing unpopular religious or political opinions, but their human rights to freedom should protect them equally with all other persons. Hence, this freedom of academics is not unique to academics.

Academic freedom proper, on the other hand, pertains to the specific professional activities of academics. It consists in the freedom to teach and to do and publish research without fear of any sanctions ranging from administrative censure through dismissal to imprisonment (and, in some places and times, death). Obviously, the right to such academic freedom is of fundamental importance to all academics as such. The question I now want to take up is, What is the nature and basis of this right, especially in relation to human rights as a whole?

I shall begin by considering two possible interpretations of the right to academic freedom. According to the first, which I shall call the *general libertarian interpretation*, the right to academic freedom is simply the universal human right to freedom as applied to academics. As we have seen, according to this universal right, all humans have the right to control their behavior by their own unforced choice and thus to act as they choose so long as they do not harm other persons by adversely affecting their well-being as I have characterized it. The action in question includes all the activities of teaching and research in which academics may engage. Because of this universal right to freedom of action on the part of each academic, all other persons have the correlative duty to refrain from interfering with this freedom, that is, with the academic's control of his or her behavior in teaching and research by his or her own unforced choice. Thus in this way we would derive the right to academic freedom from the universal human right to freedom.

This attempted derivation is unsuccessful. An important reason for its lack of success can be seen if we ask a question like the following: Does the universal human right to freedom entail that anyone who walks in off the street has the right to start lecturing in a university classroom? An affirmative answer would mean that the right to free-dom is antithetical, at least potentially, to all structured human rela-tionships that are characterized by restrictive rules and other norms. This point does not, however, show that there is no universal human right to freedom, but only that it is not an absolute right.[2] It is limited by other rights, and also, as we shall see, it is indirectly applied to justify various social rules and institutions, including those in which the right to academic freedom belongs.

The rejection of the freedom to walk in off the street and start lecturing might be explicated in terms of the prevention of harm, for the purported lecturer would be harming the interests of students by disrupting their class schedules and by presumably uninformed lecturing. Such an account of "harm," however, already presupposes a special institutional background of universities and students; it is not part of the general framework of action common to all human rights as such. Hence, the rejection of the alleged freedom, and with it the justification of academic freedom as including the freedom to lecture as one chooses, cannot be grounded, in any direct way, on the universal human right to freedom.

Nevertheless, the justification in question can be derived indirectly from this universal human right. To see how, we must first note that there are myriad other freedoms involving human relationships besides lecturing to students that also cannot be directly derived from the universal human right to freedom. Does anyone who walks in off the street have the right to start affixing nuts to bolts on automobile assembly lines or umpiring a professional baseball game or judging a case in a civil or criminal court? Such questions indicate that the rights to perform the specified actions must be earned by persons who have the relevant qualifications. Thus, these rights are not universal human rights. As Sidney Hook has said, "The right of academic freedom is not a civil right or a human right. . . . For note that we have defined it as the right of *professionally qualified* persons. That makes it a special, not a general or universal right; it is a right that must be *earned*. A human right, on the other hand, is a right that does not have to be earned. It is possessed by every human being because he is a human being, or a member of a civilized community."[3]

There remains, however, this consideration. If human rights set the justifying conditions of all other morally justified rights, and indeed of all other moral values, then the right to academic freedom, even if not directly a human right, may be a human right indirectly in that it is derivable from general human rights, especially the general right to freedom. To see how, let us ask how the right to engage in certain kinds of work is to be "earned."

A central aspect of the earning in question is contractual. It involves mutual voluntary agreements by employers to have certain persons do certain kinds of work for which they are regarded as qualified and by workers to do that kind of work. This requirement of voluntary agreement applies to all workers, and the voluntary associations that are formed thereby are applications of the universal human right to freedom.[4] For this right entails the universal right to form voluntary groups or associations whereby persons freely band together for various purposes, so that all their members voluntarily consent to belong to the respective groups and to obey their rules. But although such voluntary associations are applications of a universal human right, they may also involve various sorts of particularist exclusion. Membership in the group is voluntary in that all the members freely consent to belong and to conform to the rules, but by virtue of the purposes for which the group is formed, other persons may be excluded, even against their will. Such exclusion, however, does not prevent them from forming their own voluntary associations, and in this way the universal right to freedom is still maintained. Thus the universal right has justified a restriction or specification of the freedom to do certain kinds of work so that the freedom belongs only to voluntarily hired persons.

Can we use this restriction or specification of the universal right to freedom to account for the right to academic freedom? This question brings us to a second interpretation of this right, which I shall call the *workplace libertarian interpretation*. According to this interpretation, the right to academic freedom is not simply the universal human right to freedom as applied to academics but is a right that academics share will all other workers or employees. The right has a certain contractualist presupposition, in that all workers, including academics, must earn the right to do their respective kinds of work through having relevant qualifications as indicated by mutual voluntary agreements. In the case of academics, these agreements are made with their peers in relevant departments; administrators (deans, provosts, and others) must accede to these agreements once an opening has been declared to exist. Given this presupposition, all workers, not only academics, should be free to do the work for which they have been employed and also free to express their political and other opinions both inside and outside the workplace. This right derives from the universal human right to freedom, with the previously indicated specification, itself indirectly derived from this right, about access restricted by voluntary agreement to the respective kinds of work. Thus in this way academic freedom would be simply a part of all workers' rights to freedom; it would not be unique to academics.[5]

There is much in this interpretation that I think is sound. In particular, it serves to explicate the familiar sense of academic freedom that I have called the "freedom of academics," which is violated when administrators or public officials seek to bring sanctions against academics for voicing unpopular opinions. In this workplace libertarian interpretation, academic freedom consists in the ordinary civil liberties of expression and association. These liberties pertain to all persons by virtue of the human right to freedom. The point of stressing the workplace context is that it is in this context that the civil liberties of academics as well as of other workers may be especially subjected to negative pressures against which the right to academic freedom serves as protection.

IV. THE INTELLECTUAL PROFESSIONAL INTERPRETATION OF ACADEMIC FREEDOM

Despite its merits, the workplace libertarian interpretation fails to account for certain central components of the right to academic freedom proper. For this right not only bears on the expression of political and other views inside or outside the classroom; it bears also on the specifically academic pursuits of professors. These pursuits are predominantly intellectual in character. As such, they have two aspects, one of the subject matter, the other of method. The academic subject matter, what is taught and studied, consists in general and fundamental features of nature and humanity. Academics study and teach some segment of this subject matter with a view to understanding its basic principles and the ways in which they are instantiated in specific contexts. Their concern, then, is with basic truths. The method by which academics study and teach this subject matter involves the careful gathering and weighing of relevant evidence. In their general lineaments, both aspects of academic intellectual inquiry pertain not only to the natural and social sciences but also to such fields of humanistic research as art, literature, history, philosophy, and religion. In all these areas, the pursuit of intellectual knowledge requires certain traits of personal and social morality: such traits as honesty, truthfulness, freedom of inquiry, public communication of results, and willingness to subordinate one's own selfish desires to impartial acceptance of the facts. Without these *moral* traits of character and social interaction, the very operation of *intellectual* inquiry becomes impossible.

These aspects of basic intellectuality on the part of the academic enterprise require a third interpretation of the right to academic freedom, which I shall call the *intellectual professional interpretation*. According to this interpretation, there is something distinctive about academic freedom, as against the civil liberties of expression that belong to all persons including those who exercise these liberties in the workplace context. What is distinctive about academic freedom is that it protects academics' pursuit of basic intellectuality in the sense I have just sketched.

It may be contended that this central aspect of the right to academic freedom can be accommodated by the workplace libertarian interpretation, because on that interpretation, especially through its contractualist aspect, relevant standards of job performance must be set. These standards are more intellectual in the academics' case and perhaps more physically manipulative in the case of many other workers, but in both cases what is protected is the right, once contractual requirements have been met, to perform the relevant kind of work without threats of dismissal.

There remains, however, an important difference. Most workers, at the same time that they have rights to freedom of expression within and outside the workplace, may be subjected to careful control or supervision of their job performance: once they have exercised their contractual freedom by taking a certain kind of job, they may be told what to do and how to do it, so that their freedom within the job is limited. There have been various well-founded proposals for "worker control" in industrial occupations, but these still leave open the question of how much autonomy would be left to the individual worker, as against workers as a group.[6] In the case of the academic, on the other hand, there is far more freedom in job performance. To be sure, if she or he is hired to teach quantum mechanics or molecular biology, the academic may not spend all her or his class time discussing the novels of Jane Austen. But within their general subject matter academics must be free to pursue and set forth their results based on their careful sifting of evidence. Their results are not controlled or preordained for them in the way that carpenters or auto workers, secretaries or computer programmers, are hired to make certain determinate products or to perform certain more or less narrowly circumscribed tasks.

There is, then, a difference between violations of academics' freedom when they are penalized for expressing unpopular opinions outside their professional capacity and when they are penalized for teaching or publishing intellectual contents within their professional capacity. The former kind of freedom belongs to all workers, not only to academics; the latter is peculiar to academics and so is not only a freedom *of* academics but is, strictly speaking, *academic* freedom. Thus the difference between the workplace libertarian and the intellectual professional interpretations of the right to academic freedom bears on the objects of the respective rights, what they are rights to. In the former case, the objects that must be free comprise the modes of expression protected for all persons, including workers, by the civil liberties. In the latter case, the objects that must be free consist in the academics' specifically intellectual pursuits as academics.[7] Academic freedom in this specific intellectual professional sense is violated when, for example, a biologist is harassed or threatened with dismissal for teaching evolutionary theory, an economist for teaching or publishing Marxist theories of exploitation, a teacher of French for assigning the writings of Flaubert or Genêt, and so forth.

V. CRITICISMS OF THE DISTINCTION

The distinction I have drawn between the workplace libertarian and the intellectual professional interpretations of academic freedom may be criticized on at least two grounds. First, it may be held that the distinction involves an unwarranted, elitist downgrading of ordinary nonacademic work. The jobs of many ordinary workers do not consist merely in repetitive physical manipulative tasks; on the contrary, they have important intellectual elements, for they require various kinds of understanding of tools and equipment, including how they are to be used and what is to be accomplished by their use. It might even be possible, like Plato, to construe these jobs in dialectical fashion, as involving a conversation in which knowledge and free discourse are essential to the proper understanding of the jobs.

These contentions may be sounder in some workplace contexts than in others. The contexts vary from those of sheer repetitive mechanistic drudgery to places where considerable ingenuity and initiative are allowed and even encouraged.[8] Still, in none of these contexts is there the academics' degree or kind of purely intellectual search for basic truth wherever the evidence may lead, as against preordained tasks or goals set by others. Part of this difference is captured by Fritz

Machlup's statement that "the occupational work of the vast majority of people is largely independent of their thought and speech. The professor's work *consists* of his thought and speech. . . . In brief, freedom of speech has a very special function in the case of those whose job it is to speak."[9]

There are, indeed, other professions in which speech and other forms of expression are also central. They include journalism and law. But these may still differ from the academic profession insofar as their main aim is not to seek and teach basic truths as such but rather, in the case of journalism, to report on particular contemporary events and, in the case of law, to make or apply laws that provide authoritative guidance for actions and policies. By comparison, the concerns of academics are more basic and theoretical in their search for and teaching of truth.

A second criticism of the distinction between the workplace libertarian and intellectual professional interpretations of academic freedom emphasizes the opposite side. It holds that the vaunted purely intellectual character of the academic's work is illusory. There are two main versions of this criticism, one pragmatic, the other Marxist. The pragmatic version may take two forms. The general form holds that no work is purely intellectual or theoretical; all involve practical elements. Even the testing of scientific hypotheses requires manipulative and other experimental operations.[10] The more specific form points out that much of teaching and research, even at the graduate university level, is applicational and even vocational, as in schools of medicine, law, engineering, architecture, business, journalism, social work, and so forth. The Marxist criticisms of the intellectualist interpretation of academic work hold that such work, far from being autonomously intellectual, is rather part of the ideological superstructure of a society and, as such, reflects and supports the dominant economic power relations of the society—in our case, of capitalist society.

These criticisms make some suggestive points, but they are far from conclusive. A general reply is that they overlook that there are criteria of intellectual adequacy, consisting fundamentally in canons of deductive and inductive logic, to which manipulative and other "practical" operations must conform if they are to be regarded as means to truth. In the case of professional education at the university level, what is properly involved is not merely practical skills of manipulation or casuistry but rather the application of basic truths to general kinds of contexts in which the theoretical element is still of fundamental importance. As for the Marxist criticism, even if there are economic and political influences on intellectual work, these are not inevitable or insurmountable, and in any case there remains the distinction between such causal factors and basic intellectual criteria, which academics and other persons can recognize and to which they can conform in their methods and judgments. These criteria are autonomous both in their contents and in their value; they are not mere reflections of economic or other forces.

Academic freedom and the freedom of academics must indeed permit the incisive criticism of existing institutions from a Marxist point of view, from both within and outside the professional academic context. But especially within that context academics must be concerned not only that their intellectual activities not be interfered with but also that their criticisms and recommendations take as full account as possible of ascertainable facts, and thus of the basic criteria of intellectual adequacy. And this taking account must accord to opponents the same attentive consideration of their views as the academic wants them to grant his or her own. This requirement presupposes a general political-constitutional background of respect for and enforcement of the civil liberties. In sociopolitical contexts in which such respect and enforcement are not found or are severely threatened, including Communist and other repressive societies, the academic may face the much grimmer task of working to defend academic freedom and to establish the constitutional order in which it can thrive.[11]

Much research done in universities properly has practical aims and applications. Practicality is not antithetical to the primary intellectual-theoretical orientation of academic work so long as the research also focuses on the ascertainment of basic truth; but it must also leave open the possibility of critical scrutiny of the practical social context itself.[12] There must be moral as well as intellectual guidance here: research does and should study the problems of resource depletion, cancer, hunger, unemployment, crime, and so forth, but with a view not to exacerbating these evils but rather, in accord with the principle of human rights, to alleviating or removing them. Here, academic freedom is subject to moral limitations not as to the intellectual contents of the truths to be ascertained but as to the directions in which some research is to be pursued and the uses to which findings may be put. In one respect these limitations are common to all persons: all must avoid adversely affecting human well-being. But in another respect academics have special positive obligations here because of the potential of their intellectual research for helping to solve pressing human problems. Positive duties to help in situations of dire need pertain to all persons and groups that have the relevant abilities by virtue of the universality of human rights to both freedom and well-being. But the special contribution of academics must still reflect their commitment to and acquisition of the knowledge of basic truths. While academic freedom is subject to such moral limitations, its primary object or content is this intellectual one.

VI. JUSTIFICATION OF THE RIGHT TO ACADEMIC FREEDOM

It is the professional intellectual interpretation, then, that characterizes academic freedom in its most distinctive aspect. Why do academics have a right to such freedom? Most directly, because without it they cannot perform their intellectual function. This function, in turn, is justified by the human right to education, which is a prime component of additive well-being, that is, of the conditions and abilities that enable persons, as actual or prospective agents, to increase their levels of purpose-fulfillment and their general capabilities of action.[13] Education in this context includes the self-education whereby academic researchers pursue knowledge by inquiring into basic truths whose testing and ascertainment increase understanding of important features of nature and humanity. The general human right to freedom is here specified as the right to be free to engage in such intellectual pursuits, and thus to have intellectual freedom. At the same time, the contractual conditions noted in connection with the workplace libertarian interpretation of academic freedom also apply here as setting the context in which the academic can professionally engage in this function. But the specifically intellectual aspect of the function distinguishes the professional intellectual interpretation from the interpretation that simply equates academic freedom with the civil liberties to which workers in general are entitled.

It is sometimes held that academic freedom is justified by its value for "society"; thus Robert MacIver writes: "It is hardly possible to exaggerate the service to society of the free inquiring mind of which the university is the prime exponent."[14] It must be recognized, however, that a society may have academic freedom and yet be undemocratic and repressive; Germany under the kaisers is a famous example. On the other hand, democratic societies have sometimes violated academic freedom; one need not go back to the Athenian democracy's killing of Socrates to find examples of this. These empirical examples do not, however, disprove that there is a normative or rational connection between academic freedom and constitutional democracy. I cannot deal with this issue here in the requisite detail, but it can, I think, be shown that an inconsistency is involved in upholding intellectual freedom for academics and denying it to other persons. The argument here is parallel to that which establishes the universality of the rights both to freedom and to additive well-being.[15]

It is important, then, to be clear about what kind of "society" one is referring to when one upholds the value of academic freedom. For the rulers of some repressive societies, such freedom may in some circumstances be disadvantageous. On the other hand, for a civil-libertarian constitutional democracy, academic freedom is indispensable. But in this context, the freedom in question is common to academics and all other persons; indeed, the connection between this intellectual freedom and such a constitutional democratic society is analytic, for such a society is partially constituted by intellectual freedom. The relation is one not of end and means but rather of a certain kind of social whole and one of its constitutive conditions. What makes a constitutional democracy so valuable is precisely that it is committed to intellectual freedom and to human rights more generally.

Most fully, then, what justifies academic freedom is not simply or solely its consequences for society but rather the intrinsic value of intellectual freedom and of the kind of additive well-being involving intellectual development, especially in its educational aspect, to which all humans have rights. In this way, academic freedom is a human right despite its restriction in its professional intellectual interpretation to academics.

VII. CRITERION-BASED OBLIGATIONS OF ACADEMICS

I now want to consider the bearing of academic freedom as thus analyzed on the conflicts of criteria to which I alluded at the beginning of this essay. These conflicts bear especially on the tension between freedom as absence of constraints and academic pursuits as involving subjection to intellectual constraints. We have now seen that in the context of academic freedom proper these conflicts are partially resolved. Such freedom demands that academics not be subjected to censure or dismissal for the intellectual work they do as academics. But at the same time, their freedom does not include the absence of intellectual constraints but rather rests upon such constraints. This point raises the following question: To what extent should academics be free from censure or dismissal if they violate these intellectual constraints?

This question is sometimes dealt with by the contention that the right to academic freedom "carries with it correlative duties" on the part of academics.[16] Strictly speaking, however, the duties entailed by rights are not duties *of the right-holder* but rather duties *of other persons* to respect those rights. The logical relation between rights and duties involves what I shall call *diversity relations,* in that the subjects or holders of rights are *diverse from* the respondents or bearers of the correlative duties. The having of a right does not , as such, entail that the right-holder also has some duty. It is not the case that because some person A has a right to something X, it logically follows that A also has some duty or obligation with regard to X. If I have a right to receive ten dollars from you because of a promise you have made to me, nothing follows from this alone about my having any duty to you or anyone else with regard to the ten dollars. I do indeed have some duties in this regard—for example, I may not threaten to shoot you if you don't give me the ten dollars, and I must not use the ten dollars to bribe someone or to buy lethal drugs—but these duties are not correlative with or logical consequences of the right to receive the ten dollars from you. Rather, they derive from more general moral rights, which set correlative duties of persons *other than* the right-holders themselves. Similarly, from academics' having the right to academic freedom nothing follows about any duties of those academics themselves.

The right to academic freedom does indeed entail correlative duties, but these, as such, are duties not of the academics who have the right but rather of *other* persons who have the obligation to refrain from interfering with the academics' pursuit of their own academic work. These respondents, or duty-bearers, may and indeed do include academics themselves, but the duties of each academic then do not derive from *his or her own* having of rights but rather from *other* academics' having the rights.

A partial exception to this position is found in the case of universal human rights, for in important respects all humans are the respondents or duty-bearers as well as the subjects or holders of such rights.[17] Even here, however, each person does not have correlative duties toward other persons simply by virtue of *her or his own* having the rights but rather because other persons have these rights against her or him. The *diversity* of subjects and respondents still obtains.

Is there any way, then, in which it can correctly be held that academics have intellectual obligations that directly derive from *their own* having the right to academic freedom? The answer is that in order to have this right, one must be an academic, and in order to be an academic, one must accept and fulfill certain intellectual criteria in one's work. This is a normative conception of the academic; in actual fact not all persons who hold academic appointments in colleges and universities fulfill the relevant criteria. But the criteria provide the justification for academic work and for academic freedom in the special professional sense. Thus, by virtue of claiming, implicitly or explicitly, a right to academic freedom, academics have the duty to fulfill the academic criteria on which they base this claim.

This point may also be put more generally as follows. If some person A has or claims a right to X by virtue of fulfilling certain criteria Y, then, insofar as A claims the right, A has a duty to fulfill those criteria. For example, if A claims the right to inspect the naked body of B by virtue of A's having relevant medical expertise (as evidenced by appropriate medical training and related qualifications), then, insofar as A claims the right, A has a duty to have and use that expertise. For otherwise A's right-claim would be unfounded and hence unjustified because based on intentional falsehood and dishonesty. I shall refer to this as a *criterion-based duty*.

Now the academic claims the right to academic freedom—the freedom to hold an academic position involving research, publication, and teaching—on the basis of fulfilling relevant intellectual criteria, as evidenced by education, writings, and so forth. Hence, the academic has the duty to fulfill or conform to those criteria.

This criterion-based derivation of the academic's duties from his or her own rights also applies to other workplace contexts besides the academic one. But in general workplace contexts the criteria in question are not specifically intellectual and may include many economic and other considerations about profits and losses to the firm, which may justify dismissing employees. In the university, on the other hand, the relevant criteria are intellectual, with such of their moral concomitants as I have described.

VIII. THE CASE OF "CREATION SCIENCE"

To see the bearing of these criterion-based academic obligations or responsibilities, let us apply them to a specific case. A currently problematic area of academic life concerns the claims that have been made for "creation science." In some states, including Arkansas and Louisiana, legislators have tried to require "balanced treatment" for evolutionary theory and "creation science" in the teaching of biology in public schools.[18] The main tenet of "creation science" is that the earth and the forms of life within it are products of divine creation and are only a few thousand years old, as described in the biblical story of creation in Genesis.

It should be noted, to begin with, that "creation science" requires serious consideration in contexts like the present because its upholders include not only various legislators and religionists but also many persons who have Ph.D.'s in physics, astronomy, biology, and other scientific disciplines from leading universities including Berkeley, Columbia, Harvard, MIT, and Stanford, and who hold faculty appointments in the natural or engineering sciences at such institutions as the University of Illinois, Iowa State University, Michigan State University, North Carolina State University, Pennsylvania State University, Purdue University, and others.[19] Thus these "creationists" have the credentials that are held to entitle persons to be called not only academics in general but also scientists.

Creationism and its upholders raise many serious issues, but in the present context I shall focus, for the sake of brevity, on a statement by Stephen Jay Gould. According to Gould, the thesis that "the earth is billions of years old and its living creatures are linked by ties of evolutionary descent" is supported by "the overwhelming judgment provided by consistent observations and inferences by the thousands. . . . Science *has* taught us some things with confidence! Evolution on an ancient earth is as well established as our planet's shape and position. Our continuing struggle to understand how evolution happens (the 'theory of evolution') does not cast our documentation of its occurrence—the 'fact of evolution'—into doubt."[20] This statement, with its reference to "consistent observations and inferences by the thousands," appeals to the intellectual criteria involved in academic work. These criteria derive from the requirement that academics be concerned to ascertain and teach what is true about their respective subject matters. The ascertainment of truth requires careful consideration of relevant evidence.

Now if one holds, as a matter of literal truth, that life originated on earth only a few thousand years ago, then one disregards an immense amount of paleontological and other evidence. Thus it seems clear that teachers or professors who uphold "creation science" violate their duties based on the intellectual criteria of the academic profession.

We may also derive the intellectual duties of academics in a somewhat more traditional way from the correlative intellectual rights of other persons: the students. The university has as its distinctive *raison d'être* the pursuit and achievement of intellectual excellence. It is because academic freedom is required for this pursuit that academics have a right to their special professional freedom. Intellectual excellence, in turn, is a great human value for both intrinsic and instrumental reasons. There is an important respect, moreover, in which all humans have a right to achieve as much intellectual excellence as they are capable of. This is the respect in which all persons, as actual or prospective agents, have additive human rights to knowledge and education. These are additive rights in that knowledge and education are among the conditions and abilities that enable persons to increase their levels of purpose-fulfillment and their general capabilities of action.

Because persons have these rights, other persons have correlative duties at least to refrain from interfering with persons' having knowledge and education. A prime way of such interference is to provide false information about the age of the earth and the development of life on earth and, more generally, to obscure or falsify the kinds of intellectual procedures and criteria that are necessary conditions of genuine scientific knowledge. Thus we are returned to the conclusion that academics who teach creationism in courses of physical or biological science violate the intellectual rights of their students.

These considerations are not removed by any of the complexities that recent philosophers of science have set forth. For example, even if, as Thomas Kuhn has held, different eras of science proceed within different "paradigms," that is, different sets of basic assumptions about the subject matter, and even if scientific observations are, as Norwood Hanson would have it, "theory laden" in that the terms in which they are implicitly defined reflect the theory in which they are used, it still remains the case that all scientific theories must meet tests of intellectual adequacy that include agreement with observational and experimental data.[21] Similarly, some anthropologists and sociologists have claimed that criteria of reason and rationality are always relative to the divergent cultures in which they are maintained.[22] Nevertheless, there are ample grounds for holding that the canons of deductive and inductive logic, in the elemental senses of consistency or avoidance of self-contradiction and the ineluctableness of empirical facts, are absolute conditions of ascertaining and preserving truth. More specifically, it may also be recognized that philosophers from Plato and

Aristotle to Aquinas and Leibniz have offered arguments from divine production or creation to explain teleological features of physical and biological phenomena. But even apart from Hume's classic rebuttal of such arguments, any use to which they may be put, if it is to be intellectually sound, must be able to accommodate the immense amount of paleontological and related evidence on which the evolutionary thesis is based.

There are indeed forms of the theory of creation that interpret divine creation in such a way that it is compatible with Darwinian evolution, broadly conceived.[23] What such interpretations undertake to establish is that God's creation is itself an evolutionary process. This thesis, of course, requires interpreting the story of Genesis not as a literal account but rather as an analogical story that drastically condenses an enormously long process. But the "creationists" who figure in the antievolution controversies that are at issue here emphatically deny such compatibility and with it the empirical evidence for the fact of evolution.

Creationists who overlook or deny such evidence seem, then, to present a case in which the freedom to which academic professionals are entitled is in conflict with the intellectual criteria that underlie that entitlement by setting the intellectual obligations to which academics are subject. The solution of this conflict is that the freedom in question is not absolute; it is limited by the relevant intellectual criteria. Academic freedom in the specific intellectual professional sense requires that academics be free to teach, speak, and publish while they maintain their allegiance to these criteria, and thus that they may not be required, in their professional work, to violate the criteria. The criteria are broad enough to allow many different and indeed conflicting kinds of theses and conclusions, and thus many different understandings of how the criteria are to be interpreted and applied. But the criteria must ultimately rest on the general rational and empirical canons that govern the ascertainment and preservation of truth.

Academic freedom is violated if, as in the Arkansas and Louisiana statutes, academics are required to teach "creation science" against their own intellectual judgment. This aspect of academic freedom is emphasized by the intellectual professional interpretation of the concept, but it is not readily accommodated by the workplace libertarian interpretation. For, in focusing on the need to protect the academic's extraprofessional expression of political and social opinions, that interpretation leaves at least relatively open the intellectual requirements of the academic workplace as such. Just as employers can in general prescribe the objectives and contents of the work to be done by their employees, so the workplace libertarian interpretation of academic freedom may permit academic employers to make similar prescriptions about academic work.

The "balanced treatment" required by the Arkansas and Louisiana laws was set forth as aiming "to protect academic freedom by providing student choice" and "with the purpose of protecting academic freedom for students' differing values and beliefs."[24] On the intellectual professional interpretation of academic freedom, however, such "balanced treatment" would be unjustified, because it fails to take account of the intellectual criteria that are basic to the seeking and teaching of truth.

This conflict may be mitigated, however, in universities and other educational institutions that uphold as their chief purpose the maintenance of certain religious criteria as well as intellectual ones. Two things must be said about such institutions. First, the religious and intellectual criteria may come into conflict; when they do, a choice must be made, and if the choice falls on the intellectual criteria, then the considerations so far advanced apply to them. Second, if the institutions hold that religious criteria are their primary concern, then, to that extent, they lose the right to claim special consideration, including academic freedom proper, on the basis of the human rights to intellectual freedom and to the additive well-being constituted by knowledge and education. Such institutions can still legitimately claim the protection of the civil liberties, but these do not, as such, include the special values that the intellectual professional conception of academic freedom makes central, and "it is manifestly important that [such institutions] should not be permitted to sail under false colors."[25] Thus their claim to the specific intellectual status of universities is lost or at least significantly reduced.

In addition, none of this discussion is meant to deny that stories of creation may be taught in theological and philosophical contexts that undertake to reinterpret creation in ways that make it compatible with evolution. Even apart from such attempts at reconciliation, stories of creation may also be taught in courses of literature, philosophy, religion, and the like. But the specific intellectual criteria that are relevant in such contexts are not those of natural science, in which context the creationists with whom I am concerned claim to teach.

It seems clear, then, that academics who are creationists violate the intellectual criteria on which their claim to academic freedom is properly based. Do such persons forfeit their right to academic freedom, so that they may justifiably be dismissed from their academic positions even after they have achieved tenure? Before we consider this draconian conclusion, several serious cautions must be noted. To begin with, any such sanctions must be applied only after relevant measures of due process have been followed. Professors must be given a hearing by their peers, mainly from within their own departments, and the right of appeal to external bodies, including the Association of American University Professors, must be guaranteed.

There are strong reasons for not following through with dismissal. They bear on both consequences and antecedents. The whole idea of acting to dismiss a colleague who has gained tenure is fraught with difficulties. It infringes the collegiality that is an important value of academic life. It is open to slippery-slope dangers. If creationists are to be dismissed for violating intellectual standards, then may not similar charges be brought against Marxists who ignore the virtues of capitalism? To be sure, the empirical data that serve to invalidate creationism may be held to be far more conclusive than those to which the anti-Marxist may appeal. But in practice, once such a punitive precedent has been set, it may be abused on far less justified grounds.

There are also antecedentalist objections. Academics may indeed be dismissed or severely censured if they violate moral-intellectual norms by plagiarism or falsifying experimental data. But there is an important difference between such misdeeds and the creationists' conduct. Plagiarists and falsifiers knowingly and intentionally do wrong, whereas creationists sincerely believe that what they do is right. Thus the former, unlike the latter, are characterized by *mens rea*. But such an internal volitional state is normally regarded as a necessary condition of justified criminal punishment, and the point can be extended to the present context as well.[26] Hence, the case for punitive sanctions against the creationist is correspondingly diminished. In addition, within limits there is a right to be wrong. This right does not extend to intentionally violating other persons' rights, and it applies only at a very narrow margin to those who do wrong through negligence or incompetence. But the wrongdoer's autonomy also has a claim to be respected.[27]

My tentative conclusions on this problem are as follows: Known creationists should not be given tenure in natural science departments of secular colleges and universities, nor should teaching of their theses be required. But once creationists are given tenure, they should not be dismissed simply because of their creationism. Means should be found to reduce the intellectually deleterious effects of their teaching, including, for example, public discussions in which the relevant evidence is clearly marshaled. In this way the intellectual criteria central to the distinctive values of the right to academic freedom proper can be upheld while the effects of violating the criteria can be diminished.

In partial summary, what I have tried to show in this paper is that although the right to academic freedom is not directly a human right, it is justified by the human rights to freedom and education. The contractual aspect of being an academic is justified by the human right to freedom as specified in the right to form voluntary associations. The specifically intellectual aspect of the right to academic freedom is justified by the human right to education and thus to the pursuit of intellectual excellence, as well as by the human right to freedom as applied in such pursuit. The intellectual criteria involved in the pursuit of this excellence provide both the justification and the limits of the right to academic freedom.

NOTES

1. See Alan Gewirth, *Human Rights: Essays on Justification and Applications* (Chicago: University of Chicago Press, 1982), intro. and chap. 1 (pp. 1–67).

2. On why there is a general right to freedom despite its being overridden in certain circumstances, see ibid., pp. 15–18.

3. Sidney Hook, *Academic Freedom and Academic Anarchy* (New York: Dell, 1971), p. 35 (Hook's emphases).

4. On this application, see Alan Gewirth, *Reason and Morality* (Chicago: University of Chicago Press, 1978), pp. 282–90.

5. For a good statement and defense of this interpretation of academic freedom, see Robert F. Ladenson, "Is Academic Freedom Necessary?" *Law and Philosophy* 5 (1986), 59–87.

6. For perceptive descriptions and evaluations of movements for "industrial democracy" and "workers' control" that have tried to give workers as a group far more autonomy in their work situations, see Jaroslav Vanek, *The Participatory Economy* (Ithaca, N.Y.: Cornell University Press, 1971); Vanek, ed., *Self-Management: Economic Liberation of Man* (Harmonsworth, Eng.: Penguin, 1975); G. Hunnius, G. D. Garson, and J. Case, eds., *Workers' Control: A Reader on Labor and Social Change* (New York: Vintage, 1973); Michael Poole, *Workers' Participation in Industry* (London: Routledge and Kegan Paul, 1975); David Schweickart, *Capitalism or Worker Control?* (New York: Praeger, 1980); Martin Carnoy and Derek Shearer, *Economic Democracy: The Challenge of the 1980s* (Armonk, N.Y.: M. F. Sharpe, 1980); Robert A. Dahl, *A Preface to Economic Democracy* (Berkeley: University of California Press, 1985).

7. This distinction is emphasized by Richard Hofstadter in his book with Walter P. Metzger, *The Development of Academic Freedom in the United States* (New York: Columbia University Press, 1955), pp. 262–64; and especially in the

important essay by William Van Alstyne, "The Specific Theory of Academic Freedom and the General Issue of Civil Liberty," in *The Concept of Academic Freedom*, ed. Edmund L. Pincoffs (Austin: University of Texas Press, 1972), pp. 59–85.

8. See, for example, *Work in America: Report of a Special Task Force to the Secretary of Health, Education, and Welfare* (Cambridge, Mass.: MIT Press, 1973); and Studs Terkel, *Working* (New York: Pantheon Books, 1972).

9. Fritz Machlup, "On Some Misconceptions concerning Academic Freedom," in *Academic Freedom and Tenure*, ed. Louis Joughin (Madison: University of Wisconsin Press, 1967), p. 180 (Machlup's emphasis).

10. See, for example, C. I. Lewis, *An Analysis of Knowledge and Valuation* (La Salle, Ill.: Open Court, 1946), chap. 1.

11. See, for example, the recent report of conditions at the University of El Salvador: "In many ways the 60-acre campus scarcely resembles a university. The military looted most of the school's equipment and blew up several buildings during the four-year occupation. . . . Dr. Louis Argneta Antillion, the rector, said the university struggles just to survive. . . . 'We lost everything,' said Dr. Antillion. 'We don't want to be marching, but we have to defend our university. The mission of the university is to prepare the people for democracy. Necessarily, that's political.' He estimated that he spends half his time helping to organize demonstrations against the government and giving technical help to union organizers" (*New York Times*, September 15, 1987). The article goes on to report that earlier, "by the late 1970's, revolutionaries had seized control of the campus, turning it into an armed fort. . . . The military's tolerance snapped in 1980. It stormed the central campus and shut it down for four years." This tragic conflict, characteristic of the academic scene in much of Latin America and other undeveloped countries, indicates the difficulties of protecting academic freedom in impoverished countries with authoritarian regimes.

12. In this connection, see John Kenneth Galbraith's thesis (related to the Marxist criticism just mentioned) that what he calls the "educational and scientific estate" has come to serve the purposes of the "planning system" comprising the giant corporations of the "technostructure" (*The New Industrial State*, 3d ed. rev. [New York: New American Library, 1979], chap. 25). Galbraith goes on to recognize, however, that "the educational system" may be independent of and, indeed, skeptical and critical about the "planning system" (pp. 291–92 and chaps. 33–34; see also Galbraith, *Economics and the Public Purpose* [Boston: Houghton Mifflin, 1973]). See also the sage remarks by Edward Shils, *The Academic Ethic* (Chicago: University of Chicago Press, 1984), pp. 73–96.

13. See United Nations Universal Declaration of Human Rights (1948), article 26: "Everyone has the right to education. . . . Technical and professional education shall be made generally available and higher education shall be equally accessible to all on the basis of merit." On the human right to "additive well-being" and its relation to education, see Gewirth, *Reason and Morality*, pp. 240–49.

14. Robert M. MacIver, *Academic Freedom in Our Time* (New York: Columbia University Press, 1955), p. 259.

15. See Gewirth, *Reason and Morality*, chaps. 2, 3.

16. See, e.g., the "Declaration of Principles" of the American Association of University Professors (1915), in *Academic Freedom and Tenure,* ed. Joughin, p. 168; and Howard Mumford Jones, "The American Concept of Academic Freedom," ibid., p. 231; also George Boas, "The Ethics of Academic Freedom," in *Academic Freedom, Logic and Religion,* ed. Morton White, American Philosophical Association, Eastern Division (Philadelphia: University of Pennsylvania Press, 1953), p. 3.

17. See Gewirth, *Reason and Morality,* pp. 316–17; also Maurice Cranston, *What Are Human Rights?* (London: Bodley Head, 1973), pp. 66–71.

18. See Arkansas Act 590 (1981): "Balanced Treatment for Creation-Science and Evolution-Science Act," reprinted in Langdon Gilkey, *Creationism on Trial* (Minneapolis: Winston Press, 1985), pp. 260–65. See also "Louisiana Balanced Treatment for Creation-Science and Evolution-Science in Public School Instruction Act" (1982). Both acts were declared unconstitutional. For the Arkansas act, see "Memorandum Opinion" in *Rev. Bill McLean et al., Plaintiffs,* v. *No. LR C 81 322, the Arkansas Board of Education et al., Defendants* (U.S. District Court, Eastern District of Arkansas, Western Division), January 5, 1982, reprinted in Gilkey, pp. 268–95. For the Louisiana Act, see *Edwards* v. *Aguillard,* 107 *Supreme Court Reporter* 2573 (1987).

19. See Gilkey, *Creationism on Trial,* pp. 21–22, 238, 254.

20. Stephen Jay Gould, "The Verdict on Creationism," *New York Times Magazine,* July 19, 1987, p. 34.

21. Thomas Kuhn, *The Structure of Scientific Revolutions,* 2d ed. (Chicago: University of Chicago Press, 1970); Norwood Russell Hanson, *Patterns of Discovery* (Cambridge: Cambridge University Press, 1965). Kuhn has subsequently made many qualifications of this thesis. See, e.g., Kuhn, *The Essential Tension* (Chicago: University of Chicago Press, 1977), pp. 293–319, 321–33.

22. See *Rationality,* ed. Bryan R. Wilson (Oxford: Basil Blackwell, 1970); and *Rationality and Relativism,* ed. Martin Hollis and Steven Lukes (Oxford: Basil Blackwell, 1982).

23. See the excellent discussion by Ernan McMullin in his Introduction to *Evolution and Creation,* ed. McMullin (Notre Dame, Ind.: University of Notre Dame Press, 1985), pp. 1–56.

24. See Gilkey, *Creationism on Trial,* pp. 260, 262.

25. "Declaration of Principles" of the AAUP (1915), p. 159. See also T. M. Scanlon, "Academic Freedom and the Control of Research," in *The Concept of Academic Freedom,* ed. Pincoffs, pp. 242–44.

26. See, e.g., Glanville L. Williams, *The Mental Element in Crime* (Jerusalem: Magnes Press, the Hebrew University, 1965); and H. L. A. Hart, *Punishment and Responsibility* (Oxford: Clarendon Press), chap. 6 (pp. 136–57) and passim.

27. See Hook, *Academic Freedom and Academic Anarchy,* p. 36; Jeremy Waldron, "A Right to Do Wrong," *Ethics* 92 (October 1981), 21–39; and the exchange between Waldron and William A. Galston in *Ethics* 93 (January 1983), 320–27.

2

FREE SPEECH ON CAMPUS

Judith Wagner DeCew

That freedom of conscience and expression is protected in the *First* Amendment of our Bill of Rights is probably no coincidence.[1] Such protection has been given preferred treatment by our judiciary during at least the past fifty years. In the institutional setting of a university or college, free speech takes on even greater importance. A university provides a public forum and an educational environment where students can learn original, bold, and diverse views. A university is widely viewed as a commonwealth of learning established primarily to allow and nurture free exchange of ideas and to promote the search for truth.[2] Moreover, a major justification for granting tenure to college and university professors is to ensure their rights freely to voice or write unpopular opinions.

In his recent book, *Saints and Scamps: Ethics in America*, Steven Cahn writes:

> A university without academic freedom is unworthy of the name.
> . . . The maintenance of free inquiry requires that all points of view be entitled to a hearing. . . . no one at the university, whether professors, students, or invited guests, should ever be prevented from stating beliefs. No matter how noxious some opinions may be, the greater danger lies in stifling them. When one person's opinion is silenced, no one else's may be uttered in safety.[3]

This defense of free speech on campus invokes two familiar arguments. First, Cahn makes the utilitarian claim that on balance the harm caused by allowing expression of even the most odious opinions is less than the harm of allowing suppression. Second, the justification for the claim that the latter harm is greater, is based on a slippery-slope argument. Once suppression of one opinion is allowed, it becomes more likely that other opinions will be banned. History documents the power of the temptation to censor, and as suppression becomes more common and easier, all views are in jeopardy.

It may be that Americans overwhelmingly endorse this general principle defending free speech on campus, but Cahn is well aware that people often change their minds when confronted with concrete examples of expression of provocative or offensive opinions.[4] There are also many complex cases in which it is not at all easy to apply the principle, despite its straightforward and unequivocal defense of academic freedom. At what point is heckling an interference with speech rather than an expression of disapproval?

I shall illustrate the complexity of free-speech issues by describing a wide range of instances in which concerns over freedom of expression arise on campuses, explaining why these are problematic for faculty, students, and administrators despite current legal standards and decisions. Finally, I reconsider alternative defenses of free speech, showing why they motivate adoption of certain guidelines for educational institutions. My goal is to argue that careful policies need not censor but can help promote and enhance free speech on campus.

Let me add some comments on terminology. As recently as 1972, in *Cohen* v. *California*, Supreme Court justices disagreed over what counted as "speech" worthy of protection under the First Amendment. Young Mr. Cohen had worn a jacket emblazoned with the words "Fuck the Draft" through a California courthouse as a way of protesting United States involvement in the Vietnam War. The Supreme Court overturned his conviction of violating a California state law prohibiting maliciously or willfully disturbing the peace by offensive conduct and defended his exercise of freedom of speech. In dissent, however, Justices Harry Blackmun, Hugo Black, and Chief Justice Warren Burger argued that "Cohen's absurd and immature antic . . . was mainly conduct and little speech."[5]

A clear distinction between speech and conduct suggested in the dissent fails, however. There are some acts, such as publication of printed matter or wearing armbands to express a view, that we believe it is legitimate to protect, and there is some speech it seems legitimate to exclude as unprotected, such as Justice Oliver Wendell Holmes's famous example of falsely yelling "fire!" in a crowded theater. Thus I endorse the more prevalent view that free speech is generally a defense of "acts of expression," which can include speech, publication, displays of symbols, demonstrations, and other acts intended to convey an attitude or view. For this reason, I use the terms *free speech* and *freedom of expression* interchangeably.

Similarly, *academic freedom* has usually referred to intellectual protection for an individual faculty member for study, research, discussion, expression, association, publication, and teaching. It was first
defended constitutionally in 1952 in Justice William O. Douglas's lone
dissent against firing teachers because of previous membership in
political organizations, and by 1957 was recognized by the Court
majority.[6] But *academic freedom* can be used more broadly to encompass
the institutional autonomy of the university, its ability to make its
own educational decisions, including those concerning admission,
textbooks, dismissal, tenure, and promotion.[7] In some contexts there
are good reasons for adopting the latter usage, so that academic freedom is construed as broader and more fundamental than free speech.
For example, since free speech applies to all citizens, not merely
academics, it seems the broader use of *academic freedom* is needed to
provide the special immunity from external ideological coercion that
justifies court deference to the university to oversee its own institutional decisions and processes. Such institutional autonomy from
court intervention often sustains the integrity of the university, because those trained in a discipline are viewed as best able to judge
work in their field. On the other hand, it can also make it extremely
difficult for individuals to demonstrate they have been subject to
discrimination or unfair treatment by the university, because it shields
institutional administrative functions from outside review. Because
my focus in this essay is free speech, I shall not differentiate the
broader use and shall use *academic freedom* to mean no more than
"freedom of expression" as I have described it.[8]

I. FREE-SPEECH CONFLICTS

The most obvious sort of cases involving issues of free speech on
campus relate to college lecture series and visiting speakers. Although
the extensive activism of the 1960s has waned, controversial speakers
remain a difficult campus issue. For example, in 1983 students at the
University of California at Berkeley forced Jeane Kirkpatrick, United
States ambassador to the United Nations, to cut short one public
lecture and cancel another. That same year the moderator at a panel
arranged by the Black Law Student Association at Harvard University
refused to recognize Jewish law students who wished to question
a speaker representing the Palestine Liberation Organization. Vice-
Consul Duke Kent-Brown of South Africa was allowed to speak for
only twenty minutes at Harvard in 1987, because protesters attempted

to block the exits of the room. Former secretary of defense Caspar Weinberger was able to deliver his speech there that year, but only after many interruptions by protesters. To cite another graphic example, a Tufts University student prevented Adolpho Calero, a former Nicaraguan Contra leader, from speaking at Harvard Law School in October 1987. When Calero stepped to the podium to speak, the student charged at him, yelling epithets. Although the student was arrested, officials ended the speech, and many were left wondering after these events whether Harvard could provide a forum for free speech.[9]

Calero is the same lecturer who was unable to speak at Northwestern University in April 1985, when he was commander in chief of the Nicaraguan Democratic Forces, the largest group of Contras fighting against the Sandinista government. Calero was sponsored by two university organizations at Northwestern, the Conservative Council and the International Policy Forum, and presumably Calero was there to defend the campaign of the Reagan administration to increase support for the Contras. Students and faculty picketed and chanted around the lecture hall, monopolized the podium, and when Calero appeared, someone rushed to the stage and threw red liquid at him.[10] Undoubtedly such protests come from deep commitment to principles. The difficult question is how to protect the protester's right to free speech while also guarding the rights of those who wish to hear.

Dramatic as these cases are, they demonstrate only one of many diverse free-speech conflicts. Other instances, often less visible, occur when individuals who are part of the university community speak out on topics of interest that may also be controversial (either within or outside of class) and when groups band together to advocate particular positions or to disseminate information to which others object. Further questions arise about the role of university recognition of campus groups as different as Students for a Democratic Society and gay rights groups.

Student newspapers produce additional questions, especially when published material is viewed as obscene or offensive. Troubling and well-publicized cases arose at Dartmouth College in recent years. The *Dartmouth Review* has been criticized many times for offending blacks, women, homosexuals, and others. During October 1987 the *Review* published a satirical column likening the college president to Adolph Hitler and comparing his campus policies to the Holocaust in an analogy widely viewed as anti-Semitic.

The *Dartmouth Review* is published weekly by Dartmouth students but is not otherwise affiliated with the college; it is run independently of the *Dartmouth,* the daily student newspaper. "The fact that President Freedman is Jewish raises the stakes in a rather frightening way," wrote several faculty members in a letter to outside advisers of the *Review.*[11] Other faculty members and students, as well as the Anti-Defamation League of B'nai B'rith in Boston, condemned the column, and President James Freedman characterized it as "poisoning" the intellectual atmosphere at Dartmouth. As a result, a few students responsible were suspended. Yet the manifest depth of the disagreement was overwhelming. The editor in chief of the *Review,* Harmeet Dhillon, denied that the column was anti-Semitic, maintaining its point had been misinterpreted and twisted and expressing surprise at the reaction to it. Moreover, both the suspended students and the *Review* itself received strong support from many Dartmouth alumni as well as members of the paper's advisory board, who said the essay was heavy-handed and in poor taste but had an "underlying element of accuracy."[12]

What is the appropriate administrative response in such cases? Ought that response to differ depending on whether the paper is the "official" student paper or "independent," whether it is funded by students or the university? Should student papers be overseen by some university review board? Other student media, such as campus radio stations and flyers posted or handed out, give rise to similar inquiries about how to balance students' free-speech rights against the preservation of the academic community as civil, tolerant, and respectful of others, as a workplace where diverse individuals can function at their best.

As is clear from the Dartmouth case, issues of sexual, racial, or religious harassment are closely intertwined with campus media, and universities are struggling to articulate appropriate guidelines to prevent such harassment and to aid victims. What is the appropriate response to pornographic movies, for example, often shown on college campuses, sometimes to raise funds for illustrious and expensive speakers? Such movies raise difficult issues about sexism and offense to members of the university group.[13] Discrimination on the basis of race, sex, or religion also arises in consideration of texts used in classes and accountability for the decisions about their use.

Related cases add disagreements over international politics. For example, student and faculty protests against university investments in South Africa raise questions about the consistency of institutional support for apartheid despite public statements reiterating university condemnation of such policies. Students have also protested against recruiting on campus by the Central Intelligence Agency or other agencies that endorse moral or political views the students find objectionable and by groups that are believed to discriminate against minorities.

It might seem that free speech also protects the use of school facilities for group meetings, but the case is complicated when the group is not affiliated with the college or when there is concern the group will cause damage or risk of damage to the working or facilities of the university. Ardent animal rights groups, to cite an example, have left some biology professors fearful about the safety of their labs.

Tenure generates another classic free-speech struggle. Tenure was originally intended to free professors to say or write what they wanted without fear of reprisal, especially if the message was a political critique of national or university policies. Like the life term of Supreme Court justices, which is intended to free them from having to bow to prevailing winds, tenure is justified by what Walter Shapiro calls the American belief "in the theory that absolute job security increases the odds of independence and moral courage."[14] The catch, however, is that tenure is typically granted by those very people from whom it is meant to afford protection.[15] All admit there is a subjective element in the tenure evaluation process, and the concern remains that young professors can be punished for their politics.

In one extraordinary case, Jan H. Kemp, an assistant professor in the remedial studies program at the University of Georgia, complained many times over four years that star athletes with substandard grades were being passed to keep them in major athletic events such as the Sugar Bowl. According to an article by Ezra Bowen and C. B. Hackworth, in 1983 she was demoted and dismissed from the university by the vice-president of academic affairs for "insubordination and insufficient scholarly research. . . . In deep despair, she twice attempted suicide. Then Kemp sought a very different resolution for her anguish. Charging violation of free speech, she sued the university."[16] Athletes, administrators, and Kemp's students testified, and after a five-week trial the jury awarded Kemp a stunning $2.5 million.

Finally, free speech is also at stake in recent controversies over class "monitors," such as those from a group called Accuracy in Academia, which claimed in 1985 to have had over two hundred anonymous student volunteers monitoring and reporting on class lectures at over 160 colleges in the United States. Laszlo Csorba, executive director of Accuracy in Academia at age twenty-two, stated that the purpose of

the group was to ensure "balance and a livelier class discussion."
Academics charged in reply that the group monitored only left-wing
teachers and practiced "ideological espionage" to generate fear; they
urged the monitors "to speak up in class and freely debate their
professors instead of tiptoeing off with reports."[17]

I do not claim that these many examples give an exhaustive list of
cases in which defenses of free speech on campus become problematic.
The facts differ from case to case and the diversity of situations is
enormous. Nor do I enter into the dispute about whether all examples
I have given legitimately belong on the list. (Some have argued, for
instance, that campus recruiting by the Central Intelligence Agency is
not really a free-speech issue.)

Nevertheless, all the cases given, to varying degrees, relate to the
expression of views and involve balancing guarantees of free speech
against educational goals, safety, and concern for the university community. Free-speech rights of a speaker or group clash with rights of
listeners to hear, rights of protesters to voice dissent and alternative
views, and rights of members of the university to be protected from
fear, discrimination, harassment, and harm. All show that academic
freedom can never be taken for granted at educational institutions.[18]
Most of the types of cases I have mentioned are interrelated. In some
instances they are inextricably intertwined, as in the case of Professor
Barbara Foley at Northwestern, where both interruption of a visiting
speaker (Calero) and a decision about her tenure case were at stake.[19]

II. LEGAL GUIDELINES

There are several legal standards that aim to clarify parts of these
controversies. Some of these are general standards for protection of
free speech; others are recent decisions in which the facts are specific
to a university situation. The Supreme Court's first major encounters
with free speech arose after World War I, but they are now common
court business and a regular source of dispute. In *Palko* v. *Connecticut*
Justice Benjamin Cardozo articulated the importance of free speech,
characterizing it as a "fundamental" liberty because of our political
and legal history and because "freedom of thought and speech" is
"the indispensable condition of nearly every other form of freedom."[20]

Justice Hugo Black subsequently became an eloquent advocate of
the stronger view that First Amendment rights are "absolute," that
the charge to Congress to make "no law" abridging free speech meant
exactly that: make *no* such law. In contrast, Justices Felix Frankfurter,

John Harlan, and Lewis Powell are associated with the rival view that First Amendment interpretation requires a balancing of competing interests. Black worried, in response, that their approach would allow free-speech rights to be balanced away whenever judges found conflicting state interests.[21] Although Frankfurter rejected the view that free speech was an "absolute" right and seemed to attack statements in Court opinions asserting the "preferred status" of First Amendment protection, legal theorists maintain that he nevertheless did not completely reject "a hierarchy of values with free speech high on the list. In short, he, too, found that First Amendment rights were specially protected ones."[22]

Even if there is agreement that the right to free speech is special in some sense, alternative methods of constitutional interpretation can affect the extent to which this preferred status is recognized. One type of interpretation, in the tradition of Harlan and Frankfurter, involves *balancing* the competing claims of speaker and protester or balancing the right to speak against risk of harm, for example. This is the dominant constitutional theory, derived in large part from Justice Holmes's "clear and present danger" test.[23] Each case is evaluated individually based on the circumstances and the degree of danger; so the special weight given to the value of free speech may vary. The test avoids the extreme view that restriction of political speech is never justified, as well as the opposite extreme that a speculation of harm is sufficient to suppress speech. Yet it may be too flexible and vague to provide a very clear standard for judging which expression is allowable.

Using a second type of interpretation, *categorization,* judges define or narrow down categories of speech not protected—bribery, perjury, counsel to murder, lewd or obscene words, profanity, libel or slander, or "fighting words" (words that tend to incite immediate breach of peace)—to determine whether the speech in question fits one of these categories or, if not, is protected by the First Amendment.

Both sorts of reasoning played important roles in the *Cohen* opinion. On balance, the Court felt the words on Cohen's jacket did not pose sufficient danger or threat to viewers to justify his conviction. The Court also argued that the words might be offensive but were not obscene, libelous, profane, or fighting words.[24]

Balancing may give citizens insufficient notice of whether their speech will be allowed or not, because reasonable people can disagree in evaluating the danger. In other words, balancing appears to allow more judicial subjectivity. But it is worth noting that categorization is not always easy either. At what point does name calling and abusive language cross the line from being merely offensive to being obscene or fighting words? Moreover, categorization leaves unanswered questions. For example, if there is a hostile audience, must a speaker keep silent because of concerns for public safety, even if the words fall in none of the unprotected categories?

Perhaps because of these problems, a third way of evaluating free-speech cases has evolved. In *Gooding* v. *Wilson* it was reported that an antiwar picketer at an army building said to a police officer, "White son of a bitch, I'll kill you," and was convicted of violating a statute outlawing "abusive language tending to cause breach of the peace."[25] While his words might easily have been viewed by some courts as fighting words or as presenting sufficient provocation to danger to justify suppression, the Supreme Court struck down the statute using a third sort of theory, *overbreadth*. They judged the statute to be overly broad and hence likely, because of its vagueness, to repress too wide a sweep of language. This new way of protecting free speech is beneficial because it avoids balancing, leaves the legislature the alternative of drafting narrower legislation, and takes seriously the "chilling effect," the effect arising when banning some speech leads others to be more careful and conformist in what they dare to say. But overbreadth is never well defined; hence there is worry that it also is too manipulable a standard for consistent decision making.

Another method to help clarify decisions about freedom of expression relies on differentiating justifications for limiting speech. Because free speech is intended to protect one's right to voice unpopular opinions, justifications based on the *content* of the message (except for the clearly excluded categories) are generally viewed as illegitimate. Legitimate justifications for limiting free speech are based on noncontent features, such as *time, place, and manner.*[26] One problem, however, is that these justifications cannot always be separated to determine when speech ought to be protected. Although a sound truck in a quiet neighborhood late at night would normally be banned even when bearing a political message, if it booms information about an imminent flood or poison gas in the area, it might be allowed precisely because of the content of the message. Second, it is always possible to concoct "legitimate" justifications to stifle a particular message. Litter from pamphlets, for example, might be cited to ban distribution of political information.

In sum, whereas various types of speech have been judged to be unprotected, neither the alternative methods of interpretation— balancing, categorization, and overbreadth—nor the distinction between content and noncontent justifications for limiting speech yields definitive tests for free-speech cases. All do serve as important guidelines for judicial decisions, but courts will differ and there is substantial leeway for applying those standards in university contexts.

III. APPLYING THE FIRST AMENDMENT ON CAMPUS

Recent cases have made clear, nonetheless, that at public institutions constitutional guarantees against abridging freedom of speech are upheld very stringently. In *Tinker* v. *Des Moines School District* the Supreme Court defended students' rights to wear black armbands in school in violation of a school rule banning them:

> In our system, undifferentiated fear or apprehension of disturbance is not enough to overcome the right to freedom of expression. Any departure from absolute regimentation may cause trouble. Any variation from the majority's opinion may inspire fear. Any word spoken, in class, in the lunchroom, or on the campus that deviates from the views of another person may start an argument or create a disturbance. But our Constitution says we must take this risk. . . . In order for the State in the person of school officials to justify prohibition of a particular expression of opinions it must be able to show that its action was caused by something more than a mere desire to avoid the discomfort and unpleasantry that always accompany an unpopular viewpoint.[27]

Thus, fear, apprehension, and speculation of danger are insufficient to allow suppression even in the face of contrary school rules. Symbolic expression can be banned, according to *Tinker*, only if it would "materially and substantially disrupt the work and discipline of the school," present a clear and present danger, or exhort others to violence. This standard places a heavy burden on those wishing to impose restrictions, the burden of showing convincing evidence of disruption or danger.

Two years later, the Fourth Circuit Court of Appeals attempted to outline when institutional guidelines could be justified as prior restraint:

> Specifically, the test for the reasonableness of college regulations is whether such regulations measurably contribute to the maintenance of order and decorum within the educational system, are calculated to prevent interference with the normal activities of the

university or obstruction to its function to impart learning and to advance the boundaries of knowledge, or are important in maintaining order and normal operations.[28]

Obviously the core questions are when expression "materially and substantially" disrupts functioning of the university and whether regulations infringing on academic freedom genuinely maintain order and help prevent obstruction of the educational process. In retrospect, it may seem clear that wearing armbands does not interfere with "order and decorum," but it is easy to see that in other cases it will be far less obvious whether allowing certain forms of expression crosses the line to disruption.

A vivid difficulty of this sort arose for administrators during student protests against investments in South Africa at Columbia University in April 1985. There was a sit-in on the steps of Hamilton Hall, and two operable ground-level doors were chained shut. But offices, classrooms, and the classics library remained accessible (somewhat inconveniently) through an underground tunnel. Protesters even posted marshals and signs directing others to the route into and out of the hall. Classes and administrative work were somewhat affected, but not admissions or the fall schedule, and the demonstration remained peaceful and nonviolent. The university filed charges against the students photographed or recognized as part of the protest. When students then cut the chains, Columbia dropped contempt charges but continued internal disciplinary action.

In deciding how to treat the students, a balance had to be struck between the right of members of the university community to demonstrate as a means of expression and the right of the university to maintain the ordinary functioning of the academy. Was the student demonstration a "substantial disruption" of university functioning? Some students had clearly violated the Columbia rule prohibiting blockage of an entrance to a university building. An outside review held that chains on a classroom door represent an intolerance for the academic enterprise and that the university had the right, if it chose, to enforce such a justifiable rule against the obstruction. The students were given a one-term disciplinary warning and probation but no mark on their permanent record.

Yet many felt the students had a right to defend themselves against the charges because they had a just cause, pursued their free speech with dignity and calm, were frustrated in their attempts to use normal channels available to influence university decisions, and viewed the university as unfaithful to the principles it professed in stating its opposition to apartheid. All parties agreed that the university bene-fited in classroom discussion from the exchange of ideas generated by the protest. The students' need to demonstrate echoed a judgment from a fact-finding report of earlier disruption at Columbia that the students were not satisfied "that their views effectively entered into the process of conscience . . . [nor] convinced that the opportunities for change [were] open."[29]

The argument that a university needs to provide an environment conducive to learning helps justify the internal discipline. The strong protection of students' rights to free speech in most of the cases I shall describe, however, makes it unlikely that a court would have found the students' disruption "substantial" enough to outweigh their free-speech rights had the university pursued those charges. Nevertheless, the case illustrates the difficulty in assessing university regulations and underscores the inevitability of some balancing between ensuring freedom of expression for students and protecting and promoting institutional goals and educational prerogatives.

In another context, editors of student newspapers have claimed they are being subjected to more and more unfair pressure or outright censorship by university administrators, student govern-ments, and faculty members. Citing cases such as a cartoon viewed as racist, which appeared in a newspaper at the University of California at Los Angeles, they claim they are paying a price for publishing material that offends members of the community. Disciplinary action has included cutoff of funds and orders not to print. Moreover, a survey of eighteen campuses sponsored by the Gannett Foundation and conducted by Ivan Holmes, associate professor of journalism at the University of Arkansas, substantiated the students' claim. "Censorship was alive and well on every campus visited in this study," Holmes wrote.[30]

But a sequence of court cases shows that First Amendment rights are consistently upheld for students. The president of Florida Atlantic University dismissed three editors of the campus newspaper because he felt that: "the level of editorial responsibility and competence has deteriorated to the extent that it reflects discredit and embarrassment upon the University. I am also convinced that the decreasing quality of the . . . student newspaper . . . is irreversible under the present senior staff leadership."[31] Unimpressed, both the United States District Court and the Court of Appeals ruled in favor of the students, ordering their reinstatement and awarding them back pay and compensatory damages. (The District Court also awarded them attorney fees, but these were denied on appeal.)

Even when mandatory student activity fees are used to help finance the student newspaper, free speech has been defended. When the president of North Carolina Central University withdrew financial support from the student newspaper "because he found the newspaper's editorial comment and policies abhorrent and contrary to the university's policies as well as inconsistent with constitutional guarantees of racial equality," the Fourth Circuit Court of Appeals nevertheless found his irrevocable withdrawal of funds from the student newspaper, which held a segregationist editorial position, a violation of First Amendment protection.[32]

These cases are striking, yet the decisions are understandable in light of the constitutional standards I have articulated. Offensive expression is particularly difficult to countenance, but it has not been one of the categories of speech left unprotected. Disgusting as offensive expression may be, it has consistently been tolerated under the First Amendment. Probably the most important reason for this toleration is that there are no guidelines for determining what is offensive. Who is to decide what passes beyond the bounds of acceptability? Two other reasons offensive expression is allowed are to avoid the chilling effect, which might lead to homogenized student papers, and to avoid the slide down the slope to more repression, inasmuch as identification of what is and what is not offensive remains so elusive.

What is more difficult to understand is that obscenity is also tough to ban in a student paper, although it is constitutionally a category of unprotected speech. A University of Missouri graduate student was expelled for distributing on campus a newspaper that was characterized as violating a university rule prohibiting indecent conduct or speech. The Supreme Court noted that public institutions are free to enforce reasonable rules governing student conduct and consistent with their educational mission but concluded they "are not enclaves immune from the sweep of the First Amendment." It held in *Papish v. Board of Curators of the University of Missouri*:

> State university's expulsion of student because of disapproved content of newspaper, cover of which showed a political cartoon which depicted a policeman raping Statue of Liberty and the Goddess of Justice, which featured a headline story entitled "M ____ f ____ Acquitted" and discussed trial and acquittal of youth who was a member of an organization known as "Up Against the Wall,

M ____ f ____" were not constitutionally obscene or otherwise un-protected. . . . State University's expulsion of student because of disapproved content of newspaper, which student distributed on campus, could not be justified as a non-discriminatory application of reasonable rules governing conduct.[33]

Part of the problem is drawing the line between what is and is not obscene. That determination has been shifted from the courts to local communities; however, local guidelines vary and are no clearer than earlier federal ones. According to one dean of students, "The elements of a definition of obscenity are so obviously imprecise that a college administrator is beset with difficulty in predicting what is legally obscene."[34]

One exception to protection of student free-speech rights was the Supreme Court's 1986 decision to uphold the three-day suspension of a high school student who addressed his school assembly using "an elaborate, graphic and explicit sexual metaphor."[35] The innuendo was offensive and glorified male sexuality, but was hardly obscene, as the majority claimed. It is striking that the Court failed to cite *Papish*, but the case was distinguishable because of the disruption caused at the assembly (unlike the armbands worn in *Tinker*), the Court's concern for protecting fourteen-year-old minors in a public high school, and the "captive audience" at the assembly. Students could not avoid the speech as one could the newspaper in *Papish* or the jacket in *Cohen*.

These cases make it clear that in instances of offensive and often obscene language on a college campus (except for graffiti, for instance, which could be banned on noncontent grounds), there is in effect no balance. No legal weight is given to the effects on those in the university community who find it repugnant. Can faculty, administrators, or student groups do anything to protect those who bear the brunt of such expression?

IV. SPECIAL RESPONSIBILITIES FOR MEMBERS OF A UNIVERSITY

Even among devoted defenders of free speech, these cases must raise concern. It is not merely that some members of the university community are repelled by certain speech. As Dartmouth faculty pointed out, the stakes are higher. Group defamation theory assumes that "when stereotypes become internalized, oppression occurs, which in turn confirms stereotypes, which then perpetuates oppression."[36] License in the name of free speech appears to make the university a party to the continued oppression. The predicament is that if we restrain freedom of speech on campus to protect minorities from group defamation, we run the risk of harming minority rights to free speech.

It might be argued that although public universities must uphold constitutional guarantees strictly, private colleges could abide by less demanding principles, on the ground that they have a right to preserve the environment desired by those paying for their services. Princeton University used this defense to block a member of the Labor party from distributing and selling political leaflets on campus without the university permission required by rule. Princeton maintained that as a private institution it had the right to choose and maintain its desired atmosphere on First Amendment grounds even if that meant restrictions of activity on campus.[37]

Princeton's argument was rejected in court, and the American Association of University Professors has unequivocally defended free speech for all campuses. In 1967 the association emphasized

> that the freedom to hear is an essential condition of a university community and an inseparable part of academic freedom. . . . no more appropriate forum exists for the voluntary examination of ideas and of men than that provided by a university. [We urge] that no prior restraint be imposed on the right of members of an academic community to invite and to hear on campus any person of their own choosing.[38]

In 1983 after various interferences with speakers, the association reaffirmed through the Committee on Academic Freedom and Tenure that it:

> deplores interference with the right of members of an academic community to hear on campus those whom they have invited to speak. The right of access to speakers on campus does not in its exercise imply either advance agreement or disagreement with what may be said, or approval or disapproval of the speaker as an individual. There can be no more appropriate forum for the discussion of controversial ideas and issues than the college and university campus.
>
> [The committee] reaffirms its expectation that all members of the academic community will respect the right of others to listen to those who have been invited to speak on campus and will indicate disagreement not by disruptive action designed to silence the speaker but by reasoned debate and discussion as befits academic freedom in a community of higher learning.[39]

The Committee on Freedom of Expression at Yale, a major private university, also gave thoughtful consideration to the role of the university in guaranteeing freedom to speakers, paying special attention to offensive speech:

> Because few other institutions in our society have the same central function [as the university], few assign such high priority to freedom of expression. Few are expected to. Because no other kind of institution combines the discovery and dissemination of basic knowledge with teaching, none confronts quite the same problems as a university. For if a university is a place for knowledge, it is also a special kind of small society. Yet it is not primarily a fellowship, a club, a circle of friends, a replica of the civil society outside it. Without sacrificing its central purpose, it cannot make its primary and dominant value the fostering of friendship, solidarity, harmony, civility, or mutual respect. To be sure, these are important values; . . . a good university will seek . . . [to] attain these ends . . . [but] will never let these values, important as they are, override its central purpose. We value freedom of expression precisely because it provides a forum for the new, the provocative, the disturbing, the unorthodox.[40]

It might be claimed that in these statements the AAUP and Yale are attempting to be neutral, to say that any and all speech should be allowed, provided it is not flagrantly dangerous or overtly disruptive. Yet it might be contended that such neutrality is either impossible to achieve, because individuals who make up the university community cannot abstract from their moral or political beliefs, or wrong when it defends speech that is blatantly racist, anti-Semitic, and so on.

This argument is well worth considering, especially because universities sometimes appear to embrace free speech to give themselves the freedom to voice their own political agendas. Yet it is important to recognize that rejecting neutrality as a goal, if not a reality, requires the university to choose sides and to decide both what kind and what degree of partisanship it will embrace. If any speaker or newspaper story is to be prohibited, for reasons other than violence, the central questions always loom. Where and how do we draw the line? Who should be granted the power to decide? No reasoning compatible with the function of a university as a place of learning justifies the paternalistic stance of not letting the audience decide for itself. The university must remain confident that the speaker's credibility or repulsiveness will ultimately surface. It seems clear, then, that the university, public or private, is not only legally bound but morally committed to be a staunch defender of free speech, even in the face of offensive, noxious expression.

Nevertheless, I believe that as members of a teaching institution, educators have a duty to teach the power and oppression of words. Students must learn that offensive speech can be a pernicious weapon causing personal humiliation, fear, and destruction of an environment where all can learn and achieve to their fullest. Educational institutions exist not merely to promote free exchange of ideas and to increase knowledge but to encourage and promote the intellectual and personal development of all who study and work there. Thus, defending free speech alone, however essential, may be insufficient. The educational goals concerning speech cannot be neglected.

It was evident, according to one participant at a recent meeting of American university presidents, that "the level of conflict . . . [and intolerance on] campuses has skyrocketed in the past two years. . . . Clearly, the fabric of university life is being ripped apart by lack of shared values and lack of trust."[41] For example, in 1988 a University of Wisconsin fraternity staged a mock slave auction, complete with pledges in blackface. More recently, white male students there have followed black female students, shouting "I've never tried a nigger before."[42] Defending unabridged free speech in word, print, and deed permits insensitive, discriminatory, and embarrassing treatment of some members of the university community, which often escalates to aggressive intolerance and ridicule.

Any justifiable educational initiatives to enhance pluralism and respect on campus must be in accord with the goals of maximum protection of free speech. I next reexamine classic defenses of free speech to show how they help differentiate the purposes of free speech from its practice, so I shall be better able to propose acceptable university initiatives.

V. INSIGHTS FROM DEFENSES OF FREE SPEECH

The most common defenses of free speech are consequentialist, citing the good effects of allowing it and the bad consequences of restrictions. John Stuart Mill in *On Liberty* outlined the benefit of searching for and discovering the truth, through the correction of erroneous beliefs and the acquisition of justified beliefs. Even if an opinion is false, he argued, the truth becomes better justified by refuting the error. Beliefs are then founded on reasoned conviction. And since no opinion is completely true or false, he pointed out, allowing free expression always preserves that partial truth. Moreover, the bad effects of suppression include the possibility of banning the truth. No one is infallible, and unconventional opinion may turn out to be correct.[43] Other worrisome consequences of suppression already cited include the chilling effect on others' expression, leading to more conformity, and the potential slip to more and more suppression.

Mill's second major justification for free speech was that it is required by representative government. Less accepting of majority rule than Locke, Mill was profoundly worried about the danger of suppressing minority opinions. This argument has led commentators to focus on political speech as worthy of the highest protection. Alexander Meiklejohn has developed the fuller and more extreme view that speech affecting civic issues and self-government must be wholly immune from infringement, while "private" or nonpolitical speech, including commercial, literary, and artistic expression, is entitled to less complete, minimal due-process protection.[44] The merits of protecting political speech can be defended by the recognition that citizens in a democracy serve a political function as electors, a role they cannot fulfill adequately without access to information and the opportunity to question established views. Yet Meiklejohn's extension to less protection for other speech is incompatible with university commitments to academic freedom for all.

Mill's third philosophical basis for free expression is a nonconsequentialist and broader argument that free speech enhances and protects individual autonomy, liberty, and self-development.[45] Mill urged that eccentricity is better than uniformity and stagnation. He was at pains to emphasize the importance of personal growth and self-realization and to emphasize free speech as a vital way of guaranteeing liberty to develop one's faculties and abilities. This argument is sometimes rephrased in terms of fairness and respect for persons.

Of Mill's three central arguments, both the first and the third are essential for defending free speech in a campus context. The first argument, concerning the search for truth, supports staunch protection for speakers, newspapers, and other expression on campus. It is worth noting Mill's particular sensitivity to the rights of *all* speakers and listeners, especially those with whom one disagrees:

Nor is it enough that he should hear the arguments of adversaries from his own teachers, presented as they state them, and accompanied by what they offer as refutations. That is not the way to do justice to the arguments or bring them into real contact with his own mind. He must be able to hear them from persons who actually believe them, who defend them in earnest and do their very utmost for them.[46]

Mill's third argument emphasizes the importance of character development and personal achievement. It serves as a motivation for universities to devise ways to ensure an atmosphere encouraging that growth, and it serves as a defense of educational policies and protections that maintain such an educational environment. Individual growth cannot be ignored as an intended goal of freedom of speech. Thus the practice of the pursuit of knowledge must be coupled with attention to fostering an environment in which members of the campus community can flourish.

VI. ALTERNATIVES FOR PROTECTING THE ACADEMIC ENVIRONMENT

Some have thought that the animosity surfacing on some campuses is so outrageous, mean-spirited, intolerant, and sometimes perverse that it requires quick and decisive action by administrators to make it clear, in William Laramee's words, that "to produce, broadcast, publish a speech or work that debases, degrades, inflicts injury, or promotes animosity against traditionally defined minority groups will not be tolerated and will result in swift and severe punishment."[47] By emphasizing the two critical prongs of defenses of free speech and the recent court decisions defending students' rights, I have shown that such unequivocal regulations ultimately serve as censorship on campus and do not necessarily ensure an atmosphere where individuals can thrive. As we have seen, inflammatory speech may be viewed as slander or fighting words if reasonably regarded as a direct personal insult delivered face to face, thus likely to cause substantial disorder or violence. But general racist or anti-Semitic statements, for example, if banned on campus, would likely survive court appeal. Moreover, blanket regulations include no provision for procedural due process for offenders.

For this reason, and because of the many types of free-speech cases and the wide variety of contextual details, educational policies will have to be more specific. Thus policies on racial and sexual harassment, for example, will best be stated separately from policies protecting speakers and listeners. I cannot hope to give a full treatment of this vast topic. Nevertheless, I shall show that separate educational policies and initiatives can be devised to enhance the educational environment on campus for all and to minimize trauma for members of the university community, without jeopardizing commitment to free speech.

Harvard Law School has recently adopted guidelines for outside speakers that require speakers to respond to questions from the audience and to abide by the word of a moderator. The moderator plays a pivotal role in balancing rights of speakers and dissenters because the moderator has the power to order protesters to be ejected, to suspend the speech because of disruption, or to move or cancel the event for security reasons. Cancellation is viewed as a worst outcome, and "protest is allowed, but within limits."[48] Committee members felt these guidelines were appropriate for a law school, where questions and answers are a core element of the educational process.

Many schools have developed sexual and racial harassment guidelines. The best contain a definition of what constitutes harassment, an outline of the range of sanctions that might be imposed on offenders, informal grievance procedures, counseling, and a specific grievance procedure that includes a thorough investigation and a commitment that there will be no retaliation against a complainant.[49]

With regard to newspapers, administrators can immediately communicate to the campus community that the paper is not an official publication of the institution, can emphasize the author's responsibility and liability for what is printed, and can decry the content of any offensive or obscene piece. Offensive movies, speakers, or displays can be balanced with university-sponsored alternative events such as panel discussions, educational flyers, or exhibits voicing rival views and explicating for students the insidious harm caused by the offense.

More general positive steps can be taken as well. At Clark University this year, a new Task Force against Intolerance made a series of recommendations including:

> visible signs of commitment to the Affirmative Action office; addressing issues of cultural sensitivity in the classroom and in curriculum development; a "University Day" to discuss diversity issues both in special events and in the course of regular academic work; merit awards for faculty efforts on campus to increase understanding of these issues; and a renewed commitment to Clark's two-year-old program aimed at increasing minority representation in the student body, faculty, and staff.[50]

These are laudable beginnings, but most universities have done shamefully little to educate students about the responsibility that goes with the freedom. Even after the publicity given the poignant events in China, we might wonder how many students could explain the major justifications for free speech. Most universities have not addressed the basic issues of education, helping students understand the crucial need for free speech as well as the concerns it generates about tolerance and respect.

Policies and programs are likely to be fairest, most respected, and thus most effective, if drawn up by a bipartisan group. It should not be difficult to gather such a group. Both liberal and conservative students want to avoid harsh regulations, penalties, shutdowns of papers, speeches, radio broadcasts, etc. Committees will be most successful if they include students, faculty members, and administrators. Students must feel a part of the process, feel responsibility for the task, and learn through participation. Maximal procedures will begin with debate among all members of the institution, with the committee goal being articulation of specific, written, and publicly posted guidelines as well as innovative educational efforts. Since regulations can clearly be abused, policies should be agreed upon, public, and constructed with as much detail as possible. The guidelines need to be consistent so that once an institution opens its doors to one group, newspaper, or activity, others are assured equal treatment.

Guidelines or initiatives of the type I have described need not be incompatible with free expression in the marketplace of ideas. They may in fact guarantee access to a public forum, the ability to hear, an opportunity to protest, and essential education about the effects of speech. The practice of unbridled free speech may impede the intent of free speech in its broadest sense, including information gathering as well as the personal development of individuals. Campus regulations can, of course, be used to censor, but there are alternative ways that university policies can promote and protect all the goals of free expression without restricting academic freedom.

NOTES

Acknowledgment: I am especially grateful to Linda Jorge and Mona Olds for research assistance and discussion. I also thank the Mary Ingraham Bunting Institute at Radcliffe College and the Higgins School of Humanities at Clark University for support while I wrote this essay.

1. Archibald Cox is one constitutional scholar who believes the numerical

position is symbolic of the primacy of those rights. See *Freedom of Expression* (Cambridge: Harvard University Press, 1981), p. 1.

2. Explicit references to this familiar description appear, for example, in James O. Freedman, "President's Statement to the Dartmouth Community," February 29, 1988; and Michael W. Hirschorn, "University Efforts to Censor Newspapers Are on the Increase, Student Efforts Say," *Chronicle of Higher Education*, April 22, 1987, pp. 35–36.

3. Steven M. Cahn, *Saints and Scamps: Ethics in Academia* (Totowa, N.J.: Rowman and Littlefield, 1986), pp. 5–6.

4. Derek Bok, "Reflections on Free Speech: An Open Letter to the Harvard Community," *Harvard University Gazette*, September 21, 1984, p. 1.

5. *Cohen v. California*, 403 U.S. 15, reprinted in Gerald Gunther, *Individual Rights in Constitutional Law* (Mineola, N.Y.: Foundation Press, 1986), p. 771.

6 *Adler v. Board of Education*, 342 U.S. 485 (1952). Douglas's dissent is reprinted in *Education Digest* 17 (November 1985), 64–66. In *Sweezy v. New Hampshire*, 354 U.S. 234 (1957), the Court reversed a conviction for contempt against a professor who had refused to answer questions from authorities about the content of a lecture he delivered and about his relationship with the Progressive party. These and other cases documenting constitutional protection of academic freedom are described in Clark Rubenstine, "Academic Freedom and Institutional Autonomy: Freedom for the University," *Philosophical Studies in Education*, Ohio Valley Philosophy of Education Society, Indiana State University (1985), 76–90.

7. Rubenstine, "Academic Freedom and Institutional Authority," pp. 81–88. Rubenstine argues that cases show the institutional right to academic freedom is presumptively strong but can be overcome when there is proof of unconstitutional discrimination.

8. In "Freedom of Thought in the Ivory Tower," *Journal of Thought* 19 (Spring 1984), 27–34, Douglas Huff assesses Derek Bok's argument in *Beyond the Ivory Tower: Social Responsibilities of the Modern University* (Cambridge: Harvard University Press, 1982), that the social responsibilities of the modern university are limited by the purpose and function of a university. Huff argues that Bok identifies academic freedom with free speech and thus cannot defend the institutional autonomy of a university. Given that my topic is limited to free speech on campus, I trust there is no such confusion in my use of the terms.

9. Bok, "Reflections on Free Speech," p. 1; "Freedom of Speech Committee Focuses on Recommendations," *Harvard Gazette*, March 4, 1988, p. 3; "Harvard Law School Adopts New 'Free Speech' Guidelines," *Boston Sunday Globe*, September 25, 1988, p. 48.

10. See Joseph Epstein, "A Case of Academic Freedom," *Commentary* 82 (September 1986), 37–47, for a fuller description of events at Northwestern and one view of the effects of the incident on the tenure case of Professor Barbara Foley.

11. Allan R. Gold, "Satire by Dartmouth Publication under Heavy Fire as Anti-Semitic," *New York Times*, November 6, 1988, p. 22.

12. Ibid., quoting William Rusher, publisher of the *National Review*. According to editors of the *Dartmouth Review* the paper receives more than $100,000 in annual contributions.

13. See Judith DeCew, "Violent Pornography: Censorship, Morality, and Social Alternatives," *Journal of Applied Philosophy* 1 (March 1984), 79–94. Portions on pornographic movies on campus reprinted in *Right Conduct*, ed. Michael D. Bayles and Kenneth Henley, 2nd ed. (New York: Random House, 1989).

14. Walter Shapiro, "Government by the Timid," *Time*, February 20, 1989, p. 37.

15. See Geoffrey Cowley and Sue Hutchinson, "Down and out in Cambridge," *Newsweek*, April 4, 1988, pp. 66–67, for a description of cases in which this sort of politics is thought by many to have played a major role: tenure denials to Clare Dalton at Harvard Law School and David Noble at MIT.

16. Ezra Bowen and C. B. Hackworth, "Blowing the Whistle on Georgia: A Jury in Atlanta Calls the University Way off Side," *Time*, February 24, 1986, p. 65.

17. "Balance or Bias: A Challenge to 'Class Monitors,' " *Time*, December 23, 1985, p. 57.

18. See more examples in Kenneth Carlson, "Academic Freedom in Hard Times," *Social Education* 51 (October 1987), 429–30.

19. Epstein, "A Case of Academic Freedom."

20. *Palko* v. *Connecticut*, 302 U.S. 319 (1937).

21. *Konigsberg* v. *State Bar of California*, 366 U.S. 36 (1961), provides one classic confrontation between these two views as articulated by Black and Harlan. See Judith DeCew, "Moral Rights: Conflicts and Valid Claims," *Philosophical Studies* 54 (1988), 63–86, esp. secs. 2 and 4, for an evaluation of alternative ways of understanding rights as "absolute."

22. Gunther, *Individual Rights in Constitutional Law*, p. 646. The Court's summer 1989 decisions upholding flag burning and sexually explicit telephone messages for the "dial-a-porn" industry demonstrate the continuing preferred status of free expression.

23. *Schenk* v. *U.S.*, 249 U.S. 47.

24. It is fascinating that in this case Harlan wrote the speech-protective majority opinion and Black dissented, indicating equivocation on the absolute versus balancing views on free speech.

25. *Gooding* v. *Wilson*, 405 U.S. 518 (1972).

26. See Thomas Scanlon, "A Theory of Freedom of Expression," in *Philosophy of Law*, ed. Ronald Dworkin (Oxford: Oxford University Press, 1977), p. 157.

27. *Tinker* v. *Des Moines School District*, 393 U.S. 503 (1969).

28. *Sword* v. *Fox*, 446 F. 2d 1091 (1971).

29. The Cox Commission Report, *Crisis at Columbia: Report of the Fact-Finding Commission Appointed to Investigate the Disturbances at Columbia University in April and May of 1968* (New York: Vintage Books, 1968), p. 197.

30. Hirschorn, "University Efforts to Censor," p. 36.

31. *Schiff* v. *Williams*, 519 F.2d 257 (1975), described with the following case in Annette Gibbs, "The Student Press: Institutional Prerogatives versus Individual Rights," *Journal of College Student Personnel* 19 (1978), 16–20.

32. *Joyner* v. *Whiting*, 477 F.2d 456 (1973).

33. *Papish* v. *Board of Curators of the University of Missouri*, 410 U.S. 667 (1973).

34. Gibbs, "The Student Press," p. 17.

35. *Bethel School District No. 403* v. *Fraser*, 106 S.Ct. 3159 (1986), reprinted in Frederick Shauer, *Constitutional Law, 1987 Supplement* (Mineola, N.Y.: Foundation Press, 1987), pp. 200–208. Chief Justice Burger's majority opinion used a balancing test to weigh student rights to free speech against the interest in teaching appropriate behavior to students. One might believe the shift in court membership affected the outcome, but that seems unlikely, for it was a 7–2 decision. Justice William Brennan concurred with the majority, denying the speech was obscene, but was concerned about the disruption and the place: a mandatory school assembly. Justices Thurgood Marshall and John Paul Stevens dissented, agreeing with the district and appeals courts that there was insufficient showing of disruption and the student lacked fair warning he had violated the school rule.

36. William A. Laramee, "Group Defamation and Freedom of Speech," *Black Issues in Higher Education*, August 1, 1988, p. 44.

37. *Princeton University* v. *Schmid*, 84 N.J. 615 (1980), cited in Rubenstine, "Academic Freedom and Institutional Autonomy," pp. 84–87.

38. See p. 41 in D. Welsh, "Academic Freedom and the Rights of Speakers," *Philosophical Papers* 12 (October 1983), 39–52. The message is clear despite the unfortunate sexist lapse.

39. Ibid., p. 41.

40. Ibid., p. 40.

41. President Richard P. Traina, "The University as a Pluralistic Community," *Clark Now* 18 (Fall–Winter 1988), 1.

42. "A Step Toward Civility," *Time*, May 1, 1989, p. 43.

43. John Stuart Mill, *On Liberty*, ed. Currin V. Shields, The Library of Liberal Arts (New York: Bobbs-Merrill, 1985), pp. 43, 56, and 21.

44. Alexander Meiklejohn, *Free Speech and Its Relation to Self-Government* (New York: Harper, 1948), cited in Gunther, *Individual Rights in Constitutional Law*, p. 640. See also Cox, *Freedom of Expression*, pp. 2–4.

45. Mill, *On Liberty*, p. 71. Others who have insisted on the importance of incorporating both consequentialist and nonconsequentialist arguments for free expression include Scanlon, "A Theory of Freedom of Expression"; Fred R. Berger, "The Right of Free Expression," *International Journal of Applied Philosophy* 3 (Fall 1986), 1–10; and Lawrence H. Tribe, *American Constitutional Law*, 2d ed. (Mineola, N.Y.: Foundation Press, 1988), p. 787.

46. Mill, *On Liberty*, p. 45.

47. Laramee, "Group Defamation," p. 44.

48. "Harvard Law School Adopts New 'Free Speech' Guidelines," p. 48.

49. Compare Cheryl M. Fields, "Colleges Advised to Develop Strong Procedures to Deal with Incidents of Racial Harassment," *Chronicle of Higher Education*, July 20, 1988, p. A11.

50. Traina, "The University as Pluralistic Community," p. 2.

3

TENURE: Academe's Peculiar Institution

Andrew Oldenquist

Does everyone already have tenure? About fifteen years ago at my university an art professor made a small blue neon sign that said simply "tenure" in script and placed it in his studio window. Perhaps it counted as conceptual art; perhaps it won him tenure; I never knew. His art highlighted what professors believe is uniquely and profoundly important to their careers and their profession. The really dramatic thing about tenure is not just that it gives one security for life but that the alternative is immediate one year's notice of banishment.

Is tenure unique to the academic world, or is it universal, found under different names nearly everywhere? If it is an institution found only in colleges and universities, how does one justify it? And if tenure is justified, how should it be decided? John Silber, James O'Toole, and others have maintained that there is just as much "tenure" outside as inside the academic world. O'Toole, in the course of advocating the abolition of tenure, says it would be absurd to think colleges and universities would fire professors at will if tenure were abolished.[1] It would not be done in the academic world for the same reasons that it is not done in business. In corporations and in government, he says, people who are incompetent in one job are moved laterally to another or are more closely supervised, sometimes demoted, but hardly ever fired. Hence they have tenure in all but name. No company and no university, O'Toole says, wishes to acquire a reputation for ruthlessly firing personnel.

John Silber argues that rough equivalents of tenure are universal, because people in every business, government agency, or social entity of any kind need and desire a sense of continuity and predictability in their social environment. Hence, Silber says, the main reason for tenure is neither academic freedom nor simple job protection. He sees tenure everywhere in one form or another as the expression of a necessary and universal need for continuity and social stability.[2]

I think it is untrue that there is anything like the degree of (unspoken) tenure in the world of business that there is in colleges and universities. Silber is right about the need for continuity and community. The miniature societies people are constantly joining are an expression of our innate sociality, of our need for social identities. But the need for continuity and predictability in industry does not prevent industry from dismissing people who would be retained under a tenure system. Silber's argument cannot change the fact that business and industry let go a considerably greater proportion of their experienced people than do universities; it can only provide an additional explanation (besides the economic one) why industry is not as ruthless as we can imagine it to be, and an additional explanation why universities value tenure.

Anyone with a goodly number of nonuniversity friends knows of people in their thirties to fifties—engineers, entrepreneurs, middle-level managers, state and federal employees—who lost their jobs and had to send out dozens of resumes and go wherever in the country a new job was found. This happens fairly often, not just when a company fails or the employee is found incompetent, but it almost never happens to tenured professors. Indeed, it is inconceivable to professors how matter-of-factly people outside academia look for new jobs and cope with periods of unemployment, even in middle age. The typical academic's feelings about life without tenure are not unlike the feelings of terror and insecurity with which Soviet citizens view the American practice of job hunting after college or having to buy one's own medical insurance ("What is insurance?" a Muscovite philosopher once asked me).

In the ruthless extreme of business, which might also be called utopian meritocracy, employees are constantly compared to others waiting for their jobs and replaced the instant someone better is found. Professional athletes and coaches are subject to this continual testing; winning is the *only* criterion and the suggestion that a National Football League team should be loyal to a running back who is inferior to another available running back would be laughed at. The same may be true of first-chair players in a symphony orchestra and some corporate chief executive officers.

The system of pure meritocracy changes by degree through various kinds of jobs to workplaces where loyalty and community clearly outweigh getting the best person available. One often hears, as an excuse for applying the system of unmitigated meritocratic competition to untenured professors, than after six years of it the survivors achieve tenure. But as we shall see, pure meritocracy is not the usual situation in which untenured faculty members find themselves, and neither is it the most reasonable.

In the business world people are not let go if it can be avoided. They are laid off when contracts are lost or when economics requires it for some other reason, but they are not ruthlessly dismissed the moment a better person for a particular job is available. There is still loyalty to fellow employees and, whether conscious or not, a striving for continuity and a familiar team. This is the half-truth behind both the argument that tenure is justified because the "outside world" has the equivalent of tenure, lacking only the name, and the argument that tenure is not justified because the "outside world" has the equivalent of tenure and doesn't need it.

I. SOME CONSIDERATIONS FOR AND AGAINST

The classic statement in defense of tenure was made by the American Association of University Professors and the Association of American Colleges in 1940. They said tenure "is a means to certain ends; specifically: (1) freedom of teaching and research and of extramural activities, and (2) a sufficient degree of economic security to make the profession attractive to men and women of ability."[3] Hardly anyone talks about the second goal except when questioning the legitimacy of tenure, the AAUP today being primarily associated with the defense based on academic freedom. I shall argue, however, that providing job security has become a more important function of tenure than protecting academic freedom; at least, it is more important when integrated with communitarian goals I shall discuss.

It is understandable that professors should *like* the first AAUP goal better; the second is slightly embarrassing. It implies that tenured professors do have greater economic security than their counterparts in business and that this greater economic security is a compensation for something professors do not have. What don't they have? Presumably the better salary that "men and women of ability" can achieve in the world of business. However, people of ability do not reject university life (when they do reject it) only because of low pay. Many think of it as lethargic, devoid of deadlines, concrete results, diverse stimulation, and any significant connection with the world of public affairs; these feelings are often summed up in the contrast between "academe" and "the real world." Such people are also unexcited by the idea of grading papers, and they are unlikely to be satisfied with summers off, but some of them may be moved by tenure. In any case, the AAUP thought they might.

There are robust, bustling professors in every discipline who certainly do not consider themselves to be separated from the "real world." Other academics who see theirs as a slower-paced world like it that way and like their relative freedom to work on projects of their own choosing. But many of these, especially in the arts and sciences, also think of themselves as smarter and more knowledgeable than businesspeople who make more money and have greater decision-making power. They think of business as a high-reward, high-risk game and believe that in the academic world, in which rewards are lower, it is appropriate that the risks be lower. The most important way in which the risks can be lower is to have tenure.

There are a number of factual questions relevant to the justification of tenure about which the experts disagree. William Van Alstyne, in defending tenure against O'Toole's claim that in the absence of tenure the market will provide a new job, says that "a person turned out of one institution scarcely presents himself as additionally attractive to another in competition with other candidates."[4] Is there, however, a special inability on the part of professors who are let go to find new jobs: do they have less to offer or are they more diffident than other people? Van Alstyne is right that the "politically irksome" professor won't have an easy time in the academic marketplace. But is it the same in industry? For example, what about fired whistle-blowing engineers? It is hard to see much of a difference, except that midcareer job hunting is accepted in business. Van Alstyne also seems to assume that without tenure a university need not show cause for termination.

O'Toole, who dramatically renounced his own tenure at the University of Southern California, advocates the complete abolition of the tenure system. His main claim is that tenure is not a guardian of academic freedom but a degrading defense of simple job security, as unnecessary in academia as it is in business. As for protection from dismissal on political grounds, O'Toole argues that the law offers all the protection that is needed, citing *Ofsevit* v. *California State University*, 1978, which protected an untenured professor on the grounds that the First Amendment protects all political activity by teachers. He concludes, "As it is nearly impossible to be fired in the great corporations of America, so it would take Herculean feats of malfeasance to be fired at the great universities."[5]

What about the not-so-great universities and the community colleges, not to mention the not-so-great corporations? Would a tenureless Backwater Community College be financially as well as morally up to protecting professors who are beginning to slip and who haven't many friends? O'Toole's argument that tenure ruins young scholars by forcing them into the frantic production of trivial articles, instead of allowing them to develop a real research plan at their own pace, is not convincing. To begin with, it isn't relevant to colleges where little or no scholarship is done, and one's job is teaching. In research-oriented schools, young faculty members seldom have coherent, long-term research goals, and they need to get in the habit of productivity.

John Livingston has argued that everyone should have tenure at the time of appointment, so that incompetence may be adequately protected. Livingston says, "The unique and significant aspect of tenure in this regard is that, in contrast to the subtle and covert means by which incompetence is protected in other areas of American life, tenure does it openly."[6] The moral thing to do, he says, is to help and support the incompetent, rather than get rid of them. Livingston's position deserves to be taken seriously and then rejected. The Soviet Union has found the solution to the problem of unemployment: inefficiency. If someone is given a job with the result that seven people instead of six do what two do in the United States, and if no one is fired, there will be no unemployment. There is a serious moral point to such a system, namely, the conscious decision that guaranteeing employment is morally more important than efficiency. Americans often assume that efficiency is an intrinsic good or at least speak as though it takes moral precedence over compassion and community. Yet one certainly can argue that compassion, mutual care, and community can sometimes justify what is truly less efficient. We have a more compassionate society—some would also say fairer—when we protect the unfortunate and the incompetent even at the expense of efficiency, for example, when retarded people are given odd jobs in the neighborhood or in a sheltered workshop, when three are hired to do the work of two in order to provide near full employment, and when professors who once were good and now are mediocre are protected by tenure.

We need to strike a balance with which people can rest easy between equality of treatment, with its price of lowered efficiency, and the greater efficiency that results from meritocracy. Of course, the premise that a society that offers differential rewards has greater efficiency and productivity is challenged by utopian egalitarians; its defense requires extensive argument, and here I do no more than hypothesize it. Livingston's arguments have an intuitive appeal, but in their confrontation with merit and efficiency I believe they justify a more modest conclusion.

There are two ideologies in American society, one communitarian, cooperative, and supportive of fellow members of one's group, the other individualistic and intolerant of incompetence. Alexis de Tocqueville has argued persuasively that both characterize American society and that they exist in perpetual tension with each other. Tenure expresses the communitarian idea, supported in different ways by both Silber and Livingston, Silber stressing continuity and Livingston protection of the incompetent within one's group. These grounds for tenure need to be emphasized, for the more common stance, by the American Association of University Professors and others, is to defend tenure as a protection of the rights of the individual against the group. Focusing on the individual stresses the adversarial relations between individual and department and university, whereas focusing on the tenured body stresses the group membership and intragroup protection that tenure provides.

What if there were no tenure? Most universities have a system of annual reviews prior to the fateful sixth-year tenure decision. Departments usually put off the decision until forced by the rules to grant tenure or give notice. What would happen if the procedures of the first five years continued indefinitely (or to vary the scenario only slightly, if three-year contracts were all that could be given)? Would hopeless faculty members be strung along until things became intolerable, in year ten or twelve? Or would departments, without the magical sixth year to depend on, terminate more people earlier? It is difficult not to surmise that in a situation of annual (or even triennial) reappointment, and no tenure, fewer faculty members would be let go early, since they could always be let go later.

A tenure decision has a psychological impact, forcing department members to ask themselves whether they want to commit themselves to Jones for the next thirty years. Renewal of a term contract also gives one pause. Term contracts, however, continue into the years when many professors become tired and the likelihood of future productivity diminishes. Would young departments, seeking greatness, be inclined to be ruthless?

Since people mature and "find themselves" at different ages, should the probationary period be individually varied? Should there perhaps be degrees of tenure, implying degrees of job security, into which one gradually slides? (I don't know how this would go in detail.)

How we answer is a function of how much looseness and discretionary judgment we think we can allow without inviting too many abuses and grievances. I don't think I want to give departments and universities that much discretionary authority; there would be too many challengeable judgments of degree. No society can exist without trust and everywhere substitute rules for judgment, but neither should we expect too much of ourselves.

II. TENURE, ACADEMIC FREEDOM, AND VULNERABLE PEOPLE

There is no question that protecting academic freedom remains a function of tenure, but the importance of this particular function lies more in publicly honoring an ideal than in the number of people it saves. Today, tenure's major functions are job protection and the maintenance of a shared sense of community.

Since the grounds for terminating untenured faculty members are the same as would be used at any time in their careers if there were no tenure system, we need only look at how infrequently the termination of the untenured involves an issue of academic freedom. *Academic freedom* refers here to protection from dismissal for one's political or professional opinions and activities. At least this is one way to clarify that vague notion. It would distort the concept to include under it the protection of uncollegial or disagreeable personalities, various kinds of incompetence, or even the protection of professors' civil rights. The law protects professors' civil rights, with equal force both before and after tenure, tenure adding little or nothing to protection in this area.

Nonetheless, the number of professors tenure protects from dismissal, who would have been dismissed had there been no tenure system, may be considerable. One can only guess at the size of this group, for it depends on how loyal to one another and how communitarian a given group of professors would have been (toward colleagues beyond their sixth years) in a hypothetical world without tenure. These people saved by tenure are mostly poor teachers, negligible researchers, and disagreeable or friendless colleagues, who nevertheless were sufficiently acceptable to be reappointed through their sixth year.

The subset of these professors saved by tenure whose dismissal would have been a violation of principles of academic freedom is minuscule, for two reasons. First, among the ranks of the tenured, unproductive scholars or researchers, poor teachers, and unpleasant colleagues greatly outnumber the politically offensive and the professionally eccentric. Second, most of the professors a university is set on letting go on grounds of political or professional heterodoxy are let go anyway before or at the time of the tenure decision. Tenure can protect the academic freedom only of those who have political or professional eccentricities strong enough to make their universities want to fire them but which manifest themselves to that degree only after tenure has been granted.

It is controversial whether saving the kinds of professors tenure actually does save argues for tenure or against it. The number of professors saved by tenure from dismissal motivated by sexism or racism is a positive but not a strong consideration for the reason given: the law does a better job of protecting them than does tenure. The number of total incompetents saved is a negative consideration (except on John Livingston's view), and their number probably increases with age. But these (hypothetical) numbers are in any case very small.

But what should we say of borderline incompetents, ordinary deadwood, openly proselytizing homosexuals, rightists and Marxists who distort facts or try to have their political opponents physically prevented from speaking on campus, and people so abrasive as to drive good people out of the department? Do *these* people, who we suppose are saved by tenure (that is, who we hypothesize are not dismissed but would have been if, contrary to fact, there were no tenure), count for or against the institution of tenure?

It is very likely true that tenured professors feel freer to pursue nonmainstream and unconventional research and that this may well be a more widespread and ultimately more valuable area to protect than political radicalism. Both are kinds of academic freedom. There of course is a gray area between offbeat research and research that is marginally competent or simply not within the discipline. When I try again to envision the pool of persons who are still in the department only because of the protection of tenure, the offbeat researchers are, I think, greatly outnumbered by those who are unproductive, poor teachers, or beset by emotional and personality problems, but once again, it is impossible to prove as much. In this kind of case we cannot know for sure what would have happened if something else happened that didn't.

One thing is clear. If tenure saves a significant number of vulnerable people we think *should* be saved, "the protection of academic freedom" is a misleading characterization of tenure's role. It is a high-sounding phrase that applies directly only to a very few cases but covers under its wing a much larger number of those who are *not* heretics and gadflies. It is possible that tenure's protection of *these* people is morally more important than its protection of political extremists.

The ethical question is whether tenure is justified after we acknowledge that protecting academic freedom is a minor function. But one may protest that the principle has nothing to do with numbers; if one person, or even no one, with aggravating politics is saved by tenure, it is the principle that counts. Such a position would be perfectly silly, as silly as Immanuel Kant's condemning lying to a murderer who asks the whereabouts of his intended victim. Of course numbers count. If tenure did no good in addition to saving one Communist or Fascist a year and did great harm to the academic profession by promoting frantic, worthless publication before tenure and protecting incompetents afterward, it should be abolished.

There is no way to find out, short of abolishing tenure, whether a significant number of competent but vulnerable people who have secure jobs under tenure would be let go if there were no tenure. However, there is little doubt that a significant number of professors fear this would happen. The question whether tenure protects incompetents distracts one from the more important question whether it protects large numbers of vulnerable people who are neither political/professional dissidents nor incompetents. It is simply amazing how the tenure literature talks about the competent and the incompetent, the fit and the unfit, not only as though the boundary were sharp but also as though there were no other significant categories of people vitally dependent on tenure. Omitted from these discussions is the relatively large group of the merely vulnerable whom I hypothesize tenure saves.

Pure and ambitious meritocrats will claim that the merely mediocre, who do not demonstrate the actual incompetence necessary for dismissal under a tenure system, can and should be let go if tenure is abolished and better candidates are available. In other words, after abolition everyone should be treated as the untenured are said to be treated now. That tenure functions to prevent such meritocracy (*if* indeed the meritocrats would take power and actually do it) is the grain of truth in John Livingston's argument that tenure's proper role is the protection of the incompetent; he should have said mediocre or vulnerable instead of incompetent. Even so, one needs to answer the ambitious meritocrat and defend the position that protecting the vulnerable is by itself an adequate rationale for tenure, even if it were not needed to protect academic freedom.

One problem is that the categories of disagreeable, mediocre, dissident, eccentric, and incompetent professors shade off into one another. Meritocrats cannot fault tenure for protecting people who are vulnerable only in the sense of having personality problems, being homosexual, or being on the losing side of a departmental civil war. The vulnerable, in this sense, may be perfectly competent teachers and scholars.

But many professors in middle (or precocious middle) age also become cranky, tired of teaching, and convinced their students are dumber every year; embittered because their articles are never cited and other universities never court them; occupied with home repairs, the local AAUP, or art collecting; and professionally unproductive. They are not incompetent. When they got tenure they were as full of promise as the new generation. But the bright young men and women who want to be in a department equal to their images of themselves want to be rid of them.

What really protects these professors? Do we have a case of overdetermination, such that tenure protects them but even if it didn't they would be protected by the sense of community and collegiality we also find in the world of business, which protects marginal people there? If so, and there were no other necessary function tenure provided, perhaps we could get rid of tenure or, alternatively, get rid of community and collegiality and rely on tenure. These are both disagreeable alternatives, largely because they are not totally independent job-protection mechanisms; tenure is in part an expression of the communitarian sentiments found in nearly all segments of society.

I wish to argue that this class of vulnerable people should be protected and, to the extent there is justifiable skepticism about the protection burned-out businesspeople and burned-out professors receive independently of tenure, we require tenure. Utopian meritocrats and those who believe in constantly stirring up the pond say they would vote to dismiss professors who are maturing into mediocrity, but it is very difficult to know if the tough talk is more than just talk. Probably more dangerous than those eager to be surrounded by excellence are the intolerant, who believe that certain branches of their fields are worthless, however much they may be respected elsewhere.

It is important to see that if nothing besides tenure protected professors from constant comparison with others ready to replace them, they would scarcely be better off. Whenever we thought we could replace an associate or full professor with a better available one we could make his or her life miserable—through minimal raises, no research leaves, repetitive hated courses, 8 A.M. classes—with the aim of securing departure or early retirement. Protection from dismissal does not protect one from this sort of treatment.

That most departments are not perfectly ruthless in this way implies a commitment to colleagues that is independent of tenure and that therefore extends to untenured colleagues, although to a lesser degree. Evidently we *do* have commitments to the untenured: they are not in a constant, impartial competition with every new entry into the job market, as though they were merely another name on a dossier that just came in the mail. In a more practical vein, there is also a price to pay for making life miserable for tenured colleagues; for if they are as bad as we think they are, they can't move, and if they are too young to retire, they may be around for a long time not speaking to us and taking vengeance when they can.

Tenure remains necessary to protect professors when group loyalty and community break down because of internal alienation or too much raw ambition. It also protects them when performance falls below what the department will tolerate on grounds of loyalty but does not fall low enough to justify dismissal of a tenured person for cause. The protection of tenure covers this problematic and indeterminate middle ground. Professors see the possibility that fate may not smile on the remainder of their careers, the possibility of forced early retirement with a relatively small pension.

III. MERIT, COMMUNITY, AND BUILDING THE GREAT DEPARTMENT

One reason why tenure is a better job-protection scheme than a union is that it is communitarian rather than adversarial. (I ignore functions of a union that tenure does not address, such as salaries and fringe benefits.) A department aims to be a community of researchers and teachers, whereas a union is a pure interest group. An interest group defines itself in terms of some external goal—in the case of a union, success in contention with the employer as adversary—whereas a community defines itself in terms of a common social identity and common good.

Thus a citizens group formed to fight a new tax and a labor union formed to prevent dismissals and win higher wages from management have no *raison d'être* in addition to the achievement of those goals; if they completely succeed, or completely fail, interest groups dissolve because they have no values internal to themselves and hence no continuing reason to exist. One cannot become alienated from an interest group, for there is no sense of belonging or social identity from which to become alienated.

Ideally, a university is a community, and departments are smaller communities nested within it. Academic departments are more than interest groups. A person can be loyal to an academic department and to his or her colleagues, identify with it and share common values, and (almost inevitably) develop some sense of "insiders and outsiders," with the badge of an insider being tenure. A department can also compete with other departments and try to be the best, but it is, unless its members are totally alienated, independently a community.

We might lay out our options, ignoring variation in degree, as follows. A department can be

1. ruthless before tenure and protective thereafter,
2. ruthless both before and after tenure,
3. protective both before and after tenure,
4. protective before tenure and ruthless thereafter.

Option 4 is insane and could be part of no rational scheme, although I would not be surprised if some departments in fact follow this policy, through poor judgment, lack of mutual respect, and bitterness. There will of course be all degrees of adherence to these patterns, and with that in mind I would argue for a qualified version of option 1. But to be a meritocrat regarding the untenured is consistent with the idea that community gives us *some* special obligations toward them that complete outsiders lack, just as being a communitarian regarding the tenured is consistent with rewarding on the basis of merit. Combining these ideas implies that life before tenure is not like Thomas Hobbes's state of nature and life after tenure is not like the post office.

Tenure is the idea of a trial period followed by full community membership, a complex ritual conducted by the tenuring department leading to a recommendation of either permanent acceptance or banishment; and a department is a community of scholars and teachers who share tenure or eligibility for tenure. Tenure is much more an integral process of trial and initiation than a battle with employers, even the subsequent administrative review of departmental tenure and promotion recommendations typically involving faculty promotion and tenure committees. Tenure suits a university conceived as sets of nested communities of scholars, and suits less well a factory or cab company employing hourly workers. Tenure and department-as-community reinforce each other, whereas a union lacks the potential for this relationship.

There is a modest analogy between tenure and marriage: You choose carefully and then make a commitment for better or worse, up to a point we call incompatibility (or incompetence), infidelity (or moral turpitude). On this analogy there is implied a commitment to faculty members who are granted tenure, which by itself implies a willingness to retain people who would be let go on strict meritocratic criteria. I think that on reflection hardly anyone would accept an uncompromising meritocracy. And this impracticability is the basis of the argument that even without tenure marginal people will be protected. They will, up to a point. Couples who live together in common-law marriage share a commitment, and unless these natural commitments had existed first, humans would never have institutionalized marriage; yet for all that, a man or woman eventually wants the vow, the institutional reinforcement. So too, telling the faculty we are one big family who will take care of vulnerable people after they have been around for awhile may be true, and it may be the psychological *sine qua non* of its institutionalized form called tenure; but one still wants tenure.

Some university faculty handbooks explicitly recommend that at their annual reviews untenured professors should be compared with potential replacements from the outside, with the implication that they be let go whenever a better replacement is available. If actually practiced, this policy is not unlike situations that occurred during the Great Depression, when groups of the unemployed watched laborers from behind a fence, pointing out the slowest to the foreman. The idea that untenured professors start from scratch each year, so to speak, can be criticized on grounds of both morality and efficiency. It is much worse than a system (such as Harvard's) in which there is a clear understanding that tenured professors are almost always hired from the outside and not promoted from within. Nor is it psychologically plausible to suppose that department members could have no commitment whatever to colleagues before tenure and instantly acquire a sense of commitment toward someone at the time of tenure. We are dealing with moral sentiments, attitudes, and loyalties, which grow slowly and at the same time lie behind and animate the letter of tenure regulations.

It is more likely that a department that pursues excellence with total ruthlessness regarding untenured members will not sufficiently soften this attitude regarding its tenured members. In the extreme case, one is no more committed to the tenured than to the untenured, and as eager to replace the weakest members, but now must be more ingenious and patient, and therefore crueler. Some faculty members accept this system, caring only for the reputation of their department, intrinsically or as a launching platform for the next job. Short of the extreme, there is room for reasonable differences of opinion, some departments being strongly protectionist and egalitarian and others letting it be understood that mediocre tenured faculty will be treated with respect and helped, but will receive the lowest raises and may ultimately retire as associate professors.

Every step in the appointment process imposes some degree of commitment on us. We interview candidates and deliberate very carefully not just because we don't want to have to interview again next year but because we are opting for people, deciding on them, and giving them a chance to prove themselves. They are taken into a team, into a community, and have a claim on our help and advice in their efforts to prove themselves and earn tenure. This is why it is not right to compare assistant professors each year with the new candidates who come on the market, right through the sixth-year tenure decision, and to replace them whenever available new Ph.D.'s look better—as though our fourth-year assistant professors have no greater claim on us than the graduate students on the block at the annual professional meetings.

This is not to say we cannot let someone go at any time before tenure. And this attitude is certainly compatible with the most rigorous criteria for professional accomplishment and promise before tenure is granted. Nonetheless, the mutually supportive and collegial department is not created *ex nihilo* by tenure, as though those with tenure were insiders and those without it total outsiders.

As William Van Alstyne implied, professors feel that without tenure they would be especially vulnerable. Unlike the world of retailing, insurance, or management (it is thought), academe comprises a more or less fixed and denumerable list of academic departments a professor considers acceptable, and each (except in times of rapid enrollment increases) has a more or less fixed number of positions. The people in a given field all know of one another, and someone who is dismissed as a "vulnerable person" from one department will not easily find a position in another acceptable department. Professors will not start again at a lower rank, nor will departments appoint a former full professor at lower rank. Finally, for many it is important to their sense of success that their department be one of the best. Thus one constantly hears, "Guess what, Jones is going to X," and "How in the world did Y get Smith?" In this atmosphere and given a small number of good departments, all visible to one another and constantly being compared and ranked, professors fear that, in the absence of tenure, there would be a constant process of culling from the bottom when new people can be appointed near the top.

IV. MAKING TENURE DECISIONS

I was recently asked to help review the tenure and promotion documents of about 125 departments at my university. That I would actually do this might be taken as proof that I am quite mad—at the end of the process if not at the beginning; it was, actually, a close call. There were single-page documents that said tenure was based on good teaching, service, and research, the proportions depending on the individual, and ninety-page documents that spelled out exactly how many colloquia must be given, committees served on, and papers published in a list of journals ranked from awesome to negligible (two single-author papers in journal X being equivalent to five single-author or eight [depending on who was first author] coauthored papers in journal Y), and so on.

There were documents that left the decision to the chair, requiring only that he or she consult the faculty, and others that considered the chair a clerk who transmitted the votes of the faculty to the administration. There were Hobbesian documents that assumed a war of all against all—junior staff against senior, faculty against the chair, committees against the dean. Romantic documents, premised on a high degree of trust, said that people of good will required few rules, whereas others assumed there would be bias and abuse of power without rules that attempted to anticipate every contingency. A few departments would grant tenure and promotions only by a unanimous vote of the eligible faculty members; others required a simple majority; and some had complex, multistage voting procedures. These statements of the goals and criteria for granting tenure expressed the spectrum of political philosophies, from anarchism to class struggle to monarchy.

There was, in the late sixties through the seventies, a deep distrust of administrators. It was thought that administrators, if they could, would exercise naked power without regard to faculty and student wishes and, more specifically, would fire people for their politics, race, or gender. Faculty members had become alienated and felt that their relation to all institutional bodies was adversarial, leading them to insist on the replacement of discretionary authority with a combination of detailed rules and direct democracy that included the right of students and untenured professors to vote.

It is another kind of mistrust, deeper but apolitical, to recognize that when one's vital interests, such as salary, tenure, and promotion, are at risk, objectivity is likely to succumb to self-interest. It is this second kind of mistrust that says no one untenured should participate in tenure decisions, that conflicts of interest are real and can corrupt our colleagues and ourselves. It reflects an attitude toward the human condition, rather than an attitude toward transitory social conditions. People can grow out of biases, and to a large degree they have, but not out of self-interest. One would, I submit, have to think professors were Rousseauian noble savages and as innocent as eggs about the subtleties of rationalization to allow assistant professors to vote for the tenure of colleagues, or to allow anyone to vote for appointment to a rank higher than one's own.

The direct democracy favored in the seventies clashed with common sense about human frailty. The idea of interestedness was stood on its head and everyone with "an interest" in hiring or tenure was thought to deserve the vote, including students and untenured faculty. Yet, as the untenured ought not vote on tenure because they care too much, students ought not vote on tenure or faculty appointments because they do not care enough. They will be gone in a few years and do not have to live for the next thirty years with the consequences of their decisions. The crucial distinction is between having a legitimate interest and having a conflict of interest. Assistant professors and tenured associate professors both have a significant personal interest in a colleague's tenure, but assistant professors can be tempted to vote yes or no to increase the likelihood of their own tenure (yes, if two of them have promised to vote for each other, no, in order to ensure space for oneself or to eliminate a probable no vote on one's own tenure).

No one should vote for tenure or promotion who does not have to pay the long-term costs of a bad appointment. This rule would disqualify students, faculty in geographically separate branch campuses, and emeriti. The same kind of reasoning applies to the composition of search committees. I have seen a first-year untenured professor placed on a chairperson search committee because he was thought of as a very bright young man. He cast his weight and the next year went on to another university.

Yet, one may counter, associate or full professors may vote against tenure because they do not like the candidate's politics or because they want to make room for another analytic epistemologist instead of this candidate. Why are these reasons not disqualifying if concern about one's own tenure is? Why isn't this called conflict of interest, since the good of the department tells the full professor to vote yes and self-interest (interest in getting someone in one's field) counsels voting no?

Part of the answer is that voting no from self-love and self-preservation is a kind of corruption about which we have a clear and distinct idea, in contrast to zealotries, biases, and special interests that shade off into legitimately debatable criteria. Part is that it is impossible in practice to disqualify tenured faculty members who have apparently illegitimate reasons for opposing a candidate. And finally, part of the answer is that the tenured professors have been admitted to the club, married "for better or worse," which makes no sense if they can't vote, and the most we can do is shame them when their objections are biased or cranky. To rebut the last point one must reject the whole tenure system.

There is another reason why students ought not vote on departmental policy and personnel matters and why assistant professors ought not vote on tenured appointments. They do not know enough and are not wise enough; having an interest in the outcome is not enough. This is a correlation that holds on average and it would lead to chaos to attempt to decide individually when the young were wiser than the old. The young who are indignant at this claim should remember that they themselves expect to be significantly wiser and more knowledgeable in another twenty or thirty years.

When dean's committees evaluate candidates for tenure and promotion they count publications, look at where books and articles are published and try to appraise them, they read the chair's letter of recommendation and the outside evaluations (if there are any), and they look at peer and student evaluations of teaching. At most major universities they talk very seriously about the candidate's teaching, but negative evaluations do not weigh heavily unless the candidate is nearly catatonic in class or otherwise dramatically incompetent. Evidence that the candidate is a brilliant teacher will be proclaimed to be very important and clear evidence that the candidate deserves tenure, once the committee has already made up its mind that the candidate deserves tenure on the basis of publications. If the publication record is borderline, the brilliant teaching may be of some slight assistance to the candidate.

The hypocrisy I have implied is forced by the public stand research-oriented universities take, and most noticeably if they are publicly supported, that teaching is more important than research. Indeed, one must always list tenure and promotion criteria in the order, "teaching, research, and service." It is hypocritical because, regardless of what presidents and provosts say in public, in practice research comes first. It is also hypocritical because most people in such institutions believe that research *should* come first. They do not believe they are school-teachers, though the legislature, the undergraduates, and the public see them so; they are professionals called chemists, historians, criminologists, and so on, whose responsibilities also include teaching. In a responsible research-oriented university good researchers who are hopeless teachers will be let go with great reluctance, or they will be retained and kept away from undergraduates.

It is also true that the best researchers are hardly ever the worst teachers, and often are the best teachers. But the hypocrisy remains. There may be no remedy for it in the short run when dealing with legislators who refuse to see professors as other than teachers. Yet it is, I believe, the obligation of research-oriented universities to defend their priorities as openly and honestly as possible. They should not pretend that teaching is the most important criterion of tenure and promotion when it clearly is not. Administrators ought to defend the callings of their faculty as scholars and researchers, as well as their obligation to give students the best teachers they can. A university is not just a school. If they pretend it is, they perpetuate the hypocrisy as well as the misunderstanding of the public on which they depend for funding.

Honesty about a university's goals could require, as one solution, promoting some professors primarily as teachers, but with the understanding of higher teaching loads and possibly lower salaries. Good researchers would cost more than good teachers because there is a more competitive market for them. And there is a more competitive market because stellar individual researchers bring a university more fame, they can do more good for the world, and great research is much more newsworthy than great teaching.

It is commonly complained that when students evaluate professors they tend to give the highest ratings to the professors who best entertain them or whose personalities or looks they like. It is said, rightly, that students are rarely in a position to make worthwhile evaluations of the content or level of difficulty of the course. These considerations by themselves cast doubt on the reasonableness of using student evaluations of teaching in tenure, promotion, and merit-raise decisions. This does not mean that one should ignore the evidence of dramatic student approval or disapproval of a professor.

A matter less often raised, however, concerns a conflict of interest in the student evaluation of teaching that renders the system morally questionable. Typically, students fill out questionnaires on the last day of class, when they know all of their grades in the course with the exception of the final examination grade and the course grade. They are in no way answerable for what they anonymously write. Students have a risk-free opportunity to punish professors who have not given them the grades they believe they deserve. If anything is a situation in which duty (to rate teachers objectively) is in potential conflict with interest (getting even, "tit-for-tat"), it is the student evaluation of teaching. What is curious is that professors and administrators are disqualified if a situation presents a similar potential for conflict of interest. Why are students exempt from conflict-of-interest safeguards? Are they more moral than professors? If today we treat students as adults, it seems reasonable to treat them as liable to the vices as well as the virtues of adults.

The preceding discussion of tenure defends it for reasons that are not as solid and simple as "academic freedom." Nor can I cleanly opt for community over meritocracy. We should, I argued, be tough in appointing and in granting tenure but should accept those who survive the extended tenure ritual as members of our little tribe, to be helped and encouraged but ultimately simply protected. But not even this is a crisp dichotomy, for the untenured are not totally at the mercy of considerations of merit, "community" membership being a condition that is acquired gradually and already exists to a slight extent at the moment of hiring. The moment of hiring is rather like conception, the awarding of tenure like birth, and the six-year gestation between these events a time during which a professor is neither an "insider" nor a complete outsider who can be terminated on demand.

But do not these characteristics also justify tenure in the world of business? One possible answer is that the situations are the same and therefore either business should adopt tenure too or the academic world should abandon it. A different and optimistic answer is that each profession has evolved what is approximately right for it, different kinds of business having different degrees and kinds of job protection. A more modest answer is that each profession—colleges and different kinds of business—has the kind of job protection it was caused to have, a result partly of what is suitable to it and partly of tradition, which may express reasons that no longer apply.

There may not be any completely satisfying explanation of why what makes tenure reasonable for the academic world doesn't apply to a business. Academe's institution is de facto peculiar, to a degree relative to what it is compared with. As for whether it should remain so, I have tried to provide some reasons that, in the Tocquevillian tradition, unite meritocracy and community in a strained marriage but provide only the barest sketch of how colleges and universities are relevantly different from businesses.

NOTES

1. James O'Toole, "A Conscientious Objection," in *Three Views: Tenure* (New Rochelle, N.Y.: Change Magazine Press, 1979).
2. John R. Silber, "Tenure in Context," in *The Tenure Debate*, ed. Bardwell L. Smith et al. (San Francisco: Jossey-Bass, 1973).
3. *American Association of University Professors: Policy Documents and Reports* (Washington, D.C.: AAUP, 1984).
4. William Van Alstyne, "A Conscientious Objective," in *Three Views: Tenure*, p. 41.
5. James O'Toole, "A Conscientious Objection," p. 29.
6. John Livingston, "Tenure Everyone?" in *The Tenure Debate*, p. 59.

4

ETHICS IN ACADEMIC PERSONNEL PROCESSES:
The Tenure Decision

Rudolph H. Weingartner

Most personnel decisions—appointing, promoting, dismissing, just to name some central ones—are not at all peculiar to the academy but part and parcel of most human enterprises with a modicum of complexity. The ethics of personnel decisions in colleges and universities is a special topic only because these institutions differ from the likes of Coca-Cola bottling plants or headquarters of insurance companies in ways that are ethically relevant. To get a purchase on those ethical issues that are peculiar to decisions in the academy (and to other institutions to the degree to which they resemble it), I will begin with some comments on the ethics of a personnel decision in an artificially simple venture.

Our model enterprise is a supermarket with four levels of employees, plus the owner. The lowest level consists of workers without supervisory roles, in such categories as cashiers, packers, shelvers, food handlers, truck unloaders, clerks, and janitors. The department heads make up the next level, with some departments responsible for types of merchandise (for example, dairy products, baked goods), while others are functional (for example, maintenance, bookkeeping). The third level contains assistant managers to whom the manager assigns a variety of duties, including supervising department heads and taking turns at being in charge of the store. The manager is chief operating officer; a more distant owner functions as chief executive officer.

What are some of the ethical issues that become relevant when an assistant manager's position opens and one or several department heads are considered for promotion to that position? (Familiarity with the store, I will hypothesize, is so desirable, that the manager will hire from outside only if the qualifications of incumbent department heads fall below a certain threshold.) The broad ethical requirements—here as most everywhere—are the obligations to be fair to each candidate and to treat each of them as a person, not worrying here whether the latter principle derives from the Golden Rule or from Kant's injunction not to treat anyone as a means only.

But such general statements do not become helpful until we gain an idea of the measures such ethical treatment call for. The first five, now to be mentioned briefly, pertain to the decision process itself; the final, complex one refers to conditions that precede it. I will suggest how each of these principles would apply in our supermarket.

1. EQUAL TREATMENT. *Fairness requires that all candidates for promotion be treated in the same way, from informing eligible candidates, to gathering evidence, to the manner of consideration. Fairness prohibits playing favorites.*

In this case, all department heads need to be informed (and only they, assuming that this position is a requirement); each must be instructed regarding the procedure for applying; and the method by which candidates are considered—perusal of written material, consultation of referees, interview—must be similar for everyone.

2. THE RELEVANCE AND COMPLETENESS OF THE EVIDENCE CONSIDERED. *Every person has an indefinitely large number of characteristics and abilities. For the performance of any given job, only a subclass of these are brought into play. Fairness requires that all and only the (available) evidence for the presence (or absence) of traits that are relevant becomes an ingredient in the decision.*

This requirement enjoins the manager not to weigh irrelevant characteristics in the decision—not to be "prejudiced" against a race or hair color nor to prefer someone from the same neighborhood. That is, the employer must not pay heed to any trait that plays no role in the performance of the envisaged duties. Evidence that the candidate nags her husband is irrelevant if there is no evidence that she nags her coworkers.

3. CONSCIENTIOUSNESS OF CONSIDERATION. *Since evidence can be considered cursorily or thoroughly, one needs to point out that fairness calls for being conscientious in carrying out that task.*

Thoroughness is most likely limited to interviewing several supervisors who are acquainted with a candidate's performance, interviewing the candidate and examining evidence (tests, work samples) concerning the ability to perform skilled tasks, such as doing accounting. To give inadequate consideration is to "jump to conclusions" without making use of an appropriate quantity of evidence.

4. TIMELINESS OF THE DECISION. *Just as morality requires that justice be swift, so there is an obligation to candidates for promotion to know of the decision in a timely manner, both for the sake of mental comfort and to permit candidates to plan their lives.*

Every enterprise has its own rhythms. Here, with few candidates and a simple process of consideration, the stretch of time from start to finish should be confined to a very few weeks.

5. CANDOR. *Concern for the candidate as a person—with a life to lead and plans to make—requires that when a promotion is not granted, the candidate be provided with the reasons for this failure. The power to decide implies the obligation to be candid.*

This stipulation requires no more and no less than a conversation with each of the unsuccessful candidates in which he or she is informed about the perceived shortcomings that led to the negative decision, as well as about future prospects.

6. PROMULGATION OF CONDITIONS FOR PROMOTION. *The process by means of which it is decided whether someone is or is not promoted cannot be fair unless the candidate knows all relevant aspects of this process. Three components seem crucial.*

a. *Potential candidates need to know whether or not promotion of a given sort is possible. Promotion must not be like grace that is granted to whom it is granted, even if the grantor has good reasons.*

This principle calls for the promulgation of a policy, clearly setting forth who (what positions: department heads) are eligible for consideration for promotion to which posts (assistant manager).

b. *Potential candidates need to know what is desired in a successful candidate for promotion and what is considered to be evidence for the possession of the desired characteristics.*

It must be conveyed with sufficient clarity—however informally—what skills and experience are needed to be appointed assistant manager and what kind of references, tests, and interviews are considered relevant evidence.

   c. *Potential candidates must be apprised of how they should proceed*
      to apply for promotion, so that they can act to be considered.
      In the small enterprise envisaged, a visible display of the
      notice announcing that there is an opening and giving in-
      structions on how to apply would seem sufficient.

    I

Some of these obligations, so briefly stated, apply virtually unchanged
or in a clearly analogous way to personnel decisions in the academy;
in any case, about some of them, no further mention will be made,
important though they are. But colleges and universities are very
different from the relatively simple supermarket just considered; not
surprisingly, some of the differences impinge on the ethical considerations that govern personnel decisions about faculty members.[1] What
now follow are sketches of those characteristics of the academy relevant to my topic. And even though some of them are at the core of
what an academic institution is, only enough will be said here to
illuminate my quite specific theme.

Individual faculty members have a *complex role*, in part by virtue
of the plurality of goals of academic institutions, which cannot be
subsumed under a single heading. The conventional formulation of
this complex role refers to teaching, research, and service.

Individual faculty members have a kind of *independence* that is rare
among employees of other institutions. To a significant degree, they
decide not only on the way in which they accomplish their goals but
also on the goals themselves. With respect both to research and to
teaching, faculty members are much more like independent contrac-
tors than they are like functionaries responsible to a supervisor.

With respect to the two central functions of a faculty member—
teaching and research—a faculty member enjoys what is called *academic freedom*. One important aspect of this institution is that the entire
faculty community has an interest in the freedom of any individual,
such that some aspects of a faculty member's independence have a
quasi-juridical foundation. The granting of contracts of indefinite tenure (simply referred to as tenure in the academic vernacular) is the
most important mainstay of this freedom.

In good part as a consequence of some of the characteristics so far
cited, faculty members have a role in their own *governance*. Looked at
from the administrative side of the coin, such participation constitutes
a diffusion of authority. However, institutions vary considerably in

this respect; at the collegial end of the continuum, administrators exercise authority essentially in behalf of the faculty.

Not only are faculty members relatively independent, with some aspects of that independence juridically protected, they also differ from each other to a high degree. The *division of labor* in the academy is such that a considerable portion of the teaching and, especially, the research that faculty members engage in is importantly (and intentionally) different from that of all other faculty members.

Much administration in the academy is carried out by *amateurs*, in the sense that by and large administrators do not move up a ladder of positions of similar character (though increased scope), so that the experience in one position is often not the foundation for a subsequent administrative position. Depending on the institution, appointments at various administrative levels are for limited terms only.

Colleges and universities have *students*, whose role is different from that of the customers of a supermarket. It is inappropriate to say to students in college (or to patients in a hospital): *caveat emptor.* Students, however, are at least temporary members of the academic community, in a way in which patients do not "belong" to a hospital.

II

Many different kinds of personnel decisions are made in the academy—from appointment to removal from tenure for unprofessional conduct, from determining salary increases to disciplinary actions for having engaged in sexual harassment. Of them all, the decision to confer (or withhold) tenure is in many ways the most important faculty personnel decision.[2] Further, this is surely the decision that is most distinctive of the academy, especially if one recalls that its original function is the support of academic freedom, rather than the provision of job security.[3] Finally, the conferring (or withholding) of tenure is the personnel decision that is almost always based upon the most elaborate procedure devised by an institution—with the possible exception of the decision to *take away* tenure. For these reasons, I will use the tenure decision as the model for the exploration of ethical considerations in personnel decisions in the academy.

One is immediately struck by the multiplicity of levels involved in a tenure decision, compared to promotion in the supermarket. In the latter world, the performance of supervisors is judged in significant part by the performance of those hired and promoted by them. In this way, other, higher, managers control such personnel decisions through the evaluation of the decider, rather than by direct participation in "lower" personnel decisions. But almost all of the special characteristics of the academy I have just sketched bear on the unworkability of such a "simple" assignment of personnel responsibility to a single administrator. Instead, departmental committees recommend to departments and departmental chairs; these, in turn, recommend to the dean. Further, at some institutions a committee specifically formed to advise on a particular case so recommends, while at others, a standing committee on promotion and tenure performs that task; both function at still others. The dean, in turn, recommends to the chief academic officer—who may or may not also seek the advice of a committee—and who, in turn, recommends to the president, who recommends to a board of trustees.

The reading of such a summary induces sympathy with the non-academic's puzzlement about our cumbersome processes, since the collegial character of the academy, which accounts for so much of it, is so distant from the customs of our supermarket. But what perplexes outsiders—collegiality and complexity—also becomes fertile soil for ethical problems for participants. At worst, the process that leads to a tenure decision resembles the trial of Josef K. or an inscrutable black box issuing verdicts. Even when a procedure actually *is* fair, murkiness of process and the length of time it takes to get done are sources of anxiety to the candidate. To the degree to which unclarity and delays are unnecessary, they are immoral.

While I will discuss a number of measures that contribute both to the "objective" fairness of the procedure and to its clarity, I fear that certain causes of anxiety are well nigh uneliminable. To begin with, the academy fosters a lethal mixture, in the same head, of expectations of rationality and considerable power of vivid imagination. Scholars are brought up to be dissatisfied until they know the reasons for things; they work at making explicit what otherwise would remain hidden and opaque. In addition, the ability (indeed, tendency) to imagine a multitude of possibilities is distributed far more lavishly in the academic world than elsewhere in society, so that the scholarly ethos generates fantasies that are rooted in the human fear of failure, combined with a lack of knowledge about how the decision process functions and what it is doing at a given juncture.

Nor are complexity and the long stretch of time that elapses readily eliminated, unless one sacrifices other significant components of good decision making in a setting in which criteria are complex and collegiality is a central value. The task, rather, is to maximize clarity of role and accountability, for these measures will contribute both to the adequacy of the decisions made and to the confidence of the community that the process if fair.[4]

III

What must be clear, above all, is the locus of the decision itself. The manager of the supermarket decides who will be assistant manager. Who decides whether someone attains tenure or not? Collegiality describes only one aspect of a faculty member's relationship to the institution: even in the most collegial American colleges and universities, faculties do not wholly govern themselves—on the model of the partners of a law firm or certain health maintenance organizations, where membership, duties, and share of income are determined by the collectivity, with only details and implementation delegated to managers. Usually, a corporate model is superimposed on that of the club, in which administrators (officers) and boards of trustees (directors) are given ultimate authority.

A crucial contribution, accordingly, to the ethical acceptability of the process is the conceptual clarification that assigns to many participants the function of *advising* and *recommending*, while identifying one person as the *maker of the decision*. That person—the dean, the academic vice-president, or the president, depending on the institution—must thus regard as *advisers* all those who contributed, directly or indirectly, to the recommendation now on his or her desk and must look upon him- or herself as the person who decides, even if by custom a recommendation constitutes a severe constraint. Clarity about this division of functions has more than one serious implication for the ethics of this central personnel decision in the academy.[5]

The clear identification of a normal decision maker is a necessary condition for adequate treatment of at least four ethical issues central to this promotion process. (If only for stylistic reasons, I will refer to the deciding administrator as the dean, even though it is often another officer.) Let me state them in brief, with some elaboration to follow.

First, as decision maker, the dean is in charge of the entire process, with ultimate responsibility for the designation of the participants and the assignment and performance of their roles. This is the case even where faculty legislation "dictates" much of the procedure. Where a governance scheme does not support responsibility with authority, it must thus be seen as morally flawed.

Second, the dean, on my hypothesis, is responsible for the articulation of the criteria that function in the decision about promotion to tenure. However complex the collegial process that formulates them in the first place, they "become" those of the person applying them in a decision.

Third, the person who makes the decision is the person who must conscientiously weigh the evidence. This requirement is intimately tied to the management of the process that amasses the evidence in the first place. But it also implies that the dean cannot hide behind such a process and blame its inadequacy for the inadequacy with which the evidence might have been collected or consulted.

Fourth, the dean, like the manager of the supermarket, is the person who must give the reasons to a candidate for a failure to promote. In this way, the candidate is provided with a means for partially assessing the fairness of the judgment, not because he or she should be expected to agree with verdict and justification but because plausibility can to a limited degree reduce the suspicion of unfairness. Moreover, it helps the candidate to know the reasons for this lack of success, so as to be able to access his or her future prospects in the profession and as information for making plans. Except for certain difficulties in actually stating the reasons, the requirement is identical to that in the supermarket.[6]

IV

A certain complexity of the decision process, I have said, is uneliminable, and I have partially attributed that condition to the collegiality of the academy. The complexity of the criterion—or, if one prefers, the multiplicity of interrelated criteria—by means of which candidates for tenure are judged is also grounds for broad participation in the decision process. The components of the canonical trio—teaching, research, and service—are together incommensurable, nor are they individually quantifiable in any satisfactory way. Each is manifested differently in different fields; and even within a field, satisfactoriness and excellence have many different guises. Moreover, for many reasons, the criterion (and not just the stringency of standards) varies from institution to institution.

It is nevertheless worth bringing out one substantive and one procedural "bottom line." On the material side, recall that the institutions we are talking about have students and not simply customers in the fashion of the supermarket. They cannot turn and walk out (and try the place in the next block) the moment they don't see what they like. Students are tied to institutions vastly more strongly than shoppers to stores, and their ability to assess wares put before them is in serious ways restricted. (Not the least, readers of Plato will recall, because teaching is the kind of activity where a student cannot first read the label before deciding to "take in" the lesson.) The academy thus has a moral obligation to be concerned with the way its professors affect their students, an obligation that clearly must play a role in the process that decides about promotion to tenure.[7]

On the procedural side, the complexity of the criterion must not obscure the obligation to promulgate. Broad statements can be made to the faculty community, and such statements do convey useful information, even if its precision is limited. What evidence about teaching is considered and how much? Does advising matter, or supervising doctoral candidates? Is community service a serious ingredient and, if so, within what limitations? Do the products of research need to be published in refereed publications? Articulation on these topics characterizes the institution to its faculty—especially to newcomers— and directs faculty behavior by stipulating broad goals. As such, a fair personnel process requires conveying to potential candidates what is called for from the kind of faculty members who would be tenured.

Nevertheless, we should acknowledge that we cannot actually spell out a criterion of acceptability (including a threshold degree of excellence) in a long disjunction; we must rely instead on making comparisons, tacit and explicit, with relevant exemplary individuals who are recognized as deserving their tenured status and with the accomplishments that brought them there. And this ultimate "ineffability" of the criterion of promotability makes it most sensitive to distortion and thus puts the burden of fairness squarely on the participants in the process and on how they do their job.[8]

Before returning to a discussion of the process, I want to comment briefly on one desideratum for promotability that is particularly vulnerable to distortion. Since tenure constitutes a contract of indefinite term, how the candidate can be expected to "fit in" is a question that is inevitably asked, even if not always explicitly. However professional one's attitude, such considerations cannot be altogether purged from the criterion of acceptability. What if the would-be tenured colleague is a congenital liar and never reliable *as* a colleague? What if he or she is subject to frequent uncontrollable temper tantrums that disrupt meetings and all such common tasks as creating a collective final examination? If, then, we must pay *some* attention to the capacity to pitch in, to work with others, to cooperate in a common enterprise,[9] there is also a real danger of sliding from reasonable concern to the unethical use of irrelevant information.

It is illegal to use race or sex as a reason for not promoting: legislation prohibits it. But note that when sex or race does function as a screen in a promotion process, it does so because of an underlying belief (or feeling) that a woman, or in some contexts a man, or a black would not fit in to the group (the department, the school) as it is constituted. This illegal behavior, it is worth remembering, is also unethical. It bases a judgment on traits that are not relevant for the performance of the job under consideration, precisely because it is not the candidate's ability—to cooperate, say—that is under scrutiny but the potential discomfort (if that's what it is) of the existing group's members to do the cooperating.

No doubt this explication is much oversimplified, but a lesson can nevertheless be derived for the ethical application of the criterion of "fitting in." Just as there is prejudice against women, so there is prejudice against people who tend to be grubby; just as there is aversion to blacks, so there is aversion to very fat people. The moral obligation of those who decide on tenure goes beyond behavior that is legally proscribed: only those characteristics that play a role in the performance of a function—even a most complex one—may be considered in the formation of a judgment. Such characteristics, moreover, must have relevant institutional consequences, where "relevant," again, must be job-related. When failure to "fit in" is not dependent on the candidate's (predicted) behavior or institutional impact, but simply on the views and feelings of the group, morality rules it out from consideration.[10]

V

This brief sketch of the difficulties with a single component of the complex criterion used in the decision to promote merely reinforces the claim that the participants in the decision process are responsible for the ethical acceptability of tenure decisions. While most aspects of this procedure have ethical implications, actual or potential, I want in particular to focus (and on a fairly abstract level) on three issues I take to be central.

First, some observations about the selection and organization of the individuals who will participate in the decision. To begin with, institutions vary greatly in the number and kinds of faculty levels that play a role in a tenure decision. By no means do all such differences have ethical implications, but it very much does matter that there be more than one faculty level, with the "higher" representing a broader constituency than the "lower." In this way a wider perspective is introduced, capable of serving as a potential check to parochialism, a limitation that tends to give too much prominence to personal traits of marginal relevance.

With respect to the selection of participants at different levels, considerable variations may still make no ethical difference. It does however make a difference, from a moral point of view, that the *method* of selecting participants be the same for each class of candidates. Arbitrariness in the designation of those who help make judgments is the enemy of fairness.

It also matters that those who are selected to stand in judgment of the candidate are appropriate for that role. That faculty members of the same or lower rank should not be party to the formulation of a recommendation is widely understood. Actual or potential competitors cannot seem to be fair judges, even if in fact they are capable of the requisite objectivity. There is, by way of interesting contrast, more disagreement about the role students should play, with both extremes—full participation and no role at all—finding passionate defenders. The introduction of a criterion and of a distinction will be helpful in sorting out this controversy.

Those who appropriately participate in the recommendation on a promotion should surely be qualified to do so. While another sense of "qualification" will be taken up shortly, we have no choice but to assume that credentialed colleagues are qualified. Students, on the other hand, lack those credentials. They are generally unable to judge a faculty member's research and service, if only because they have not acquired the experience of dealing knowledgeably with testimony and letters of reference on such topics. Even if one assumes, then, that students are capable of determining the effectiveness of a faculty member as a teacher, the handicaps just mentioned would make them very unequal participants in the formulation of a judgment to be based on so much broader a criterion.

But students have a perspective—derived from knowledge and concern—that is not possessed by faculty colleagues in equal measure. And as "consumers" of education, their perspective is relevant to providing a full account of the work of a faculty member. The reconciliation of the "no" of the previous paragraph and the "yes" of the current one must then be achieved by means of the distinction between participant and consultant. Just as departmental and other committees

consult scholars throughout the world about the quality and importance of a candidate's research (without having those scholars participate in the formulation of the summative judgment), so the faculty
can turn to student committees and to records of the evaluation of
teaching by students to obtain advice from this constituency of the
academy.

But there is an additional aspect to being qualified which, though
of considerable ethical relevance, is nonetheless often ignored. Credentials are a necessary but not a sufficient qualifying condition for
taking part in deciding. Justified participation must be informed participation; no voice should be permitted to speak unless its owner has
done the homework that entitles. We know that the academy subsists
on paper: for every candidate, a massive amount of it is collected into
a dossier, which then becomes the primary evidence for the verdict to
be given. To participate in deciding without having a grasp of the
material that was systematically collected to serve as the basis of the
required judgment introduces an element of arbitrariness at best and
irrelevant prejudice—for or against—at worst. Managers of the promotion process have a duty to ensure that participants are qualified
by being prepared.

Although I believe the third issue to have great moral relevance,
it is nevertheless frequently ignored. Fairness (not to mention good
decision making) requires that each group that functions in the recommending process engage in face-to-face discussions on the issue of
the merit of the candidate. Members of departmental committees,
departmental senior faculties, ad hoc committees, promotions committees—whatever the units—must not simply be polled for a count of
votes; rather, its members must have been present during an informed
discussion of all aspects of the case. Absence must imply disenfran-
chisement and a reduction, at best, to the role of (nonvoting) consultant.

Two reasons support this thesis: one follows from the complexity
of the criterion of tenurability and the other is a corrective to the
dangers of unfairness in a process that is mostly conducted behind
the veil of confidentiality. Some reflections on confidentiality will
follow; a few comments here will surely suffice to spell out an implication of what was earlier said about the standard by which candidates
are judged. That criterion is multifaceted, incommensurable, non-
quantifiable. It is complicated in exactly the way that calls for the
deployment of more than one mind if all aspects are to be adequately
seen and weighed. This kind of personnel decision—far more than

most meetings academics busy themselves with—justifies the time taken by groups of people engaged in informed discussion. There is here a reasonable expectation that the picture of a candidate that emerges at the end of a discussion will have greater verisimilitude than any that might have been produced by one participant alone.

Yet still more important than this positive result is the efficacy of discussion for dispelling misapprehensions and jumps to conclusions of all kinds. Mill's *On Liberty* points to the necessity of open discussion if, on a larger canvas, we are to make progress toward the truth. Similarly here, the clash of opinions in discussion tends to combat error and unwarranted assumptions. No one *eligible* to vote on the fate of a candidate (and of the institution) should therefore have the *right* to vote without having participated in a discussion with informed peers.

VI

Unethical behavior is possible in broad daylight, but no doubt the risks become greater under the cover of confidentiality. Mostly we know when we do something wrong; having other people in a position to find out has a tendency to discourage us—at least in such polite circles as the academy. *Prima facie*, an ethical case can be made against the practice of confidentiality in personnel decisions: an open process is more likely to be fair to the candidate being considered. Moreover, the lifting of confidentiality would certainly eliminate much of the anxiety that is engendered by the opaqueness of the decision process.

But clearly, more is to be said if one reflects on some of the reasons for the practice of confidentiality. Leave aside the important (and ethically relevant) consideration of protecting the candidate from public exposure—from a display of actual inadequacies to expressions of half truths, surmises, and occasional lies about the person. Surely, confidentiality is practiced because it is believed that if assured of privacy, participants will make "more honest" (here meaning "harsher") assessments of candidates and will in this way better serve the institution.

I have no doubt that this is so. The academic world is not a tough world, populated by strong egos ready to "mix it up" in personal slugging matches. Further, collegial participation is in good part voluntary and constitutes an often unwelcome intrusion on the central activities of the teacher-scholar. Certainly the referee who gives time to a sister institution by making and conveying judgments about the work of a candidate does so as a volunteer, often a reluctant one. Given these underlying truths, it is highly likely (though subject to empirical testing) that decisions made by means of a process that eschews confidentiality will be "softer" and lean somewhat more toward the candidate and away from the standards of the institution.[11]

But the point to be made about this observation, assuming it to be true, is that such leaning away from the interests of the institution is not ethically neutral; it cannot be granted that the ethical field belongs entirely to the candidate, so that anything that might improve his or her chances of success constitutes moral improvement.

The impersonality of the term *institution* is misleading. Talk about standards of that entity must be translatable, if we are to make sense, into talk about ways in which colleagues, and students—present and future—are affected and how a decision impinges, in a world of finite resources, on future candidates for the same status. Reduced propinquity, relative to the palpable presence of the candidate, might call for some differential weighing; in no way, however, can the effect of a decision on an institution be considered to be morally neutral. If, thus, confidentiality makes the process fairer to the institution, that too has ethical relevance.

In any case, if in any institutions confidentiality is accepted as a fact of life, it should be observed that several of the measures earlier stressed will act to reduce the likelihood of negative ethical consequences. A nonarbitrary way of selecting the participants in a process, including the thoughtful designation of scholar-consultants on the candidate's work, becomes important. More important still is discussion at all levels, where distortions stand a chance of being revealed and countered. Crucial, finally, is the assumption of responsibility by the decision maker for the integrity of the process as a whole.[12]

VII

One is strongly tempted to go on and provide more detail regarding the ethical issues that have been raised, to continue with additional ethical implications of the tenure process (and there are such), as well as to put forward more elaborate justifications for the various claims and suggestions made. No doubt, the source of that pressure—here to be resisted—is the recognition that personnel decisions in the academy are like life, where much of our behavior has ethical implications and we are very frequently called upon to decide what is right, what is better, and to justify our decision. Institutions, however, even colleges and universities, have a way of veiling the fact that we are moral agents by permitting us to hide behind rules and procedures that were formulated by anonymous administrators or legislated by faculties acting corporately. One is lulled into the belief that as one plays a certain role assigned to one in a given process, one does so detached from the fact that one always remains a person.

I hope that this sampling of ethical issues in the tenure process has exhibited some heuristic truths. In the end, *individuals* decide, *individuals* act and the fate of *individuals* is determined by personnel decisions, including present and future students, present and future colleagues. Since significant roles in the personnel processes of the academy are assigned to administrators and to faculty members, they bear a responsibility both for the ethical acceptability of the procedures used and for the way in which they are implemented from case to case.

To be sure, for each degree of seriousness of an undertaking, an appropriate degree of conscientiousness is required. Some decisions call for most scrupulous care, while many others do not demand similarly elaborate cogitations. But in our human world, there are no oases in which the obligation to be conscientious has been repealed. The examples here given of some ethical implications of various steps in the tenure process should show that ethical reflection is relevant and makes a difference. We should resolve, therefore, to think of all personnel decision in the academy as taking place in a world in which the actors are moral agents who have ethical responsibilities.

NOTES

1. Perhaps ethical considerations pertaining to personnel decisions about secretaries, grounds keepers, or cafeteria workers, etc. are modified by the fact that they work in an institution of higher education. However that may be, I shall here be concerned only with decisions about faculty members.

2. Conventional wisdom certainly has it that the tenure decision is the most important. Years of observing and administering have led me to the belief that the decision to appoint has a still more important effect on the institution (not to say the individual), since those *considered* for tenure have to have been appointed and since more of them (in "regular" positions) receive it than not. Exempted from this generalization are those institutions where the decision to confer tenure is fully analogous to the decision to appoint.

3. I say "original" function, because today the primary role of tenure is held to be that of providing job security. But when faculty members will once again be in short supply—and assuming no millennial changes in the political

climate inside and outside the academy—the issue of security will wane, and tenure is again likely to stand above all for academic freedom.

4. One way in which much unclarity would be dispelled in one fell swoop is with the complete elimination of confidentiality in the decision process. To that topic I will turn toward the end of these comments.

5. That in virtually all colleges and universities there are "higher" powers who have the right to overturn the "decision" made "lower" down should not be permitted to confuse the point just made. There is a *normal* decision maker—the dean, for example—who has certain duties (yet to be discussed) if the process is to be ethically acceptable. Nothing is changed by the possibility that provost, president, or board of trustees *might* overrule and that sometimes they do. It merely follows that when (and only when) a higher authority actually *does* overrule, a limited number of duties normally assigned to the normal decision maker—such as providing reasons for a negative decision to the candidate—are transferred to the person who made the final decision. (Note that all these comments pertain to the original decision process and not to an appeal from a decision made, a quite different matter.)

6. The American Association of University Professors has made a recommendation (*Academic Freedom and Tenure, 1940 Statement of Principles*) that is appropriate in other contexts as well. An administrator is advised to provide reasons for nonpromotion only if asked and in writing only if asked in writing—and in any case only confidentially to the candidate. This suggestion is sound, since it should indeed be up to candidates to decide how much he or she should "know" when potential future employers make inquiries about what happened. And it is certainly not up to a third party to let a wider audience know what the candidate's shortcomings are thought to be. As to the difficulty of providing reasons that are thought by the candidate to be *satisfactory*, see note 8.

7. One need hardly protest that the relationship of teacher to student is a major issue, since it includes not only the tricky one of teaching effectiveness, but such still broader ones as the teacher as nurturing support and as role model. To open up these topics, however, would be to permit the tail to wag the dog: a concern about the process of personnel decisions must not become the occasion for an essay on the central topic of the role of the faculty member in higher education. What these comments do say, however, is that at any given institution, pieces of such an essay must be written, so to speak, if its members are to become clear as to what they are doing when, among other things, they consider the promotion of a colleague.

8. These characteristics of the criterion for promotion contribute significantly to the frequent dissatisfaction of unsuccessful candidates with the reasons given for their rejection. Situations arise not unlike that of a student who asks why a paper graded B+ was not given an A. This demand is hard to satisfy, since the same lack of originality, depth, spark, or whatever that led to the B+ underlies the inability to discern the difference between what was accomplished and what is better. Salieri, in *Amadeus*, is an exception when he recognizes in just what way his music is inferior to Mozart's, while remaining unable to emulate him.

9. The academy must be more tolerant of eccentricity than most institutions; it must have room for the "mad genius," when society stands to benefit

from the work of that genius, even though the madness exacts a price. At the same time, it has to be admitted that the institutions vary in the degree to which they can *afford* to tolerate certain eccentricities. In tight places, most everyone is needed to pitch in; in plusher institutions, there is more give. Not everyone can afford to create a separate department for the impossible person whose books are seminal!

10. The concern here with the ethical characteristics of a *process* has required me to remain essentially neutral with respect to substantive criteria, with the obligation remaining for individual institutions—assumed to differ markedly from each other—to develop their own goals and criteria. To take up such issues, I have maintained, is to look—in a way that is inevitably distorting—at the main business of colleges and universities under the heading of a procedure. The matter of affirmative action, which I have tacitly raised, is another topic that is bigger than the framework here provided. Besides here noting that what has been said is not intended to be incompatible with affirmative action in faculty recruiting, I want to draw one obvious consequence that *is* here germane. Criteria that operate in recruitment or promotions activities must be made known to those affected.

11. I ignore altogether the complication that open processes provide the opportunity for another kind of politicking that also has ethical implications.

12. The practice of confidentiality is under legal and legislative pressure from a variety of sides. It is not inconceivable that in a decade or so, it will, for all practical purposes, have disappeared from personnel decisions in the academy. My optimistic speculation has it that after a dip in the quality of decision making, the academy will slowly make a transition to adulthood and its citizens will learn to accept public scrutiny of tough decisions. No doubt the fact that faculty jobs will soon be plentiful again will aid in this transition.

5

THE RESEARCH DEMANDS OF TEACHING IN MODERN HIGHER EDUCATION

Theodore M. Benditt

In the past few decades institutions of higher education have demanded greater research efforts from their faculties. Actually, this has been a phenomenon of higher education for most of this century, but there is probably a perception among college teachers that the pace has quickened in recent years. Some have applauded the strengthened emphasis on research, while others have thought it a regrettable departure from the proper mission of higher education, which, as they see it, is teaching. Many professors think that research is appropriate for certain universities, but do not think it an appropriate emphasis for their own, middle-level institutions. This article will argue, to the contrary, that research is a proper and necessary adjunct to responsible teaching in higher education. The first half of the article will sketch the history of the American college and university, characterizing the kind of institution the American university has become, and will provide a context for the argument that follows.

I. THE HISTORY OF THE AMERICAN UNIVERSITY

The early American college both before and after the Revolution was structured on the model of Oxford and Cambridge. It was, for the most part, set in the countryside, away from population centers (of which there were few). Such siting required living accommodations and naturally encouraged the paternalism (*in loco parentis*) that still lingers, although sharply diminished, as a feature of many American colleges. The colleges ministered to students' moral and religious lives through required daily morning and evening prayers and frequent revivals.

If the early American college encouraged moral discipline among students in keeping with its parental role, it also strove to instill its peculiar notion of intellectual discipline. In its earliest days the American college was under the influence of scholasticism, which penetrated college study in the form of the disputation, the use of deductive techniques to establish the validity of universal truths. Yet the colonial curriculum also reflected the Renaissance interest in literature and belles lettres and in the humanistic ideal of classical scholarship. Latin and Greek were central in the curriculum; indeed, until 1745, when arithmetic was added at Yale, Latin and Greek were the only subjects in which there were college entrance requirements. All other studies—logic, rhetoric, ethics, metaphysics, science, mathematics, and moral philosophy—were conducted in Greek and Latin.

The disputation was not designed, however, to encourage free thinking, and neither was either the curriculum or the mode of instruction in the early American college. Through all of the nineteenth century, even at institutions where sectarian ties were weak, professors were hired not for their scholarly ability or achievement but for their religious commitment. Scholarly achievement was not a high priority, either for professors or students. Colleges were concerned with supposedly inspired teaching aimed at molding young men of good character, young men who would become clergymen and statesmen. To this end, order and discipline, not inquiry, were considered essential. Students were tracked according to when they entered college—each class of freshmen, sophomores, juniors, and seniors was taught as a bloc, with no differentiation made on the basis of either ability or interest. Instruction consisted of daily classroom recitations of memorized portions of textbooks to ensure that students had read their assignments. It was assumed that the information content of the curriculum was adequate and appropriate—simple, indubitable truths purveyed by kindly, righteous professors and absorbed by dutiful and disciplined students. There was certainly no idea that students should use libraries or consult original sources rather than textbooks. Colleges had virtually no libraries at all, and those they had were limited mostly to religious books. And anyway, exposure to conflicting ideas would only undermine the inculcation of superficial truths students were meant to learn.

Sectarian interests very much informed the orientation of the early American college. Indeed, most early colleges, particularly after 1800, were founded by religious denominations eager to provide higher education for their adherents rather than see them attend the colleges of rival sects. But higher education was also religiously oriented in a general, not simply a sectarian, sense. College professors were often clergymen or at least had some theological training, and until the end of the nineteenth century college presidents were almost invariably clergymen. Piety, rather than scholarship, was one of the primary goals of higher education, holding a higher place in the scale of values than intellect. Indeed, some denominations did not believe in an educated clergy, and others, though believing in an educated clergy, thought that the purpose of education was to instill appropriate Christian virtues, if not to train young men for the clergy.

In addition to being pious, the early college was aristocratic, though these orientations were not unrelated. First, the early college was aristocratic in its focus and rationale. It took its justification to be the serving of social ends. President Joseph McKeen of Bowdoin College expressed it thus in 1802:

> It ought always to be remembered that literary institutions are founded and endowed for the common good, and not for the private advantage of those who resort to them for education. It is not that they may be able to pass through life in an easy or reputable manner, but that their mental powers may be cultivated and impressed for the benefit of society. . . . [W]e may safely assert that every man who has been aided by a public institution to acquire an education and to qualify himself for usefulness, is under peculiar obligations to exert his talents for the public good.[58]

Second, the early college was aristocratic in its clientele: it served the aristocratic elements of society, and sometimes even of English society. To be sure, being American, it was expected to be more democratic, but for a variety of reasons, financial and otherwise, it was not. For one thing, few could afford a college education. And finances aside, there was not much interest in being college educated. There were few positions for which a college education was a prerequisite. More important, the colleges were not interested in offering the practical sort of education that many Americans wanted. The colleges thus had a real problem. Although they had their own ideas of what education should be, they needed students in order to stay in business.

Challenges

A number of forces were producing pressure for changes in higher education. First, there was, consistently throughout the colonial period and into the nineteenth century, a desire on the part of many for more practical education, meaning business, agriculture, technology, and more modern science. These were not compatible with the classical approach for a number of reasons. First, they were not part of the Renaissance idea of an educated person. Second, to the extent that higher education was focused on social purposes, it was meant to train for leadership, which was thought to require cultivated, well-rounded individuals having "large and liberal views" that would give them greater distinction than the mere possession of property. Third, the primary orientation of colleges was not this-worldly; they really cared more about success in the next world than in this one.

The second force at work against the American college was dissatisfaction with the methods of teaching, spurred in part by doubt about the faculty psychology on which such methods were held to be based. The mind consists, in this view, of a number of mental faculties—the senses, the memory, reasoning, the mathematical, the poetical, and others—all of which need to be cultivated, and the right way to cultivate them is by rigorous and disciplined training of the mind. Furthermore, since everyone is the same, the same discipline, including the same course of study, is appropriate for all. By the middle to late nineteenth century this view of the mind and its powers, with its implications for education, was under attack from the new experimental approach to psychology.

Finally, the German model of education was beginning to have a significant impact on American thinking. Universities in Germany were faculty oriented, not student oriented. They offered specialized branches of instruction and graduate studies. They prized intellect and scholarship, promoting free inquiry rather than received truths. And they had *standards*. They sought excellence, not mediocrity. This orientation stood in sharp contrast to the lowest-common-denominator type of superficiality practiced in American colleges, which rested on classroom recitation of lessons from simplistic textbooks.

Early Efforts at Reform

At a number of institutions in the 1820s and 1830s there were attempts to change the character of college education in two ways, namely, to make it serve more people and to make it more intellectual. Harvard, Vermont, Amherst, the University of Nashville, and Thomas Jefferson's Virginia instituted such reforms as sectioning students according to ability; offering elective courses; offering education in manufacturing, agriculture, and finance; introducing more advanced courses; and teaching modern foreign languages and United States history. Actually, quite a number of institutions were willing to offer new subjects in order to appease demand and attract students, but the purity of the curriculum was preserved by not allowing such studies to count toward the degree.

In the end, these reform efforts were not widely accepted, withering even at the institutions that experimented with them, and the American orientation toward education was effectively set for at least another generation by the publication of a report in 1828 by the president of Yale on behalf of its faculty. In this extremely influential document the Yale faculty rejected the suggestion it had been hearing "from different quarters . . . that our colleges must be *new-modelled;* that they are not adapted to the spirit and wants of the age; that they will soon be deserted, unless they are better accommodated to the business character of the nation" (132). A superior education, it held, must rest on a proper understanding of the human mind, by which it meant faculty psychology and its accompanying psychology of learning. The study of modern foreign languages it regarded "as an accomplishment rather than as a necessary acquisition" (133). Those interested in careers in trade or manufacturing or agriculture would, it argued, be best served by the classical curriculum. The Yale Report even found that education by textbook and recitation was to be preferred to the use of original (and conflicting) sources, for "the diversity of statement in these, will furnish the student with an apology for want of exactness in his answers" (134). Frederick Rudolph sums up the report and its impact thusly:

> The Yale Report was a magnificent assertion of the humanist tradition and therefore eventually of unquestionable importance in liberating the American college from an excessive religious orientation. In the meantime, however, the report gave a convincing defensive weapon to people who wanted the colleges to stay as they were. The inertia of social institutions, the simple ordinary laziness of men, would of course support the Yale professors and their disciples. They were joined by men of profound religious conviction who were disturbed by the suggestions of the reformers that colleges should prepare men to meet the needs of this world, rather than the needs of the next world. They received encourage-

ment from the pious, for whom the excessive concerns with matters of intellect had always seemed a threat to the true faith. The privileged orders were pleased that Yale chose to withstand the demands for a more popular and practical education, demands that threatened to unleash the multitudes. And these—the religious, the very pious, the privileged—were the people who ran the colleges, people who also knew that the American college was running on a shoestring and that the old course of study, while the best, was also the cheapest. [134–35]

The Rise of the University

It was not until after the Civil War that significant changes in education occurred, driven by the rise of science and the land-grant movement. Among other things, the rise of science increased pressure for scientific and technological education, including agriculture and engineering. A number of private institutions were founded to serve these ends, and the new land-grant colleges also provided an outlet for public demand for a more practical type of education.

But while new institutions were being created that would teach new subjects, the character of virtually all American colleges was also about to change with the development of a university movement and its orientation toward intellectual excellence. Daniel Gilman, president of the University of California in 1872 and soon to become president of the new Johns Hopkins University, held that "the university is the most comprehensive term that can be employed to indicate a foundation for the promotion and diffusion of knowledge—a group of agencies organized to advance the arts and sciences of every sort, and train young men as scholars for all the intellectual callings of life" (333). Higher education was beginning to be interested not only in vocationalism and practical education but in knowledge, scientific truth, research and scholarship, free inquiry, and an understanding of the world—this world, not the next one. Critical to the new conception was the idea that an institution of higher education should be concerned with finding new truths and that it should adopt the attitude that knowledge (or, rather, what we think we know) is speculative, contingent, and subject to revision in the light of new evidence. This attitude toward knowledge was implicit in the new evolutionary ideas of the period, ideas that were fairly readily accepted in the colleges. "The conflict over Darwinism in the colleges was less a matter of whether evolution was true than a matter of whether the old regime or the new regime would prevail, whether piety or intellect, whether authority resting on received truth or on scientific evidence" (347).

Within society at large there was an interest in new knowledge fueled by the rise of science. More to the point, this interest found a natural home in institutions of higher education. Institutions that at one time thought their role was to instill received wisdom and turn out classically trained leaders were now beginning to connect education with the acquisition of knowledge. Students were not only to be taught what was known, they were to be taught that it was known based on evidence and subject to alteration in the light of new evidence. That is, they were to be taught in a context of inquiry and scholarship, in a context of conflict of ideas, in a context in which they might be encouraged to participate in the development of new knowledge.

Within the colleges the mechanism of reform was the elective course. The elective was a significant break with the old curriculum. It allowed students and professors to pursue what most interested them. In so doing it bespoke both a new psychology and a new philosophy of education—that, on the one hand, people are different in their interests, their abilities, and the ways they learn and, on the other hand, that the ancients did not know everything worth knowing and that people who know different things can equally count as educated. The elective principle led to a number of ideas and institutions that ushered in a new concept of higher education. It encouraged depth of knowledge, as opposed to superficiality, and with this the notion that intellect, inquiry, and scholarship are important. In the classroom the effect was that standards of performance were no longer set by the slow students. The elective principle encouraged the accumulation of knowledge and, following upon this, specialization and the understanding that no one can know everything worth knowing. Finally, the elective led to the departmentalization of knowledge and its institutional manifestation, the academic department, "a symbolic statement of the disunity of knowledge" (399), and to faculty control over appointments. Close behind came the development of traditions of academic freedom and their institutional embodiment in the tenure system, made necessary because the orientation toward inquiry and knowledge often brought academicians into conflict with important interests in the community propped up by ideas no longer held sacrosanct.

II. RESEARCH AND THE MODERN UNIVERSITY

Higher education now takes place in institutions that have become the main focus of the acquisition of new knowledge. Corporations are involved in research and development, as are private and publicly supported research foundations and agencies of the federal government, but much if not most of the research in the United States is carried out in universities, and many of the significant research findings and breakthroughs have occurred in the universities.

Colleges and universities serve many functions. Even with respect to teaching there is not simply one purpose. Almost every college and university offers both general education and specialization and requires of its students that they fulfill requirements in each. As the foregoing historical sketch has shown, specialization is now an integral part of higher education, and it is hard to imagine modern academics arguing with the idea of specialization or with the psychological, epistemological, and social values that underlie it, although many might take issue with certain kinds of specialization or with the current balance between general education and specialization. The training of all academics involves a higher degree of specialization culminating in the doctoral dissertation, and most academics want to teach specialized courses to students. Their competence to teach such courses rests on their training as graduate students and, to a lesser degree, on specialized knowledge acquired since then.

These remarks should not be taken to minimize some of the problems associated with specialization and the compartmentalization of knowledge that goes along with it. At some point one wants to see a synthesis of some sort, a bringing together of the knowledge acquired in the disciplines. The recent push toward interdisciplinary instruction and research, waning now to some extent but still important, is the outcome of this desire. Nevertheless, it is widely conceded that interdisciplinary work cannot simply replace disciplinary work and that good interdisciplinary work must be based on good disciplinary work. Furthermore, it is unlikely that many professors would want to give up teaching their specializations altogether.

Teaching advanced subjects to upper-level students imposes on a professor certain obligations that everyone will easily recognize. It requires at a minimum that one keep current with the field; obviously, one may not simply teach, twenty years later, which is mid-career for most academics, what was learned in graduate school. Although important, however, keeping up with one's field is hardly adequate. Advanced, upper-level courses, even at the undergraduate level, inevitably demand a research effort in support of such teaching.

What exactly is it that a professor teaches? A professor can either teach material developed by others and found in the literature or his or her own material or, of course, some combination of these. Obviously if a professor teaches his or her own material, not only thought but also research and scholarship will be required. For in the nature of any academic pursuit ideas do not arise in a vacuum. They have a context provided by the history of thought about a subject and by prevalent ideas about it. The professor must not only present his or her own ideas, but show how they respond to problems not answered by older or competing ideas or how they in some other way constitute an advance. One does not invent ideas simply to hear oneself talk. There is a context that gives ideas their point and their significance; one can advance new ideas only by showing how they function in that context. Doing this is, of course, engaging in research and scholarship. Thus, teaching his or her own ideas commits the professor to a program of scholarly activity.

Typically, however, a professor will primarily teach ideas developed by others. He or she reads the literature, attends lectures, learns the leading current ideas in the field, and presents them in class. This is a perfectly legitimate professorial activity, but it does not absolve the professor of the obligation to conduct his or her own research and scholarship. For one thing, there are invariably a variety of ideas available in a field, so that inevitably one must select among them. We select the material we present to undergraduates either on the ground that a particular set of ideas is more nearly correct than another or on the ground that it is more interesting or important to study than another. When it is the former, the professor is again committed to a research activity, for it is necessary to evaluate the ideas in question. Evaluation entails reading additional literature in order to see what the problems and objections might be and how they might be answered, but of course, *simply* reading what others have said *is* insufficient; one must at some point come to one's *own* conclusions.[1] One might, however, choose certain material to teach not because one judges it more nearly correct but because it is interesting or important to study or widely hailed in the field. Still, a professor who is doing a worthwhile job in the classroom cannot escape the research task. For one must understand *why* it is worth paying attention to or at least why *others* think it worth paying attention to. One must also understand what is wrong with the ideas being taught, since our hypothesis is that the professor thinks the ideas interesting or important but *not* the most nearly correct ideas in the area. And in any event the professor must understand the ideas well enough to deal with problems and objections that might be raised, even if only by students.

The brunt of the foregoing line of argument is that teaching cannot be dissociated from claims to truth; that is, a professor cannot stand in front of a class, present a lot of material, and then step away from representing any views of his or her own as to what is true and what is not. Thus, a professor cannot teach conscientiously while escaping the need to conduct what amounts to a research program. Let me clarify by means of an example, not necessarily involving upper-level teaching. In many ethics courses contemporary moral and social issues are discussed. Some professors teach by taking stands on the moral issues, letting their students know which positions they think correct and why. Others simply make critical presentations of the arguments on both sides but refrain from taking stands on the moral issues in question. Does this practice constitute stepping away from representing the professor's views as to what is true and what is not? No, because, while not taking a stand on the moral issue, the professor does take a stand on the main thrust of his or her teaching, which is whether the arguments that are used on either side of the issue are good arguments or not.

It is sometimes maintained that one of the important goals of undergraduate teaching is the passing on of an intellectual tradition. One has only to be reminded of the great medieval European universities to be aware of the important role universities play in perpetuating an intellectual tradition. This role continues in the modern university, where it is our responsibility to perpetuate the tradition in what we teach to our students in each generation. Though it may not be articulated, it is my impression that in some disciplines professors think that this is a particularly important, even dominant, goal of teaching, and it may be what many have in mind when they decry what they believe is the modern preference among academicians for research over teaching. This approach, if used to drive a wedge between teaching and research, is, I believe, mistaken, for the perpetuation of an intellectual tradition itself makes scholarly demands. The concept of "a tradition" or "the canon" or "past culture" or whatever it is we seek to instill in the next generation is not very precise; indeed, it changes over time. At one time there is a prevailing idea of, say, the literary canon, the body of literature that is most important in defining a culture or a period, which we and our students must study if we are to understand that culture or period. But then comes a group of scholars arguing that we do not properly understand that culture or period because this or that has been omitted, and the canon must be redefined to set things right (and, frequently, to allow us to come to terms with the biases of our own time that have been responsible for misidentifying the canon). Since the tradition or the canon is subject to change, a professor must inevitably exercise some judgment about what bits of the past to project into the future. As before, a professor's commitment must ultimately be to his or her idea of the most nearly correct set of ideas, and not to a prevailing set of ideas or a set of ideas either left by others or developed by one's contemporaries. In the case of the literary canon a professor does not, in teaching Melville or Dickens, have to represent their ideas as correct. What he or she must represent is, first, that the analysis of them is correct and, second, that they are indeed important and worth studying.

The idea of teaching as passing on a tradition, and of being a good teacher by doing a good job of it without engaging in scholarship, is tantalizing but unworthy. The only way to divorce it from any scholarly demands is to believe either that the tradition is unchanging and that we are sure we have the proper perspective on it or else that it does not really matter what we teach our students so long as it somehow makes contact with our past, is interesting, and gives our students the patina of education. Without putting too fine a point on it, this is similar to the approach of the early American college and suffers from many of its defects. In the modern university, however, passing on a tradition does not absolve one from the responsibility for taking a critical, scholarly attitude toward it.

Thus far I have maintained that a professor has an obligation to engage in research and scholarship because these are integral to conscientious teaching. A professor at the very least must make choices about what set of ideas is most nearly correct and therefore worth teaching, and research and scholarship are required in making such choices. There is yet another reason, of a different sort, for connecting research and teaching. Part of the educational enterprise is to promote the growth and development of students. The role of colleges and universities, as we have seen, has come to include the advancement of knowledge, and accordingly, the colleges and universities are in an especially good position to show students how knowledge advances. In the contemporary world, gaining some understanding of how knowledge advances is an important part of students' growth and development. Therefore, students should be shown, as part of their education, how knowledge advances, and the best way for professors to do so is to demonstrate it, to show themselves to students as engaged, in small and appropriate ways, in the advancement of knowledge. It is one thing to recite historical examples of the development of new ideas, but even though the ideas are likely to be considerably less influential, it is in its own way more impressive, and certainly more educational, to show the development being done by one's own example. Historical figures, however important their discoveries, will hardly seem to most students to be people they can expect to emulate, but a student's own (dare I say?) nonimportant professor can serve for some as a powerful role model. We always teach in our courses the big, important discoveries and innovations, but a student can probably gain much by being shown firsthand examples of how ideas come about and are examined and tested. Students should be shown where and how ideas really come from and that they can be developed not only by the giants but by people not unlike themselves. In order to do this kind of teaching, professors must be engaged in research projects.[2]

The aim of teaching in the early American college was to groom students to take their places in the world adequately fortified with received wisdom. There was, to be sure, the sense that students so educated would be appropriately alert to social needs and adept at leadership. Contemporary colleges and universities in fact function in some measure to develop leaders, and part of this function may well involve inculcating an updated set of received truths. But few people, and virtually no educators, would hold that this is the primary proper function of higher education. Educators and the public at large believe that one of the main roles of higher education is to develop critical abilities, including the capacity to deal with the constant barrage of new information and, generally, the pressures of a changing social and physical environment not only on a national but on a global scale. In fulfilling this role educators and others have to cope with an uneasiness about how to foster such abilities without capitulating to relativisms of knowledge and values. Yet even so, there are few who would opt for the teaching program of the early college. The life of the modern college and university is tied to the acquisition of new knowledge in a changing world, and the professor cannot escape by pretending that teaching can be done without research. Even if there are eternal verities, the main business of higher education lies elsewhere.

Having said this, however, I must acknowledge that not all teaching is going to have a research component. There are subjects, frequently technical in nature, that are noncontroversial, universally accepted as central to a discipline, and in which there is no room for the infusion of one's own ideas. Obviously, good teaching of such a subject does not require a research orientation. Nevertheless, the case for the scholarly obligations of professors is not affected, for such courses are not the main or even a significant focus of college and university teaching. For one thing, they tend to be lower-division courses. For another, few professors can devote all or most of their teaching careers to such courses, and no professor *should* be teaching such courses exclusively. Certainly it cannot be the existence of courses such as these that supports the case for augmenting the teaching focus and diminishing the research emphasis in higher education. Indeed, if such courses were the main focus of education, we would not need colleges and universities. Higher education is "higher" because it involves a level of complexity and subtlety that goes beyond mere information; it reveals the thinking, the theoretical framework, and the discarded alternatives that lie behind the facts presented. As Kenneth Minogue notes, "Technical subjects, as such, are not academic and only become so as they are seen to invoke a higher degree of abstraction than is technically useful."[3] The college curriculum needs such courses, but they are only the beginning of a college education.

If the role of professor as teacher inevitably carries with it a commitment to research, what is the case for *publishing* the results of that research? The research effort is a search for truth. In speculative matters truth is not easy to come at. Operationally, we try to get at it by testing our ideas—putting them forward for consideration and examination. We know, or should know, that we often fail to see deficiencies in our own ideas. Most of us depend on others to help with the critical task; we find that our ideas are often best worked out in the course of dialogue with others. Sometimes a professor will rely on students to provide criticism, and sometimes, particularly in graduate education, presenting our ideas to students is a good way to test them. Even in undergraduate settings students can provide valuable insights or at least provoke the professor to further thinking and revision. Nevertheless, undergraduates are not usually up to the critical task, and even the input of graduate students is usually of limited value. Interaction with colleagues and peers is almost certainly going to be needed. Informal interchange with one's local colleagues is good, but frequently, their insight is not as searching as that provided by other specialists in one's field. Thus, professional, public interchanges at conferences and in the journals is best.

This testing before our peers is something that we owe our students if we are going, as we inevitably must, to put our ideas before them. There is something most unseemly about professors who will parade before their students their wisdom and the (as it may seem to them and their students) overpowering persuasiveness of their ideas and arguments, but will not present these ideas for their peers' consideration, let alone defend the ideas before them. The classroom is a safe place and the professor has a lot of power there. Asking professors to advance their ideas to the profession at large will not prevent the abuse of power that consists of using the classroom as a platform for demagoguery, but it will help prevent the damage done by carelessness and incompetence.

Inasmuch as incompetence and carelessness can do damage of a sort, it might be worth commenting on a phenomenon common in many other fields but unknown in higher education. Secondary education and a great many professions, such as law, medicine, engineering, architecture, and others, not to mention welding and cosmetology, require some kind of professional certification and frequently demand continual upgrading of one's skills and knowledge. I would guess that professors escape this kind of regulation because there is no sense of risk to public welfare in higher education as there is in many other fields, including secondary education. And in any event there is probably a general feeling that completion of a terminal degree is a sort of certification, and also a general expectation that people at that high a level of a field will be motivated to keep up without the need of public regulation. Finally, the idea of upgrading one's skills and knowledge cannot be as clearly defined in higher education as it can in other professions. Keeping up as a practitioner in engineering or law means learning the latest developments that have become part of the corpus of knowledge expected of any competent practitioner. In an academic discipline, however, there is little new knowledge that is as widely accepted as that. Most new developments are speculative and much debated, requiring discernment and judgment about what to accept and leaving room for differences of opinion. What this means is that incompetence in higher education is harder to detect and that keeping current in a discipline is mostly left to the professor's integrity. We demonstrate this integrity by continuing to do that which we were educated to do and which convinced our various institutions of higher education that they could responsibly entrust us with the education of undergraduates.

There are other reasons, in addition to the testing of ideas, for the professor to publish his or her ideas. New ideas should be shared, even if they are only small accretions to knowledge. Few of us are going to make significant breakthroughs or write monumental treatises. Most of us do "normal science" or its equivalent, normal social science or normal humanities. Why should our findings not be shared with others? They constitute advances; someone may benefit from them. If they are worth making available to our students and our local colleagues, why should they not also be shared with others?

There is a related point. Everyone would agree, I believe, that scholars have a responsibility to preserve and perpetuate knowledge left by others. Historically this has been one of the most important things that universities have done; our understanding of our traditions and the antecedents of our culture have depended on it. But the responsibility of scholars is not only to preserve knowledge left by others but to preserve the knowledge they themselves possess. A tradition is not just the past; it grows and changes. For future generations tradition includes *us*, includes who we were and what we did and thought. Therefore these things must become part of the record. Future generations can decide what is worth preserving and what is not. For us, the task is to preserve the ideas that constitute part of the ongoing tradition, by presentation or publication or other forms of reproduction that will be available to others.

NOTES

Acknowledgments: The first part of this article is based largely on Frederick Rudolph, *The American College and University* (New York: Knopf, 1962), and to a lesser extent on Burton R. Clark, *The Academic Life* (a Carnegie Foundation special report) (Princeton: Princeton University Press, 1987), chaps. 1 and 2. Parenthetical page references in the text are to Rudolph.

1. "The duty of giving lectures is a pressure upon the academic to rethink what he takes to be the fundamentals of his subject. . . . This fact is a clue to the nature of universities, a clue which is worth following because many people have been seduced by such metaphors as that of 'the frontiers of knowledge' into believing that universities are pre-eminently places where 'advanced' studies are pursued. This manner of thinking suggests that way back in the 'centre' of knowledge there is something secure and fixed. This is a superficial and popular view. The real distinction of universities is that they are unusual combinations of 'advanced' work, on the one hand, with the continuous rethinking and restatement of many things which, for all practical purposes, we take for granted. They deal as much with simplicities as with complexities. The ordinary lectures for the undergraduates . . . force scholars to re-examine their subject as a whole. . . . [I]n academic terms, to teach a subject is to rethink it." Kenneth R. Minogue, *The Concept of a University* (Berkeley: University of California Press, 1973), pp. 57–58.

2. In an interview conducted by the Carnegie Foundation "a biologist in a leading liberal arts college explained that: If you are not doing research you really are only masquerading as a scientist, I think. That is my own prejudice: Technically, you won't keep up; and I have seen plenty of horror stories of

people who haven't kept up as soon as they stop doing research. . . . [And] part of your teaching is directing student research and really serving as an example to students who ultimately want to become biologists. If you aren't doing anything, you don't provide that example. You are just somebody who lectures to them and stuffs their heads with information, but you don't serve as a model. I think [that] in the humanities it is more the model thing that is important." Quoted in Clark, *The Academic Life*, pp. 82–83.

   3. Minogue, *Concept of a University*, p. 72.

6

THE TRUTH, THE WHOLE TRUTH, AND NOTHING BUT THE TRUTH

Paul D. Eisenberg

Whatever may be true of them in other aspects of their lives, academics in their professional work and lives face some particularly knotty problems about truth telling. The difficulty is compounded by the many different areas of teaching and research, and even service work, in which such problems occur. In this essay I shall concentrate on some of the problems that arise in the areas of teaching and service; or rather, since the kinds of service work I have in mind may well be regarded as adjuncts to one's classroom teaching, I shall consider teaching and service together. Before turning my attention to these areas of one's academic life, where, it seems to me, problems about truth telling arise both more frequently and in a more troublesome form than is the case with research, I should like to say a few words, for comparison's sake, about truth telling in research.

There one encounters, for example, the kind of case, already much publicized, involving a researcher—usually young or untenured—who deliberately falsifies his data in order to obtain impressively new and interesting results, and thereby to gain tenure or to become a much stronger candidate for a major research grant. Perhaps we academics tend to think of this kind of falsification as quite new, and certainly in this "high-tech" age there are ways of falsifying data that *are* new. The basic problem is no doubt much older, however. Thus in *Gaudy Night*, first published in 1936, Dorothy Sayers makes much of the (fictional) case of a brilliant historian who deliberately suppresses evidence in order to make his own novel argument persuasive. Although that incident is fictional, its plausibility presupposes that Sayers and others in the academic world of her time knew of real incidents of that kind. And on the Continent in that same year, some German scholars were, presumably, quite deliberately suppressing information or otherwise falsifying their accounts in order to make themselves and their works attractive to, if not indeed usable by, the Nazis.[1] In this essay, however, I shall deal only with the present-day situation and, yet more particularly, with the situation now in nonsectarian American colleges and universities. Accordingly, there is, I like to think, no need to mention here the obverse case of someone who, like Descartes with Le Monde, has come upon an important scientific truth or, at any rate, has written a work in all sincerity that he nonetheless dares not publish because of the fear of reprisals from the church or the university itself. In small church-affiliated schools that problem may persist, however (just as it is not unlikely that even today a less daring counterpart to J. T. Scopes may be unwilling to advocate in the classroom or, perhaps, even to introduce into it a highly unpopular view that he accepts.)

In the major colleges and universities, however, subtler pressures may—indeed do—exist that lead to suppressions of the truth, suppressions that, if not so blatant as those to which I have just referred, are nonetheless real. Sometimes, for example, a junior colleague may be unwilling to confess her interest in such and such a field or line of research—let us say, applied ethics or women's studies—because she knows her senior colleagues look with disfavor upon it. Or such a person fears to make, much less to publish, a rebuttal of a senior colleague's view lest her attempted cleverness cost her her job or, at least, lest it bring an end to the good will and support of the colleague in question. Senior scholars, however, sometimes face quite similar problems. I have heard of one distinguished researcher who, although he was prepared to acknowledge in private the force of a less well known scholar's objection to an aspect of his view, was unwilling to make the same acknowledgment in print or publicly to abandon the view that had made him famous.

Although such contemporary situations as I have just described do present the persons involved in them with difficult choices, it seems to me that "we" (that is, fellow academics) already know how at least most such cases should be resolved. From our (external) point of view, the ethical problems that such cases raise do not seem to be particularly difficult. Do we not think that in such cases the truth, the whole truth, should be told, and indeed nothing but the truth? For if one is "really" an intelligent person, one will (eventually) make one's way in the academic world even if one fails to get this or that important grant (there are always others), even if one loses (temporarily) the favor of this or that colleague (one has other colleagues; there are or will be other jobs), etc. At any rate, however sticky such problems may sometimes be in practice, they have typically one feature in common—one that, I think, tends to make them, as a class, less difficult cases for ethical theory than those that I am about to describe in the areas of teaching and service. That is, most of these problems confront "isolated" individuals who are tempted to do what (they themselves know) most of their colleagues in the academic world do not or would not do. It is because most of us do not deliberately falsify data, do not fail to make public acknowledgment of powerful objections to our (former) views, etc., that the behavior of those who do such things strikes us as so clearly reprehensible.

In other areas of academic life, things are not so clear-cut. Again, let me consider several examples:

1. One is teaching an introductory course in, for example, philosophy. One very much wants to tell one's students the truth about whatever topic one is discussing, but how much of the truth should be told? The whole story, one knows, is very complicated; and telling it would both confuse most of one's students and leave one with too little time for presentation and discussion of other topics that one had announced would be included (which would give the course as a whole proper balance, which one knew the students were more likely to be interested in, etc.). Incidentally, one may be concerned not to displease one's students for the further reason that their evaluations of the course will subsequently be considered in recommendations concerning one's annual salary increase or one's tenure or one's promotion; but here and in the subsequent cases, I wish to consider such a case in, so to speak, its pedagogical purity. Accordingly, then, how should one decide which portion of the truth to tell and which to leave untold? And should one tell one's students that one is simplifying (at the risk of appearing to condescend to them), or should one act as if there were no more to be said (at the risk of leading some of the students to think that indeed there is no more to be said)?
2. A particular undergraduate student, although apparently conscientious, has written a very poor paper or exam. In one's written comments on the assignment or in one's subse-

quent remarks to the student, should one tell him more or less bluntly what one thinks of the work? If one does not, the student may well think that the work is, after all, pretty good and, hence, that the very low grade he has received on it is unwarranted. On the other hand, being candid with the student may hurt his feelings and, yet worse from a purely pedagogical point of view, one may thereby discourage the student and, hence, weaken his motivation to try harder in the future.

3. Indeed, will one dare to give such work the low grade one thinks it deserves? (Grading should here be thought of as "standing in" for a verbal assessment; so that, although the number or letter assigned cannot itself be deceitful, what it implies about the instructor's assessment of the work can be.) In addition to the considerations just mentioned under example 2, one knows also that other instructors—one's departmental colleagues among them—would not grade the work in question very low. Setting aside (if indeed one is able to do so) one's concern not to be regarded as a crank even by one's colleagues or to be unpopular with the students, one is still left to wonder whether one can justify, even to oneself, giving a very low grade to a student who chanced to take one's course but who might equally well have enrolled in another section of the course and received from the instructor in it a much higher grade. Is it not unfair to penalize the student, in effect, for taking one's own rather than some apparently quite similar course? Or perhaps one's departmental colleagues share one's standards but instructors in other departments do not. Should students be penalized for enrolling in elective courses in one's own department when they might equally well have taken something in another department?

4. A student relatively unfamiliar with the faculty of one's department asks one's advice about taking such and such courses with certain of one's departmental colleagues. However much one may admire those colleagues' research in certain areas or their teaching in certain courses, one has good reason to believe that this one among them has very little knowledge and, worse yet, is quite confused about a subject which he nonetheless confidently teaches to undergraduates, or that that one is doing more or less mechanically

and for the nth time a course the lectures for which she carefully prepared a decade ago but about which she has thought very little in the interim. Should one tell the student what one really thinks? Or in a spirit of loyalty to one's friends and colleagues, should one enthusiastically recommend their courses (even as, one hopes, they will recommend one's courses to their present or past students)? At least, should one describe the courses in question somewhat more favorably than one thinks they deserve? Or should one pretend to know nothing about those particular courses? Or should one deviously seek out reasons other than one's real ones for not recommending those particular courses—say, that the subject matter in such and such another course is more likely to interest the student or that the student will be able to take those courses (or ones very much like them) some other time but has meanwhile the special opportunity to study with such and such an illustrious visiting professor in the department or with such and such a distinguished pedagogue in this, the last year before her retirement?

5. The present case is, admittedly, a variant of example 2, but nonetheless, it may be thought worthy of mention in its own right. A senior who has majored in one's department but, so far, has not shown much talent or originality asks one's advice about whether she should think seriously about pursuing graduate studies in one's discipline. Should one tell the student exactly what one thinks? Or should one fall back on other reasons for being discouraging—for example, that jobs in that discipline are still very hard to get? Or should one think that a person ought not to be discouraged from at least trying to do what she most wants or what most interests her; that, after all, other departments are not so demanding as one's own; that sometimes students bloom late? And with such considerations in mind, should one proceed to recommend to the student various departments where one thinks she has a decent chance of being admitted and even of performing, if not at a distinguished, at least at a passable level?

6. A graduate student who has worked closely with one is now ready to look for an academic position elsewhere and has asked one to write a letter of reference for her. She is very good but not indeed wonderfully talented and she still has

a long way to go on her dissertation. She is really quite worthy of getting a good academic position, however. One knows that people from other schools and many in one's own department are prepared to write greatly inflated letters about *their* students. Should one, then, exaggerate some-what about her ability, too, and, moreover, straightfor-wardly aver that she will have completed all work on her dissertation by the start of the next academic year (and thereby make her seem to be a no less attractive candidate than many others with whom she will be competing and who, one suspects, are no more talented or further along in their dissertations than is one's own student)? Or should one describe her and her situation exactly as one perceives them and thereby run the risk of making her appear a far less attractive candidate than she actually is?

It should be noted that in none of the six cases just described is one contemplating a choice between a clearly moral alternative and one that is merely self-seeking. In that respect also these cases differ from the ones I described previously. (Granted, one might be able to *redescribe* at least some of those earlier cases so that they were seen to involve a conflict between competing moral concerns.) Perhaps it is precisely because in these latter cases one is forced to choose between competing goods, neither of which is merely prudential or self-aggran-dizing in character, that they are so problematic.

They are not, however, equally problematic. Thus really conscien-tious pedagogues may always feel a bit bad about presenting a deliber-ately simplified account, but they are likely to be able to find, or to have already found, a way of doing so which is more or less satisfactory to them; and similarly with several of the other cases presented. I do not mean to say, however, that in these cases there is a single right approach that will work equally well for all concerned teachers. In fact, it seems to me that these matters have to be decided by the individual instructor, and on a case-by-case basis. Thus, clearly, the extent of simplification required in an introductory account of Des-cartes's philosophy may well be less than that deemed appropriate in an account of Spinoza's philosophy, inasmuch as Descartes's philoso-phy is, in some more or less obvious sense, easier to understand than Spinoza's.[2] But whether one should decide to devote equal time to presentation of the two philosophies, or more to Spinoza's because it is indeed the more difficult, or less to it for that very reason—all this depends on the teaching style of the individual instructor and his purposes in a given course, in a given quarter or semester. I say "a given quarter or semester" to indicate that one may want or need to rethink these matters and, hence, to structure the contents of a course differently at different times in one's teaching career, in response to a variety of factors: for example, changes in one's own interests, perceived changes in students' interests, the availability of attractive new versions of certain texts.

In the matter of deciding how much to say about a given topic in one's classroom or what to say in one's comments on a student's paper or in advice that one gives a student about other courses or about pursuing a graduate degree in one's own field (and so on), one (very likely) has at least the relative advantage of *not* needing to consider what others are already doing. I mean to say that in these matters there is no already prevailing practice that one takes to be reprehensible or unsatisfactory, but which one cannot immediately change and which one must somehow take into account if one is to reach a morally acceptable conclusion about what one is to do. In contrast, what grade to give a student or how to describe a student in a letter of reference are examples of matters where one's conscientious decision must take into account prevailing practice—in other words, widespread grade inflation and inflation/exaggeration in claims made about prospective young academics.

Traditional ethical theories have *nothing* (helpful) to say about the former sort of cases; what is called for is casuistry (in the best sense of that term) and individual judgment. Traditional ethical theories do have something to say about cases of the latter kind, but such theories do not speak to us with one voice. On the one hand, Kant tells us that the knowledge of what other people generally do *in fact*, if it is not morally acceptable, should carry no weight whatsoever with the individual moral agent as she sets about deciding how to behave. In contrast, classical utilitarianism invites—indeed, requires—us to consider what others are already doing as we set about our own ethical decision making; for a situation of a type in which most other people are already behaving in a certain way (albeit a way that is ethically shabby or reprehensible) is one in which one's own decision/action will very probably have consequences significantly different from the consequences of one's decision/action when either there is no relevant prevailing practice or the prevailing practice is not ethically reprehensible. Thus a Kantian in Nazi Germany, for example, would tell the truth, whatever the cost to oneself and one's family; an (act-)utilitarian in the same situation might very well reach an opposite decision, since the contribution that the consequences of one's truth telling would make to the well-being of those concerned might well be less than the cost of a lie that helped to preserve the lives and the liberty of oneself and one's family.

My present concerns relate to situations that are "merely academic" and, hence, likely to be much less dire than those to which I have just alluded. Granted, one could, easily enough, somewhat increase the moral intensity of the cases with which I am concerned. For example, it might be true that if I give such and such a student a low grade in my course, that student will not get into medical school, whereas a student who in other relevant respects is equal to mine and who indeed has performed in approximately the same way but in another section of the course, where the grader is quite generous, stands a much better chance of being admitted. Or because I write a wholly truthful account, my student fails to get a job in academe, whereas another student whose career I have followed and whom I know to be on the whole less able than my protégé gets various people to write quite glowing letters and, on their basis, is offered a good position. But whenever one gives a low final grade to a student or writes a candid assessment in a situation where others are not proceeding similarly, *something* is likely to be hanging in the balance. At the very least, it seems that an injustice of some sort has been done the students who get only the grade or the assessment that they "deserve" when others who have performed no better and perhaps have performed even less well get a higher grade or a much stronger recommendation. Is it proper, then, for me, the instructor, to consider only the matter of fidelity to my own standards (which I have examined and reexamined and which I find to be quite acceptable) and thereby to be *true to myself;* or should I not, rather, have an even greater concern for my students, a concern that will sometimes lead me to put my devotion to justice and well-being for them before my devotion to the truth itself and truth to myself?

It is clear that different but equally conscientious instructors have answered and continue to answer that question differently. As I come to reflect upon it once again, I find myself reaching the same conclusion as I have done previously; now I should like to share it with you, though (I can imagine) you may well disagree with it. I am inclined to think that one should regularly reexamine the acceptability of one's standards but that while one does find them acceptable, one should use them and only them in reaching one's decisions about the grades to assign to one's students and the strength of the recommendations to write on their behalf. I think so for several reasons. First, one usually cannot be sure that anything else affecting the student's long-term well-being really does hang on this grade or that letter, whereas one can be sure when one gives the student an inflated grade or recommendation that the truth (as one sees it) has not been respected and that one has therefore been untrue to oneself.

Second, it is not clear, on balance, that one's student, if graded/ assessed honestly, is then being treated unjustly (vis-à-vis comparable students who have happened upon more "generous" instructors). I mean to be speaking here not of instructors who in all honesty have adopted standards less demanding than one's own (we shall never reach consensus in such matters, and that is a fact of the world which all of us must recognize); I am referring to those others who one knows or has good reason to believe have standards very much like one's own but who have "given in" to the pressure of widespread academic inflation. The matter of (in)justice here is itself very complicated. Granted, there is something amiss when my student gets, let us say, B− for the same level of work to which you give an A but which, you admit to me privately, is "really" worth only the lower grade. My student is at a disadvantage in an obvious respect. In a less obvious respect, however, so too is yours. For your student is not getting from you one thing that she or he deserves—namely, your honest evaluation of her or his work. Not to give students what they deserve is to do them an injustice!

Moreover, it seems to me that in our role as academics—more particularly, as teachers—we serve our students as role models, whether or not we wish to. We in academe have the opportunity—or is it not indeed the duty?—to be, and to present ourselves as being, disinterested servants of truth (as we see it). Or rather, since, like Nietzsche, I think that, strictly speaking, there are and can be no disinterested human actions, let me say, instead, that we have the opportunity, if not the duty, to be and to present ourselves as being interested in discovering and conveying the truth. Why set such a high value on truth and truth telling? The question is age-old and very important. There is a sense, however, in which no (serious) academic should be asking that question, for if the academic life is or ought to be concerned with any one thing preeminently, surely that thing is truth (in its many manifestations and guises).

Finally, just as one is, willy-nilly, a model for one's students, so is one also for one's fellow academics. Thus, for example, if some of them see me writing in a manifestly honest way about my student, they may not only appreciate my honesty with them but may come to think that they ought to write no less honestly themselves. If, however, I am afraid that my merely truthful letter will be taken to be a weak recommendation (either because the exaggerations or partial truths in others' letters have not been recognized for what they are or because it has been presumed, in view of the widespread practice, that my statement, for all of its qualifications, is itself inflated), I can take the trouble to comment in the letter, or in a covering letter (a sort of "metaletter"!), on the significance of my letter-writing style. I can also join with other like-minded academics in urging our various professional organizations to produce official statements condemning various types of academic dishonesty.

There may be other measures I can adopt as well. What I must recognize, however, is that such problems as I have raised in this essay do not have easy answers; that despite my academic's desire to reach a decision quickly so that I can get on with other aspects of my academic life (in particular, my research), they deserve careful attention; and—by no means least of all—that I do not need to meditate on these questions in solipsistic splendor but can and should discuss them with interested colleagues, of whom there will always be many.

NOTES

1. Cf., for example, Walter Kaufmann's discussion of this matter in his chapter "The Master Race," in his by now classic study *Nietzsche: Philosopher, Psychologist, Antichrist,* 4th ed. (Princeton: Princeton University Press, 1974).

2. The question of why one philosophy is easier to grasp than another is an interesting one to consider in detail. Is it a matter of the vocabulary and typical sentence structure, the extent of agreement with various prephilosophical intuitions, the extent of the antecedent absorption of the philosophy in the general culture, or some combination of these and yet other factors? This, however, is not the place to engage in detailed investigation of that question; our business lies elsewhere.

7

THE ETHICS OF GRADUATE TEACHING

Robert Audi

Teaching is many things. It is conveying information, developing skills, and imparting modes of thought. It is imposing exercises, eliciting ideas, and encouraging imagination. It is creating attitudes, practicing communication among persons, and building citizenship. It is the modeling of personal styles, techniques of speech, and patterns of thought. It is a job, a profession, a passion, and, for some, a sacred trust. The moral responsibilities of teachers toward their students are numerous and far-reaching, particularly for teachers of the very young. Elementary school children, for instance, are highly impressionable. But even adult students are often deeply influenced by their instructors. This situation clearly occurs at the graduate level, where faculty often have years of close or even intimate contact with their students. Even if we consider only graduate teaching, there are too many ethical problems to address in a single essay, and I must be selective. My main concern will be four broad areas of professional activity; competence, modeling, advising, and befriending. In dealing with these, however, it may be possible to say much that counts toward a general theory of the ethics of graduate teaching.

I

The ethics of graduate teaching may be usefully approached from the perspective of models, in the sense of broad conceptions embodying a view of the professorial role in relation to the student. Four models seem to me common, natural, and especially well suited to focus some of the main moral problems that confront teachers of graduate students. I shall call these the didactic model, the apprentice model, the collegial model, and the friendship model. It will be apparent immediately that they can be combined, and that there are other models which overlap one or another of them in some way. There are, for instance, prophetic, dramatic, contractual, and conversationalist models, as well as a pair of Socratic ones: the gadfly model, which emphasizes the challenging of received views, and the dialectical model, which centers on the technique of example and counterexample, definition and refutation.

The first four models will each be briefly sketched in this section. Section II will consider their relation to some moral questions important in graduate teaching, and section III will compare the results and, on that basis, draw some general conclusions about the ethics of graduate teaching, particularly teaching in Ph.D. departments, though much of what I have to say applies also to teaching in many professional schools as well. In setting out the models, my focus will be on ideals of good teaching rather than, say, the rights of professors or students. For the most part, rights will come into this essay only indirectly, because my aim is to formulate moral guidelines and ideals for the day-to-day activities of professors in relation to their students, rather than the minimal standards of propriety set by rights. I shall not be considering the adversarial situations that most naturally evoke reference to rights. It goes without saying that morally responsible teachers do not violate their students' (or colleagues') rights; but teachers who do no better than this are at best ethical without being morally admirable.

If the didactic model has a motto, it is: Listen to me. The professor is to be an expert, students are to absorb all they can in class. The professor can be kind, even personable; but the main task is to get across a proper version of the relevant truths concerning the material. Lecturing tends to be the favored pedagogic mode used in this model, but it need not be. If there is discussion, however, as in seminars, the professor must have a good idea where it should lead. Plainly, if this is one's model, one should be highly competent in the field and quite up-to-date on developments in its literature. The standards for competence and currency will vary, of course, both from one level of graduate study to another and from one institution to another. But the conscientious didact will try to achieve excellence on both counts.

The apprentice model is perhaps no more modest, but it is oriented more toward developing skills than toward imparting information. Its motto might be: Follow me. It is as though the professor were an Aristotelian *phronimos*, a person of practical wisdom, and one could acquire the crucial wisdom only by imitation, practice, and criticism.

This model allows professors to do whatever they think needs modeling. It may be lecturing, doing experiments in a lab, proving theorems on a blackboard, holding an informal class or seminar discussion, conducting a survey interview, or operating a complex machine. Unlike the didactic model, this one makes it natural sometimes to criticize, in front of one's students, even one's own performance. But even those who unsparingly note their own deficiencies still need sufficient competence to illustrate well the skills they are trying to develop. One's ideals may exceed one's capacities, and one may say so with less embarrassment than the didact is likely to feel in administering self-correction. Nonetheless, only a few students will learn well from merely observing a teacher's skills being exercised at a low level of competence. In addition, seeing those capacities in action is still only part of what students need; a conscientious use of the apprentice model also requires ability to explain oneself clearly and in detail, and to comment critically, but constructively and kindly, on one's students' performances.

There is a sense in which both the didactic and apprentice models are authoritarian. By contrast, the collegial model is more nearly egalitarian. Its motto might be: Be my junior colleague. This model is most likely to shape the graduate teaching of professors fresh from their own Ph.D. training, but it may fit certain personalities so well that it remains with them, at least to some degree or in some contexts, throughout their teaching careers. This model is perfectly compatible with lecturing, but the lectures that accord with it have a different tone from those done by, say, a didact. It is in seminars, laboratories, and individual consultations with students that this model is most influential. In these informal settings, students are drawn out, treated as if their ideas are worth taking seriously, and corrected without an authoritative tone or, more subtly, by such devices as the gentle suggestion of an alternative. They may be invited to criticize the professor's work and may be asked to serve as coauthors on papers in their joint areas of specialization. This model prevails more often in the sciences than in the humanities, and it is certainly more common—as obviously more natural—after students become candidates for the Ph.D. Clearly, there tends to be less student pressure on professors using the collegial model, perhaps in part as a trade-off for the authority they give up. But these professors still need to be able to guide and correct, to illustrate techniques, and to respond to problems in the students' research.

It is a short step from the collegial model to the friendship model.

122 | ROBERT AUDI

Here the motto is: Be my friend. Again, this is most commonly exhibited by faculty who are newly arrived from their own Ph.D. programs,
particularly if they are not married or similarly attached. The friendship model is superficially much like the collegial one, but there is an
important difference. The former has a professional relationship, that
of colleague, at its center; the latter does not. Granted, normally the
professor still must grade the student, but doing so is, as the professor
may even acknowledge to students, an awkward matter felt to interfere with the relationship. The class or seminar is an experience of
shared learning; lunches, casual hallway conversation, and recreation
are a normal part of teacher-student activities; and first names are the
standard mode of address. To be sure, first names may occur in
relationships dominated by the other models; but by and large, among
those three only the collegial model makes it natural for students to
use them. Typically, didacts at most tolerate being called by their first
names, and apprentices must earn the right to use them, even if some
professors grant it quite readily when the time comes. Certainly we
can learn much from our friends, and friendliness in a relationship
reduces anxiety and can thereby facilitate learning. But it is very
difficult to evaluate one's friends objectively and, when one sees
them regularly, to avoid burdening them with some of one's personal
problems. The friendship model is thus very difficult to realize without
compromising one's moral obligations to one's students—those who
are friends and, especially, those who are not.

Reflection on any of these models will quickly bring us to two
very general moral principles that should be acceptable to professors
regardless of which of these, or other prima facie reasonable models,
they favor. First, there is *a competence principle:* professors should be
competent in their subjects. Second, there is *a fairness principle:* professors should be fair to their students and colleagues. I have already
suggested that standards of competence vary, but I take it that there
is, in most disciplines at least, a body of methods, concepts, theories,
and major figures with which anyone teaching graduate students
should be solidly familiar. Similarly, there is an obligation to keep up
with a subset of developments in these areas, for example by reading
professional publications, attending lectures and conferences, and
conducting some research of one's own. As to fairness, it requires,
minimally, treating one's students equally in one's evaluations and
doing those evaluations conscientiously using reasonable, previously
explained standards. The standards should be neither unrealistically
high nor unchallengingly low. Previous explanation does not require

that examination questions be revealed in advance, but it does entail making sample questions available, describing the assignment in adequate detail, and the like. Responsibilities to colleagues (which are only a secondary concern in this essay) are often defined in detail in institutional documents, but clearly each department or unit should have a clear understanding of the responsibilities of its faculty, and professors should do their share without prodding by colleagues. This obligation is owed to colleagues, but is also crucial for the efficient, harmonious operation of a department necessary for optimal treatment of its students. An uncooperative professor is a detriment to the departmental teaching effort.

II

The four models I have described—and combinations of them—work differently in different fields. Consider, for instance, a laboratory science versus mathematics or a humanities discipline as compared to the performing arts. The sciences may require faculty-student teamwork in a way the humanities do not; the performing arts require individual instruction in ways the humanities do not; and some disciplines, such as archaeology, require that professors and their students travel together, often in close quarters. In what follows I must ignore many differences among fields. In order to deal briefly with some central issues concerning graduate teaching, I shall simply raise each of four major issues in relation to each model. This approach will bring out the bearing of the model on each issue and will help assess the models as points of departure for academically sound and morally responsible graduate teaching.

The problem areas I want to concentrate on are these: grading, including recommendations for jobs or other degree programs; modeling, including professorial demeanor, professional relationships, and personal style in speech, dress, and other respects; advising, whether on papers or dissertations or placement; and befriending, taken to include both social relations and close professional ties. Some of the models to be considered bear distinctively on only some of these problems, and I cannot treat each case in detail for each model.

The Didactic Model

The responsible practice of the didactic model, like that of the other three, requires a commitment to fairness in grading. None of the models frees a professor of the obligation to treat students equally and by reasonable standards that are explained in advance of assignments or exams. Didactic instructors, and to some extent professors using the apprentice model, may be individual or even idiosyncratic in setting their standards; but they may be so in any pedagogical framework, and within the limits of competence in the subject and fairness in grading, idiosyncracy is acceptable. There is, however, an obligation to keep abreast of what other teachers in the same field are doing, if only for purposes of comparison. This is especially important in doing recommendations. For here one's students are compared not with each other or even with one's own standard but with others who are applying, from different institutions, for the same positions. Thus, one's appraisal should reflect not only a grasp of the student's absolute level of competence by one's own standards, but also a sense of what is expected of applicants in the relevant competition. This is not to suggest inflation of one's appraisal; that should be avoided almost as assiduously as deflation. The point is in part that referees should do their best to take account of the context in which recommendations are assessed. If one's standards are higher than those of one's profession generally, one's students should not suffer for it by being mistakenly thought less prepared than they are; and if those standards are lower, others' students—as well as perhaps some of one's own—should not suffer for it either.

Regarding the matter of modeling, the first obligation of the didact is to model *that* role well: above all, to impart correct, valuable information and ideas, and to do so effectively. But students absorb much from their professors, and there is surely a general moral obligation to behave in a way that is both professionally admirable and appropriate to a moral agent interacting with others. One cannot be a *pure* didact, and one is obligated to behave responsibly in the other aspects of one's behavior as well.

When it comes to advising, the didact must bear in mind what we might call *the principle of the priority of the student's point of view:* that the relevant point of view is that of the student. Thus, while it would be appropriate to lay out what one thinks are the best topics or jobs to pursue, one should adapt one's thinking to the needs and capacities of the student. A student may be temperamentally unsuited even to an exciting topic on which one can give excellent guidance. Students may also be unsuited to exploring uncharted territory, even if one promises to light their way and can project easy publication for the much-needed dissertation that fills the yawning gap. There may be a related principle for advisers here, *a consultation principle:* the more important the question facing the student, and the stronger one's opinions on it, the greater one's obligation to urge seeking the advice of someone else as well.

Finally, on the question of befriending students, the typical didactic professor may have no special temptations; there may indeed be a danger of being too impersonal. Still, it is important not to allow a teacher-student relationship to be *dominated* by friendship, as can happen with students whose uptake is especially good or who stay after class to hear more. However, for many a didact it may be desirable to go to some lengths at least to develop a friendly manner toward students. This topic will soon come up again.

The Apprentice Model

Where the apprentice model prevails, the points just made about grading and recommendations hold equally. There is, however, a tendency to identify with a student whom one treats as an apprentice. This may lead to bias and, especially, inflated recommendations; it can produce jealousy of other faculty members who work with the student; and it may restrict the student's options by inspiring fear about one's reactions to activities perceived as unlikely to carry one's approval. The impulse to create protégés is, of course, not restricted to those adhering to the apprentice model, but it must be monitored very closely by any responsible professor who works from the model.

On the apprentice model, it is natural that the obligations of good modeling should come to the fore, and here more than with any of the other models the teacher has a moral obligation to do well the things being stressed to the apprentice. If the aim is to develop skills by doing the relevant tasks with or in front of the student, they should be done skillfully, with their main features in high relief. Where the professor has any reasonable doubt about the execution, other professors (or authors) who are good models should be suggested. And where there are no doubts, it may be a good idea to entertain some.

Similarly, in advising an apprentice there may be a need to allow others to help. If the matter is the topic of a seminar project, there may be little if any need; but with a choice of dissertation topic or of the sort of job to pursue, some advisers might be morally bound, under the consultation principle, to urge their advisees to see other faculty members. Much depends on the maturity of the student, the closeness of the student's interests and abilities to the professor's areas of competence, and the availability of other faculty members who can help. Another variable is the extent to which professors following this model intend to keep their apprentices to themselves. Some do so more than others. The more one expects to do so, the greater the obligation to see to it that if a student chooses to work with one—especially on a dissertation—it is on the basis of a free and adequately informed choice.

The dimension of friendship must also be handled carefully in such relationships. It is hard to be an apprentice to an unfriendly professor, or even to one whose warmth or tolerance wear thin when the going gets hard for the student and help is needed. On the other hand, an apprentice relationship is likely to fail if it becomes dominated by friendship (as may also happen when graduate teaching is dominated by the collegial model). What is wanted is professional closeness combined with emotional distance.

The Collegial Model

Much of what needs to be said about how the collegial model bears on our four problems is already implicit. Fair grading may be harder to do than on the first two models, but it is equally obligatory. Recommendations, too, may be difficult to balance, yet are subject to the same standards.

Given the collegial character of the relationship, modeling is likely to be slightly awkward; but a good senior colleague can serve as a role model to a junior professor without condescension, and the same should be possible for a faculty member in relation to students treated as junior colleagues. It should in fact be easier given the classroom opportunities and private discussion meetings built into the academic side of the relationship. What must be resisted is a tendency to let the friendship dimension of the relationship dominate in a way that makes the professor feel free most of the time to drop the leadership role, which is needed in professors even by the majority of advanced graduate students. Even the most advanced students need criticism; and it may be less effective if delivered in the roughly egalitarian way often used in criticizing the work of colleagues. On the other hand, when tact is stretched into indirectness or transformed into perceptibly calculated gentleness, if may render criticism ineffective and offend the intended beneficiary.

When it comes to advising, professors who think of a graduate student as a junior colleague may find it especially easy to work from their own experience; freely relating it can help and, within limits, any adviser can draw on personal experience for concreteness and realism. But if thinking of a student as a junior colleague makes it easier to be candid, it may also facilitate identification with one's students and may lower the threshold for reading their experiences or prospects in terms of one's own. Again, the crucial principle is that one should think one's way into the point of view of the advisee—or at least the reconstructed point of view, corrected for misinformation or certain biases. If this sounds parentalistic, that may be because advising is perhaps intrinsically so up to a point, but there is surely no more parentalism required by this strategy than a graduate student who is clearheadedly seeking advice could countenance. One should not, then, simply figure out what one would do in the same general circumstances; the task is to help advisees figure out the best strategy from their own considered perspective.

If, in the collegial relationship as imagined here, there is already a personal connection and a sense of shared role, the dangers that friendship with students will supplant the professor's faculty obligation loom up. They must be resisted here as on the other models. It is not just that we may do too much for our friends relative to those to whom we owe similar obligations; consciously or unconsciously, we may also exploit their understanding of our own preoccupations and thereby do too little for them. Some of the problems posed by faculty-student friendships will be noted in connection with the friendship model.

The Friendship Model

The friendship model presents the greatest challenge to the morally responsible professor. If I play ball, lunch out, and regularly socialize with my students, I will find it hard to give them low grades or, even more, to decline to recommend them for certain opportunities they want to pursue, or to rank them below others who are appreciably better but not my friends. I can, to be sure, *face* such a conflict between friendship and professorial duty and still act professionally. But how do I know that when I am in such a situation I will always face the conflict? Surely one's judgments can be biased as well as one's conduct: even someone incapable of ranking B over A when judging A to be better might *judge* A better in the first place as a result of friendship; and praising more warmly than the record warrants is still more likely to arise because of friendship than a biased ranking. It need not be that the friendship produces an assessment one could not professionally defend; that degree of bias is probably not the most common and is not my main concern. The more difficult problem is how to be fair to students not widely different in overall merit. Sometimes one can defend a judgment favoring B over A only because one knows more about B as a result of friendship. B thus benefits over other students from a nonprofessional access to a faculty member. Granting that because of shyness, industry, and other factors, inequality of access cannot be eliminated, it is easily intensified unfairly by faculty-student friendships.

The area of modeling also presents difficulties here. Even if one's student friends consider one more knowledgeable than they on a major subject, one may feel pretentious in conducting oneself so as to illustrate professorial demeanor. The difficulty is not insurmountable, but even if one succeeds admirably, there may be less tendency to act accordingly if one is respected only as a kind of peer, or even just viewed mainly *as* a peer. While peer behavior is certainly influential, there is much benefit to graduate students in being taught by people they feel they must *aspire* to equal.

Concerning advising, advisers who are friends of their students may not be able to achieve the proper *detachment* from them, though to be sure the professor may know the advisee better than would be the case where any of the other models prevails. For this very reason, however, a professor may find it hard not to hear out, and even try to help in solving, quite personal problems, including some that are better dealt with by psychologically trained professionals or others with special qualifications. This sort of discussion may be detrimental to the student and, in any case, may take the professor far into conversations that supplant some of the academic work that should be primary in the relationship. Perhaps there is a prima facie obligation to bring others not so close to the student into the advising process, particularly so when advisers identify too closely with the advisee and may be projecting their own desires where they should be working from the advisee's point of view. Such loss of detachment is a common price of close friendships with students.

Loss of detachment is an inevitable price where friendship grows into love, as it often and naturally does. Romantic relationships between professors and their graduate students, like other emotionally charged relationships between them, are thus to be avoided. It is not only detachment that is lost; there can also be pressure on the student to support the professor and on colleagues to accord special treatment to the student. Indeed, the very invitation to join a professor in a purely social activity may be felt to be hard to refuse, or even coercive.

If there is to be such a suggestion, it is better that it should come—spontaneously—from the student. Even then, because of differences in status and power, any resulting relationship is likely to proceed on an unequal footing. In the light of all these liabilities, a professor should avoid romantic relationships with a student even after the course is over, so long as the student is pursuing work in the department. Once students leave a department, the situation is quite different. Even here, however, the *thought* of a romantic relationship *after* a course may still bias a professor's treatment of a student *in* it.

III

I want now to speak more generally about the ethics of graduate teaching. A number of points emerged in connection with more than one of the four models explored, and of course any two or more of those models can be combined to yield still others. Indeed, one reason for my focus on them is that they are all, to some degree, natural in one or another phase of graduate teaching. There are at most a few graduate professors who do not have a bit of the didact. Most of them must, after all, lecture here and there even in seminars, save for a very few at a truly professional level where discussion has both its own momentum and adequate focus. And how many professors can do full justice to a dissertation student without indicating how they do things themselves? At the dissertation level, and even before, is it not natural to treat at least the more mature students as junior colleagues, at least from time to time and especially when they assist in undergraduate teaching? And for most professors it is hard to be as friendly as is natural with graduate students one knows well—particularly if they assist one in teaching or research—without becoming in some way a friend.

Friendliness and support are also important in another way. Students must feel fully free to raise questions, and to contribute to discussions, without the fear that merely by making errors they will harm their prospects. Yet even apart from such fear, they may not adequately participate in discussions without being pressed to do so. This pressure works best when the professor is neither too close nor too distant and the teacher-student relationship is neither too hot nor too cold. One might think that maintaining this delicate balance undermines the love of one's students that is a mark of many devoted teachers. But nothing I have said precludes either professors' loving their students or students' loving their professors, and such mutual affection is often both a natural response to shared inquiry in an atmosphere of respect and an incentive to good learning. This kind of love, however, is neither romantic nor exclusive.

Different tasks make different roles appropriate, and a successful graduate teacher is likely, at one time or another, to work at least in the spirit of each of the four models I have considered. It may be a professional responsibility to acquire facility in at least the first three. This approach implies friendliness and a supportive attitude toward one's students. That capacity is the best element in the friendship model, and it is not necessary, though it is surely desirable, for professors to be able to shift fully into the friendship model on certain occasions, such as departmental social functions.

We might usefully distinguish between a model that is *dominant* for a teacher and one that, at a given time, is *prevailing*. My most general point is that different models should prevail at different times and none need be dominant. If one model is, it should not be dominant to the extent that the professor cannot shift out of it. A seminar should not be a lecture course. Some professors need to keep this point in mind, especially if their dominant model is didactic. Moreover, a tutorial session should not be a friendly chat. If one's dominant model is the friendship one—or even the collegial—this difference must be consciously observed.

Given these points about the uses of the models in differing circumstances and their combinability in almost any teaching situation, let me consider some of the broad principles and ideas that have emerged. First, I have stressed the obligation to be professionally competent: teachers, especially graduate teachers, should have something to say; it should be worth saying; and it should be said well. Second, I have emphasized the integrity of the grading process: fairness is essential, and it must be achieved using adequate professional standards (another place where competence is crucial). A third, related point concerns fairness in doing recommendations. That they should be neither overstated nor understated has already been said, but there is a further obligation. Students are entitled to presume that a letter requested as a *recommendation* will be, on balance, positive unless the professor indicates otherwise. Thus, however difficult it may be, professors should find a way to decline to do a recommendation if it cannot be positive, unless an understanding about its range can be worked out with the student. My fourth point concerns faculty relations: professors must be fair to their colleagues. This obligation has many dimensions not directly related to graduate teaching, but I have stressed in that connection the need to avoid jealousy of colleagues and indeed to urge students to draw on them. Moreover, professors should generally keep their personal differences with colleagues out of their discussions with students and should avoid undermining colleagues' authority or credibility on academic matters. This is another reason why the collegial and friendship models may lead to unethical behavior: in relationships of those two kinds it is hard to conceal attitudes toward, and even personal disagreements with, colleagues.

The modeling obligations, as we might call them, deserve separate mention. Here one must remember that educational institutions are preparing their students for citizenship as well as for a special field. I do not mean to imply that citizenship should be taught in every field, but conscientious professors should keep in mind their wide-ranging influence over those they teach. Any aspect of their conduct can be seen to set a standard or at least a precedent. One is never *just* a teacher. One is always an advocate of a point of view, a critic of certain positions, an exemplar of someone trying to communicate, a purveyor of images, a practitioner of behavioral standards, a person dealing with others in common tasks—whether in the intimacy of tutorials and advising situations or in the lecture and the seminar. One may have a *right* to be unconventional and even eccentric, so long as one is fully competent and a decent person; but one's *ideal* as a professor should be to conduct oneself as an admirable human being: just, kind, tolerant, competent, committed, and good-humored. The former, rights conception is associated with a minimal ethic; the latter, professional ideal expresses an ethic worthy of aspiration. We may insist on the former, but we should strive for the latter.

Both modeling obligations and those appropriate to the collegial model bear on a special domain not yet mentioned: coauthorship. Coauthorship is more common between faculty and graduate students in the sciences than in the humanities, but it occurs in all major fields. It is of the greatest importance that faculty not take undue credit for the work of graduate students. The converse point is also important, but faculty members are in a better position to protect or defend themselves, and in part for that reason student excesses are probably fewer. Here again, fields differ. In the sciences, work done by graduate students may form a very substantial part of the publications of their faculty; faculty members are morally obligated to see that its scope and importance is duly recognized and, if possible, evident in the published version. In the humanities, the same may happen, but it is perhaps more common than in the sciences that ideas of advisers or other faculty members are a major influence on research or publication by their students. Here students should give due acknowledgment. It must be added immediately, however, that measuring people's relative contributions to joint projects is difficult; a conscientious effort must be made, but to be excessively quantitative about the matter—or suspiciously possessive—is neither sanctioned by ethics nor conducive to creativity.

These cautions plainly apply to supervising dissertations. Neither advisers nor their students should take undue credit, or even fail to acknowledge significant help from one another. But there is something subtler. Particularly for advisers with many ideas, it is often easier to help a student along by suggesting structure and even content than to provide the patient guidance best suited to eliciting the student's own best work. Indeed, it may be easy to make too many such suggestions even to students not having any particular difficulties. Care must be taken here. Professors using the apprentice model should be especially cautious, but all research supervisors should carefully consider the matter and concentrate on helping to develop the best work their students can produce.

The breadth and complexity of the ethical ideals appropriate to graduate teaching raise the question whether graduate programs should make a point of teaching academic ethics. Certainly, most disciplines have some special moral problems that should be thoroughly discussed with Ph.D. students; and much of what I have said also applies to law, medical, and other students in professional schools that do not generally grant the Ph.D. There are problems about dealing with human and animal research subjects; difficulties with chemical wastes; possible warlike uses of discoveries in physics; problems of properly crediting other for ideas in philosophy; and many other special problems. But I do not see that structured courses in academic ethics must be a part of every Ph.D. program, though it is certainly arguable that properly educated *undergraduates* should all have some systematic training in ethics. On the other hand, if not a course, then at least discussion of some of the moral issues confronting a discipline should be conducted at some point in graduate education, preferably fairly early in the program. The specific problems, level of detail, and manner of discussion depend on the field. Moreover, a high ethical standard should be exhibited whenever possible in graduate teaching: in one's treatment of students, faculty members, and others; in one's honesty in presenting research findings; in one's balance in appraising authors and texts; and in one's general sense of responsibility—academic, personal, and social.

One of Immanuel Kant's formulations of the Categorical Imperative applies especially to the ethics of teaching, whether at the graduate level or at any other: Always treat humanity, whether in your own person or in the person of any other, never solely as a means but always as an end. Students are never to be treated merely as a means— say, just an essential element in a successful academic career—but always as beings with a certain dignity. They are, by implication, to be treated with respect and, at times, their teachers must become advocates for them, whether internally in relations with administrators or other faculty members or externally in helping them secure a position. The same applies, of course, to students' treatment of professors, who are not to be viewed as merely means to a degree or a career. Much—though by no means all—of what I have said in clarifying the ethics of graduate teaching can be viewed as an application of Kant's principle. The principle serves as an important constraint on all four models, and surely on others that may be useful.

There is no one specific way to do graduate teaching. There are many good ways, and I suspect that the best is a complex and variable combination of a number of techniques rarely used in their pure form. Highly competent and optimally responsible professors need agility in graduate teaching. They must go from lecture to discussion, from the crowded classroom to a quiet office for consultation, from the formality of writing a student about examination results to the informality of discussing a proposed seminar paper; they must shift from the encouraging tutor to the gentle critic, from technical points in the literature to short presentations of results for first-year graduate students, from teacher possessing the right answers to adviser hoping to elicit them; and, ultimately, they must pass from professors teaching students to former teachers relating to mature alumni. In a single office hour, a professor may do snippets of lecture, express friendly support, criticize a paper, compose at the blackboard, engage in Socratic dialogue, try to inspire the dispirited, and, for much of the time, listen patiently to thoughts in the making. Each situation can raise moral problems. Not all of these problems are predictable, but the framework and principles laid out here may help us to anticipate many of the common kinds, to move toward their resolution, and to articulate worthy ideals for the conduct of graduate education.

8

PROFESSORS, STUDENTS, AND FRIENDSHIP

Peter J. Markie

"Do they want us to be their *friends*?!" That's how a professor once reacted when the graduate students in his department complained about the faculty's insensitivity to their concerns. I'm not sure that the graduate students wanted the faculty members to be their friends, but would it have been inappropriate for them to want that? Is it inappropriate to praise professors for being not only teachers but also friends to their students? It is generally agreed that the best college professors are caring, sensitive persons whose concern for their students extends beyond the classroom. Shouldn't they let their interest in their students extend so far that they are open to friendships with them?

I believe that professors should not become friends with their students, and my intention here is to argue in support of this prohibition. I shall begin, though, by clarifying it.

I

When I say that professors should not become friends with their students, I do not intend to give a piece of practical advice about how professors ought to behave to gain certain ends I suppose them to have, such as avoiding embarrassment and maintaining their colleagues' respect. Refraining from friendships with students may help some professors achieve these goals, but that is not what interests me. I also do not take my claim to be a description of the conventional or institutional obligations that define what it is to be a professor. To be a professor is to occupy a particular institutional role, and that role may be defined by certain duties so that claims attributing those duties to professors are analytic. I do not think the duty to refrain from friendships with students is a defining duty of being a professor, and my claim that professors should refrain from such friendships is not intended to be analytic. My claim is a synthetic proposition about the moral obligations of professors.

There is an important difference between moral obligations and prima facie moral obligations. When we have a moral obligation not to do something, it is morally wrong for us to do it. We have a prima facie moral obligation not to do something when there is good reason to think we have a moral obligation not to do it. Not every prima facie moral obligation is a moral obligation. If I make conflicting promises, I have a prima facie obligation not to violate one promise and a prima facie obligation not to violate the other, but I can only honor one of my prima facie obligations and the one with the most moral weight in the circumstances is the one I should honor; it's my moral obligation. The other is a prima facie moral obligation but not a moral obligation. When I say professors should not become friends with their students, I am in the first instance, concerned with what is prima facie morally obligatory. My claim is that it is prima facie morally obligatory for professors to refrain from friendships with their students; in other words, in the absence of moral considerations that override those that count against faculty-student friendships, a professor is morally obligated to refrain from such friendships. We shall see that the moral considerations against faculty-student friendships are very strong and so very unlikely to be overridden. In all but extraordinary circumstances professors are morally obligated to refrain from forming friendships with their students.[1]

Exactly who counts as a professor's student? Do professors have a prima facie moral obligation not to become friends with anyone enrolled in the college or university where they teach? Some seem to endorse this extensive an obligation, but I do not.[2] The moral considerations against faculty-student friendships do not give us any reason to think that I, as a philosophy professor, have a moral obligation not to become friends with my neighbor who is an advanced graduate student in physiology. I am a professor and he is a student at the same university, but there is no professional relationship between us that can generate a prima facie moral obligation for me to abstain from developing a friendship with him. I claim the following obligation for professors: they have a prima facie moral duty not to become friends with those students they are presently teaching or likely to teach in the future.[3] My argument for this claim will also support a related one:

professors have a prima facie moral duty not to teach students who are their friends.[4]

It is important to appreciate what friendship does and does not involve in this context. Three necessary conditions for friendship are crucial; an appreciation of them will help us see through some mistaken objections to the prohibition on faculty-student friendships.[5]

First, we are friends with someone only if we share or have shared an activity with that person. We can become friends with someone we have never met, say through correspondence, but we can't become friends with someone with whom we have never done anything. The shared activity that is the basis of friendship can take a variety of forms, but as friendship develops, it will involve the mutual communication of otherwise private information. A friend knows things about us that others don't; others are at best "merely acquainted" with us.[6]

Mutual affection is a second aspect of friendship. We may not enjoy every moment of everything we do with a friend, but we generally enjoy our shared activities, and more important, part of what we enjoy is doing those things *with that person*. We also value a friend's welfare because of whose welfare it is. Someone who adopts the attitude of universal benevolence will value our friend's good simply because it is someone's good, and a very religious person may value our friend's good because our friend is one of God's creatures. We value our friend's good because it is his or her good in particular.[7]

A third aspect of friendship is that friends acknowledge their mutual affection through expectations and commitments. We expect our friends to place a special value on our welfare because it is ours, and we commit ourselves to honoring their corresponding expectation. Because our friends place a special value on our welfare, we expect them to give us special guidance, and we are committed to giving guidance to them. The guidance we exchange with friends requires the very personal level of communication associated with friendship.[8] The commitments that develop as part of a friendship have moral weight. As promises, they are prima facie moral duties of fidelity, and since most, if not all, involve benefiting someone who has already benefited us, they are prima facie duties of gratitude.[9]

This account of friendship has some important implications. Being friends with someone isn't the same as liking that person to a particularly high degree, and it isn't the same as acting toward that person in a friendly way, by, for example, extending greetings, sharing jokes, and so on. Friendship involves mutual liking and friendly behavior, but it also involves a mutual exchange of otherwise private information, a mutual concern with each other's interest because of whose interest it is, and mutual expectations and commitments. All these elements of friendship admit of degrees. I shall not attempt to specify just how great the communication, enjoyment, valuing, expectations, and commitments must be for friendship to exist.[10]

We have a limited control over who our friends are. We cannot make a friendship happen. Even if we share an activity with others and provide them with otherwise private information about ourselves, we can't make them freely provide us with such information about themselves, and we can't make ourselves or them feel the affection of friendship. The most we can do is act in ways likely to lead to friendship. We can prevent a friendship from happening; here we have a great deal of control. We can avoid sharing an activity with others that includes the exchange of otherwise private information about ourselves, and even if we feel affection for others, we can refrain from acknowledging that affection through a commitment to them to give their welfare special consideration because it is theirs.[11]

Friendship, as I've explained it, can exist between persons who are very different in age, experience, and interests. Some have a more restrictive conception. Cicero requires that friends be virtuous and share "a perfect conformity of opinion upon all religious and civil subjects."[12] Montaigne requires that friends hold everything "in common between them—wills, thoughts, judgments, goods, wives, children, honor and life."[13] Not surprisingly, Cicero decides that each person can at best have two or three friends, and Montaigne decides that each can have only one.[14] They may have captured an important relationship that may sometimes exist between people, but they haven't captured our ordinary conception of friendship. We ordinarily think that even people who are not extremely virtuous can have friends and that each person can have several friends and share different interests and activities with each.

Friendship necessarily involves attitudes often thought to be valuable, such as regarding someone else's welfare as an end in itself, and G. E. Moore's well-known isolation test can be plausibly interpreted as yielding the result that each friendship is intrinsically good.[15] Consider a friendship between two people in isolation from all other states of affairs and without regard to its consequences. Is the world better for the existence of that friendship with the aspects of affection and commitment that it necessarily involves? It is plausible to believe the answer is yes and hence that the friendship is intrinsically good. Friendships clearly differ in their extrinsic value (the amount of intrinsic good and evil they produce in the world), but it has been plausibly argued that the general practice of forming friendships is extrinsically good.[16]

In all, then, friends share an activity that includes the mutual exchange of otherwise private information. They have a mutual affection that consists in their enjoying each other's company and valuing each other's welfare because of whose company and welfare it is. They acknowledge their affection through a series of shared expectations and commitments; the commitments are prima facie moral duties. The extrinsic value of friendship will vary with the circumstances, but it is plausible to believe that each friendship is intrinsically good. Now let us consider why professors should not enter into this sort of relationship with their students.[17]

II

We can use our understanding of friendship to see through some mistaken objections to the claim that professors have a prima facie duty to refrain from friendships with their students.

Some may object that professors don't have a duty, because people are never obligated not to do what they are incapable of doing in the first place, and professors and students are too unequal in their interests, abilities, and experiences to be friends. This argument is attractive if we conceive of friendship in the way Cicero and Montaigne do. Few, if any, professors have students who agree with them on all religious and civil subjects or share all their thoughts, judgments, and acts of will. Yet, this conception of friendship is far too restrictive; seldom will any two people be so perfectly matched. The objection also gains plausibility from our tendency to think in terms of stereotypical images of professors and students. The "average" professor is middle-aged, sedentary, has one child, one home mortgage, two car payments, thinks of the period from Monday to Friday as the work week, and is interested in fine literature and music. The "average" student is nineteen, active, beginning to break free from parental authority, lacks burdensome financial commitments, thinks of the period from Monday to Friday as five days in which to find a date for the weekend, listens to top-forty radio through an ever present Sony Walkman, and reads only to pass tests. A survey of any college campus will reveal how inaccurate these stereotypes are. Professors and students share interests in intellectual pursuits, social causes, and athletic activities. All these activities can provide the basis for a friendship. The differences between professors and students are especially few in the case of graduate students and junior faculty.

Others may object that professors can't be obligated not to become friends with their students, because they, like the rest of us, can't help who their friends are; we like some people and dislike others just as involuntarily as we like some foods and dislike others. This objection gains its plausibilty from our tendency to think of friendship as merely liking someone to a great degree. It may well be that we can't control whether we like someone. Yet, we can control whether we share an activity with someone in such a way that the mutual affection associated with friendship develops and is acknowledged through commitments and expectations. What is important here is not so much the activity as the way people engage in it. Teaching can be done in a way that gives rise to friendship; it can be done in a way that does not give rise to friendship. The difference lies in whether the participants just share the activity or also share themselves through the activity, for example, by exchanging personal information about their hopes, concerns, and so on. Professors can avoid becoming friends with students by refusing to let their teaching activities become the occasion for the sort of sharing of personal information, commitments, and expectations of which friendships are made. They need only maintain a professional distance from their students.

Still others may object that professors can maintain this professional distance only by being so cold and formal in their dealings with students and so insensitive to their students' needs and concerns that they cease to be good teachers. This is clearly not the case. Professors who act toward their students in a warm and friendly manner and are sensitive to their student's needs and concerns must be interested in information about them, but they need not be willing to share personal information about themselves. They must value and give special consideration to each student's welfare, but they can value each student's welfare because it is the welfare of one of their students rather than because it is that student's welfare in particular.[18]

Finally, some may argue that faculty-student friendships are morally permissible, since every friendship is intrinsically good and a friendship between a professor and a student gains further extrinsic value by enhancing the educational relation between them. The problem with this objection is that even if every friendship is intrinsically good and a particular faculty-student friendship is extrinsically good, it may still be morally obligatory that the professor not maintain that friendship.[19] We are sometimes morally obligated not to engage in activities even though they are both intrinsically and extrinsically good. Suppose that every act of beneficence is intrinsically good and that a particular act of beneficence open to us is also extrinsically good. We may still be morally obligated not to perform the act. The act may, for example, require us to violate some previous commitment that is important enough for the wrong of its violation to outweigh the considerations of intrinsic and extrinsic value. Professors are in a similar position. We'll soon see that they can develop and maintain friendships with students only at the cost of violating more weighty commitments they have made.

In all, then, professors are capable of forming friendships with their students, and they are capable of avoiding such friendships by maintaining an attitude of professional distance. They can maintain this attitude without ceasing to act in a friendly way toward their students and without losing their sensitivity to their student's needs and concerns. Even if all friendships are intrinsically good and some faculty-student friendships are extrinsically good, it may still be morally obligatory that professors refrain from them. It's now time to show that professors are indeed prima facie morally obligated to refrain from friendships with their students.

III

Critics of faculty-student friendships sometimes argue that if a professor and a student become friends each will be likely to exploit the other. The professor may exploit the student by getting the student to help on some research project without any recompense. The student may exploit the professor by getting the professor to raise a grade when it does not deserve to be raised. This line of argument contains a serious problem. Suppose a professor and a student are friends, and one of them does a favor for the other. Is the one who does the favor simply honoring a proper request from a friend or being exploited? If it's the former, we haven't found anything wrong with their friendship. If it's the latter, then the one who is doing the exploiting is not acting as a friend, since friends don't exploit their friends, and we still haven't found a problem with their friendship per se. If they had really remained and acted as friends, the exploitation wouldn't have occurred. In short, appeals to the possibility of exploitation can't show that there is something wrong with faculty-student friendships that are successful frienships.[20] I think there is something wrong with faculty-student friendships even when they are successful, and I shall try to show what it is by an alternative line of argument.

If engaging in an activity is likely to limit severely our ability to honor one of our moral obligations, then we have a prima facie moral obligation not to engage in that activity. Establishing and maintaining a friendship with one or more students is likely to limit severely a professor's ability to honor his or her moral obligations. Hence, each professor has a prima facie moral obligation not to engage in such friendships. That's my argument; let's consider the two premises.[21]

The first premise is the general principle that we are prima facie obligated not to engage in any activity likely to limit severely our ability to honor our moral obligations. This principle is behind many familiar judgments about the obligations of professionals. We believe, for instance, that lawyers have a prima facie obligation not to represent both parties to a dispute; they have this obligation because a lawyer who represents both parties will attempt to identify with the interests of each and will be unable to honor the moral obligation to give each adequate representation. Psychologists have a prima facie obligation not to become romantically involved with their clients, since to do so will severely limit their ability to honor their moral obligation to give adequate care.[22] The argument for the general principle is quite straightforward. If engaging in an activity is likely to limit severely our ability to do what is morally obligatory, there is a good reason to think that it is morally obligatory that we not engage in that activity, namely, that it is likely to keep us from doing what we are morally required to do. Since there's a good reason to think it is morally obligatory that we not engage in the activity, we have a prima facie moral duty not to engage in it.

My second premise is that establishing and maintaining a friendship with one or more students will severely limit a professor's ability to honor other moral obligations. What other moral obligations? To begin with, each professor has a prima facie duty to give all students equal consideration in instruction, advising, and evaluation. Any instructional or advising opportunities, such as extra help after class, that a professor makes available to one student must be made available to all students, unless a relevant difference between them justifies different treatment. Any opportunities a professor makes available to some students in the evaluation process, such as a makeup exam, must be made available to all students, unless there is a relevant difference between them. This prima facie duty is a duty of justice. It is also a prima facie duty of fidelity; in the context of the current understandings between professors and students, a professor who offers a course implicitly promises to give those who take it equal consideration. This prima facie duty, like any prima facie duty, is open to being outweighed by conflicting ones, but such an occurrence is extremely rare. In the general course of events, professors are morally obligated to give their students equal consideration in instruction, advising, and evaluation, and when they fail to do so, they not only violate a prima facie moral duty, they violate their moral duty; they do something morally wrong.

How is the activity of forming and maintaining friendships with students likely to limit severely the ability of professors to give students equal consideration? Note first that no professor will be friends with every student in a class, for even if a professor tries to become friends with every student, some students will not be interested, and a friendship won't develop. Recall some of the aspects of friendship. Friends feel a strong mutual affection for one another. Each values the other's welfare just because of whose welfare it is, and each makes a commitment to the other to give the other's welfare special consideration. Hence, professors who become friends with their students, become friends with only some of them, and thus adopt a special attitude of concern for, and a special commitment to, the welfare of some of their students but not others. They are then likely to give those students who are their friends extra opportunities in instruction, advising, and evaluation, even though being a friend is not a characteristic relevant to the distribution of these opportunities. They are likely to violate their moral obligation to give all students equal consideration.

Friends make special allowances for friends. Requests to hand in a late paper, take a makeup exam, or receive a letter of recommendation are much more compelling when made by a friend in need. When grading exams, professors will be more inclined to be sympathetic to a friend's attempts and to work harder than usual to appreciate what the friend is trying to say. They will be inclined to use professional contacts to aid students who are their friends, even though they do not use those contacts to aid other students who are not friends but equal their friends in interest and ability. Friends give advice to friends and discuss what they have in common. Professors are likely to give students who are their friends extra advice with regard to a course of study and career. Their conversations with their friends are likely to include the subject matter of the course, since that is one of the main interests they are likely to share, and in such conversations, the professors will give their friends instruction that isn't given to the other students. These are some of the more obvious ways in which professors who become friends with their students are likely to violate their moral obligation of equal consideration.

Professors who become friends with students are likely to violate another one of their moral obligations. Professors do not simply evaluate students; they offer their evaluations to students and to others as evidence of the student's abilities. Rightly or wrongly, one of the things students want most from professors, and one of the things professors present themselves as able and willing to provide, is a credible evaluation of students' abilities. Professors have a prima facie moral obligation to students not to act in a way that will lessen the credibility and so the worth of their evaluations. Professors who establish and maintain friendships with students violate this prima facie obligation. They bring about a state of affairs that constitutes good reason to doubt the objectivity of their evaluations, namely, that they were friends with some but not all of those they were evaluating. It is not necessary that a friendship actually cause a professor to favor some students over others; the appearance of favoritism is enough to lessen the credibility of a professor's evaluations.

IV

Several objections are likely to be made against my argument.

First, the strong inclination of professors to give unwarranted consideration to students who are their friends does not imply that they will actually do so or be likely to do so. By carefully monitoring their own inclinations and behavior, professors can ensure that their friendship for some of their students doesn't prevent them from giving equal consideration to all their students. They can avoid giving a friend's request for a late paper, makeup exam, letter of recommendation, or the like special consideration. They can avoid being unduly sympathetic in their evaluation of a friend's exams and papers. They can make any extra advice or instruction that they give their friends available to all other deserving students or they can refrain from giving their friends such extra advice and instruction. In short, careful professors can form friendships with students but refrain from treating those students as friends in the course of their professional relationship with them. They can thus be friends with their students without violating their moral obligation to give all their students equal consideration.

This objection asks us to believe that in relating to students who are their friends, professors can display a willingness and ability to control their inclinations that we don't attribute to other professionals and don't even attribute to professors in other contexts. We require even the most respected jurists to excuse themselves from hearing cases that involve the interests of a friend, and we do so because we doubt their ability, if not their willingness, to control the strong inclination to favor a friend. We require letters in support of promotion and tenure to be solicited from professors who are not friends of the candidate; we treat letters from the candidate's friends, even from friends who claim to be giving an objective evaluation, as likely to be biased. In short, we generally believe that people are seldom both willing and able to control the strong inclination to favor a friend, and we have no reason to believe that professors will be an exception where their students are concerned.

This objection to my argument also ignores the moral obligation of professors not to act in a way that lessens the credibility of their evaluations. Even if professors do not favor students who are their friends in the evaluation process, and so honor their moral obligation of equal consideration, their friendship with some of their students creates the appearance of favoritism and so lessens the credibility of their evaluations.[23]

A second objection to my argument is that I've misunderstood the nature of a faculty member's obligation to give each student equal consideration in instruction, advice, and evaluation. Professors are obligated to treat students alike unless there is a relevant difference between them, and in some cases being the professor's friend is a relevant characteristic. Professors who have already given all their students the basic level of instruction and advice to which they are entitled do not do anything wrong if they then give extra instruction or advice to students who are their friends. They do not do anything wrong if they use their professional connections to help those students who are their friends but do not use them to help otherwise equal students who aren't their friends. In these cases, professors make an extra effort and give some students more than they are required to give them; they act properly when they make the extra effort for their friends but not for other students. Indeed, they would act improperly if they failed to make an extra effort for their friends.[24]

This objection misses the main point of my argument. Even if professors should sometimes favor students who are their friends simply because they are their friends, there are still cases in which professors should not do so, and professors who become friends with students are likely to violate their obligation of equal consideration in those cases. The evaluation of students is clearly an activity in which being the professor's friend is not a relevant characteristic. Suppose I have my teaching assistant grade all the exams, and I then add ten points to each exam written by one of my friends. Having assured each student of an initially objective evaluation, I then make an "extra effort" on behalf of my friends. My extra effort is obviously improper. The moment I give my friends ten extra points, I deprive all the students of a fair evaluation. Whether a student's exam receives a fair evaluation is determined in part by how it is treated relative to the other ones; if it is treated differently when there's no relevant difference between it and the others, the evaluation procedure is unfair. Being the professor's friend is not a characteristic that entitles one to extra ten points.[25]

Another problem with the objection is that it is far from clear that being the professor's friend is ever a relevant characteristic relative to the obligation to give all students equal consideration. Since it's not a relevant characteristic in the evaluation of students, how can it be relevant with regard to the activities of instruction and advice? What difference between these activities could make being the professor's friend a relevant characteristic with regard to instruction and advice but not with regard to evaluation?

Perhaps the difference is this: when we evaluate students, we judge their performance relative to certain goals, and the only relevant criteria are those directly related to those goals. Being the professor's friend is not such a criterion; the exam is not, we may suppose, an exam in how well one can be the professor's friend. We are engaged in a different sort of activity, when we instruct and advise students. We are providing them with a service and so long as we provide this to a certain agreed upon level to all, we do nothing wrong if we then give an extra amount to our friends. Suppose I agree to give each of five people a place to sleep. I do nothing improper if I give the best bed to the one person who is my friend and the remaining four beds to the others who aren't my friends. So too, professors who give extra instruction and advice to their friends, while giving their other students an appropriate level, do nothing improper.

The difficulty with this suggestion is that when we instruct and advise students, we are doing more than providing them with a service. Our students are competing for class rank, honors, and job opportunities, and we are running the competition. We both evaluate their competitive performance and offer them preparation for that performance. Whether the competition is fair is determined not just by how much preparation—instruction and advice—each student gets, but by how much each gets relative to the others. Each must get the same amount unless there's a difference that justifies giving one a competitive advantage. Being the professor's friend doesn't entitle a student to a competitive advantage in preparation for the competition any more than it entitles the student to a competitive advantage in the evaluation of the competition itself.

A third objection to my argument is that I still have not found a problem with faculty-student friendships per se. My argument, like the reasoning that appeals to the possibility of exploitation, does not apply to faculty-student friendships in which the parties act as friends should. Suppose I favor a student who is my friend in the evaluation process and in doing so violate my moral obligation of equal consideration. I have not acted as a friend should, for I have actually harmed, rather than helped, the student. I have given the student and others a false impression of the student's capabilities. If I had acted as a friend, I would have given the student a correct evaluation. If professors become friends with their students and really understand what the duties of friendship require, they will honor their duty to give all students equal consideration.

It is far from clear that professors harm students when they unjustly favor them in the evaluation process. Some have argued that they do not.[26] I want to focus on another flaw in the objection, however. Even if professors harm students to whom they give an undeservedly high grade, they do not ordinarily harm students by giving them extra advice and instruction or by making an extra effort to use their professional contacts in their behalf. All these activities are ones professors will be inclined to do for students who are their friends, and they can all constitute appropriate behavior for a friend. Nonetheless, they also constitute inappropriate behavior for a professor, for they constitute a failure to honor the moral obligation of equal consideration.

Finally, some may object that arguments analogous to mine can be given for false conclusions such as that senior professors should not become friends with the junior professors they'll be evaluating for promotion and tenure and that department chairs should not become friends with those colleagues they evaluate for raises. This objection is half right; arguments analogous to mine can be used to show that senior professors and chairs have these prima facie moral duties. Yet, what is wrong with that? The critic needs to give us some reason to believe that senior professors and chairs lack these prima facie duties; I know of no reason to believe this.[27]

V

I conclude, then, that the activity of friendship, for all its intrinsic value, is morally out of bounds for professors where actual and potential students are concerned. Instead of trying to be good friends to our students, we can and should use our energies to be good teachers to them.

NOTES

1. A professor's prima facie obligation to refrain from friendships with students will be overridden when the professor, the student, or a third party will be greatly harmed if the professor and student refrain from developing a friendship as long as their professional relationship exists. There are, I believe, very few such cases.

I shall not deal with the further question of how a college faculty should encourage its members to honor this obligation. Some moral obligations of professors are so serious that failure to honor them constitutes grounds for dismissal even for tenured professors, e.g., the moral obligation to employ honest research practices. Violations of other moral obligations are not so serious, e.g., the moral obligation to help one's colleagues entertain visiting lecturers. I suspect that violations of the obligation not to become friends with one's students generally fall somewhere between the two extremes.

2. Steven M. Cahn, *Saints and Scamps: Ethics in Academia* (Totowa, N.J.: Rowman and Littlefield, 1986), p. 36, writes: "When a student is graduated or no longer enrolled in the school, whatever personal relationship may develop with a professor is up to the two of them. But during the years of undergraduate or graduate study the only appropriate relationship between teacher and student is professional. It is in everyone's interest to maintain these bounds."

3. I take teaching to include such activities as the supervision of independent research and the designing and grading of graduate comprehensive exams.

4. Suppose I become friends with a graduate student in another program whom I am not likely to teach; I do not violate my prima facie obligation not to become friends with students I teach or am likely to teach. Then, against all likelihood, I am asked to be the outside reader on the student's doctoral dissertation. If I accept, I violate my prima facie duty not to teach my friends. The prima facie duty not to teach one's friends can, of course, be overridden in unusual cases. Suppose a professor's friend has a great need to take a certain course and the professor is the only one who can offer it.

5. Since these necessary conditions are generally acknowledged, I shall present them with a minimum of argument. Excellent contemporary discussions of friendship are contained in Lawrence Blum, *Friendship, Altruism, and Morality* (London: Routledge and Kegan Paul, 1980); and Elizabeth Telfer, "Friendship," *Aristotelian Society Proceedings* (1970–71), 223–42. The most excellent classical discussions include Cicero, "Laelius; or, An Essay on Friendship," in *Cicero's Offices*, trans. John Warrington (New York: E. P. Dutton, 1909); and Michael Montaigne, "Of Friendship," in *The Complete Works of Montaigne*, trans. Donald M. Frame (Stanford, Calif.: Stanford University Press, 1948).

6. Montaigne, "Of Friendship," p. 136, appeals to this aspect of friendship to explain why parents cannot be friends with their children: "Friendship feeds on communication, which cannot exist between them because of their too great inequality, and might perhaps interfere with the duties of nature." James Rachels gives an excellent discussion of the value of privacy and its relation to friendship in "Why Privacy Is Important," *Philosophy and Public Affairs* (1975), 322–33.

7. Telfer, "Friendship," pp. 244–25, gives a fine description of this aspect of friendship. Consider too Blum's discussion of the relationship between friendship and beneficence in *Friendship, Altruism, and Morality*, pp. 43–66.

8. Consider Telfer's discussion of this point in "Friendship," p. 230; see too Montaigne, "Of Friendship," p. 138.

9. See Telfer, "Friendship," pp. 231–37, for an extended argument against the view that friendship does not involve moral duties.

10. See Blum, *Friendship, Altruism, and Morality*, pp. 67–72, for examples of friendships that involve different degrees of affection and commitment.

11. Consider Telfer, "Friendship," pp. 229–30; and Montaigne, "Of Friendship," p. 137.

12. Cicero, "Laelius," pp. 176–77.

13. Montaigne, "Of Friendship," p. 141.

14. Cicero, "Laelius," p. 177; Montaigne, "Of Friendship," p. 141.

15. Consider Blum, *Friendship, Altruism, and Morality*, pp. 140–168; and G. E. Moore, *Principia Ethica* (Cambridge: Cambridge University Press, 1903), p. 187.

16. See Telfer, "Friendship," pp. 238–41.

17. It should also be apparent that two people can be sexually or romantically involved without being friends. For this reason, a prohibition on faculty-student friendships does not, in and of itself, entail a prohibition on faculty-student romances or sexual relationships. This is not, of course, to say that there is no other basis for a prohibition on romantic and sexual relations between professors and their students. It is just that such a prohibition cannot be established by arguing that professors should not become friends with their students and that every romantic or sexual relationship between a professor and a student is a case of friendship.

18. That good professors can maintain a professional distance from their students is even more obvious if good professors need only concern themselves with the educational needs of students and not with any other psychological needs they may have. I think this view of a professor's obligations is mistaken, however. While a good professor must not try to become a student's psychologist or confessor, he or she should maintain a concern for each

student's general psychological needs, at least to the point of being willing to encourage obviously troubled students to seek counseling. A professor can maintain this concern without being open to friendships with students.

19. Some faculty-student friendships have consequences that make them extrinsically evil. I concentrate on the extrinsically good ones, since I want to answer the claim that the intrinsically and extrinsically good cases of faculty-student friendship are morally permissible.

20. G. Robinson and J. Moulton, *Ethical Problems in Higher Education* (Englewood Cliffs, N.J.: Prentice Hall, 1985), pp. 91–94, raise the issue of exploitation. While the possibility of exploitation does not provide the basis for an objection to faculty-student friendships per se, it may provide the basis for an objection to those romantic and sexual relationships between professors and students that are not also cases of friendship.

21. Cahn, *Saints and Scamps*, pp. 35–36; and Sidney Hook, *Education for Modern Man* (New York: Dial Press, 1946), p. 189, also pursue this line of argument, though neither develops it to the extent that I do here.

22. Those who object that a psychologist can give adequate care to patients with whom he is romantically involved do not, even if they are right, have a good objection to the general principle I am defending, namely, that if an activity is likely to limit severely one's ability to honor a moral obligation, then one has a prima facie moral duty to refrain from the activity.

23. Some professors work so hard not to favor students who are their friends that they are actually more demanding in evaluating their friend's work than they are in evaluating other students' and they do not provide their friends with the extra advice and instruction they give to other students. These professors are still violating their duty to give all students equal consideration.

24. Consider Blum, *Friendship, Altruism, and Morality*, p. 48.

25. The injustice done in this example is thus a case of comparative, as opposed to noncomparative, justice. Consider Joel Feinberg, "Comparative and Noncomparative Justice," *Philosophical Review* (July 1974), 297–338.

26. Consider Feinberg, "Comparative and Noncomparative Justice," p. 306.

27. One other point deserves at least passing consideration. It is sometimes suggested that since there are far more white, male professors than female or minority professors, female and minority students are at a competitive disadvantage relative to white, male students. White, male professors are far more likely to strike up friendships with white, male students than with female or minority students, and those friendships provide white, male students with extra instruction, advice, and professional connections that give them a competitive advantage. It is also sometimes suggested that the way to rectify this problem is to increase the number of female and minority professors and so increase the opportunities of female and minority students to develop and profit from friendships with professors. There are good reasons to increase the number of female and minority professors, but this isn't one of them. The initial problem is not that female and minority students do not have faculty friends available to them; it is that white, males students do. Instead of compounding the problem, we should correct it by having white, male professors honor their obligation to give all students equal consideration even though it means refraining from friendships with their students.

9

SEXUAL HARASSMENT IN THE UNIVERSITY

Nancy ("Ann") Davis

The notion of sexual harassment entered public consciousness in the United States with the publication of a survey on sexual harassment in the workplace conducted by *Redbook* in 1976. More than nine thousand women responded to the survey, and almost nine out of ten reported experiencing some sort of sexual harassment on the job.[1] Unsurprisingly, these revelations stimulated a lot of discussion in the news media, the popular press, and academic journals.[2] At about the same time, sexual harassment was found by the courts to constitute a form of sex discrimination and thus to be illegal under the terms of Title VII of the 1964 Civil Rights Act, which prohibits discrimination on the basis of race, sex, religion, or national origin.[3] Shortly thereafter, the same sorts of protections were held to extend to the educational sphere.[4] Title IX of the Education Amendments Act of 1972 forbids sex discrimination in all public and private institutions that receive federal money from grants, loans, or contracts.

Though sexual harassment in the university began to receive attention in the media in the late 1970s, it was not until 1986 that educational institutions themselves really began to sit up and take notice. In that year, in *Meritor Savings Bank FSB* v. *Vinson*, the courts held that it was possible for an employer to be found guilty under Title VII if an employee's harassing conduct created a "hostile environment" for the harassed employee, and it allowed individuals who were the victims of sexual harassment to sue employers that did not have a policy that clearly prohibited sexual harassment.[5] These findings have been held to be applicable to educational institutions, and though many institutions had initially been slow to react, most were not slow to draw the obvious moral, namely, that it was not just an individual harassing instructor who might be liable to prosecution but the university that employed that instructor as well.[6] Most educational institutions have formulated or are in the process of formulating policies concerning sexual harassment.

In addition to being illegal and in opposition to expressed policies of many (if not most) educational institutions, sexual harassment is condemned as unethical by the American Association of University Professors, and by many of the myriad professional organizations that most faculty members are associated with.[7] It is difficult to produce a comprehensive, uncontroversial definition of sexual harassment,[8] or a philosophically watertight account that explains just what it is about the different kinds of behavior that have been described as sexual harassment that makes them all of a piece unethical. Though, as we shall see, these difficulties pose problems for attempts to formulate fair and effective policies concerning sexual harassment, they pose no serious impediment to the achievement of consensus about the more blatant forms of sexual harassment. In the classic *quid pro quo* case in which an instructor puts unwelcome sexual pressure on a student and makes it clear that the student's academic evaluation or professional advancement is contingent on her yielding to that pressure, what the instructor does is obviously coercive, unjust, disrespectful, and discriminatory.[9] It is an abuse of power and a betrayal of trust. And it is inimical to the existence of a healthy educational environment in a number of ways.

Yet surveys conducted at college campuses around the nation reveal that a sizable proportion of female college students—somewhere between 25 percent and 40 percent—report they have been subjected to some sort of sexual harassment on the part of their instructors,[10] and anecdotal evidence provided by female students, faculty members, and administrators corroborates those findings. Surveys may be difficult to interpret and compare, for they do not all employ the same definition of sexual harassment, and anecdotal evidence must always be treated with caution, but it is clear that sexual harassment and other forms of sexually inappropriate behavior are no rarity in the university.[11] Any serious participant in higher education must be puzzled and distressed by this fact.

Commentators have identified many different sorts of factors as contributing to the prevalence of sexual harassment in the university. Some have emphasized that the university was and remains a male-dominated institution whose ground rules and procedures were fashioned by men. Traditionally, the influential teaching and administrative jobs in the university have been occupied by men, and it is men who have made the policies and interpreted the rules of university governance. Though things have changed considerably in the past decade or so, most of the senior faculty and administrative positions are still occupied by men. And women remain significantly in the minority in most, if not all, academic fields. This situation is thought, in itself, to be a problem. It is women, not men, who are almost always the victims of sexual harassment and men, not women, who are almost always the harassers.[12] And men are likely both to operate with a narrower notion of sexual harassment and to have lower estimates of the incidence of sexual harassment on campus than women do. They are also likelier to view the incidents of sexual harassment they acknowledge do occur as isolated personal incidents, rather than as the expression of an institutional (or broader) problem. Commentators thus often cite the dearth of senior women and the associated inexperience and insensitivity of academic men as among the principal factors contributing to the prevalence of sexual harassment on campus. If women were less of a minority on campus or if they occupied positions of power that enabled them to have greater influence on rules, practices, and policies, then (it is thought) the incidence of sexual harassment on campus would decrease.

The women's movement and other associated movements have led many women—and many men—to question received gender stereotypes. But it is clear, nevertheless, that those stereotypes continue to exert a powerful influence on people's views about the relations between male professors and female students. Although it is a truism that social attitudes about status, gender, and sexuality frame people's expectations about "proper" relations between the sexes, most of us are blind to many of the effects of those attitudes, and implications of those expectations often go unnoticed.[13] Though fewer people may now regard liaisons between experienced and influential older men and inexperienced, comparatively powerless younger women as the ideal sort of relationship, such liaisons are still widely thought to be acceptable (if not simply normal). And the persistence of romanticized Pygmalionesque views of the educational process appears to legitimate such relations between male professors and female students. It is clear that gender stereotypes and associated differential social expectations contribute in a number of ways to the incidence of sexual harassment on campus.

Until we have a better understanding of why there has been so much sexual harassment in the university, we are not likely to be able to arrive at a solid understanding of what can or should be done to curtail it: the formulation of a cogent and successful sexual harassment policy thus requires more reflection on the factors that have contributed to the existence—or persistence—of sexual harassment in the university. Commentators are correct, I believe, in citing both the dearth of senior women in the university and the persistence of conventional gender expectations as significant contributing factors. But rather than cover the ground that may be familiar from other discussions of sexual harassment, I want, in this essay, to focus on some of the contributing factors that have received less attention, and on factors whose significance and implications have not been fully appreciated. This will be the task of sections I and II. In section III, I will sketch some suggestions regarding the implications of these observations for the formation of a sound and workable sexual harassment policy.

I. PROBLEMS IN DEFINING SEXUAL HARASSMENT

Most universities' sexual harassment policies incorporate definitions of sexual harassment that are closely modeled on the Equal Opportunity Commission's Sex Discrimination Guidelines, which have been taken to be legally applicable both to the workplace and the university.[14] According to those guidelines,

> unwelcome sexual advances, requests for sexual favors, and other verbal or physical conduct of a sexual nature constitute sexual harassment when (1) submission to such conduct is made either explicitly or implicitly a term or condition of an individual's employment, (2) submission to or rejection of such conduct by an individual is used as the basis for employment decisions affecting such individual, or (3) such conduct has the purpose or effect of unreasonably interfering with an individual's work performance or creating an intimidating, hostile, or offensive working environment. (sec. 1604.11)

This definition is obviously an inclusive one, covering a wide range of behaviors.[15] Sexual harassment has been taken to include conduct that is not personally targeted, though it may be tasteless and offensive, such as sexist remarks and jokes and the (unnecessary) use of sexually explicit material in the classroom or other academic settings, and conduct that is both personal and offensive, such as comments on a student's body or physical appearance, and overtly salacious leers, offensive remarks, and personal inquiries (for example, comments or queries about the student's sex life). (Both of these forms of conduct may be taken to violate clause 3 of the EOC Guidelines). It includes conduct that is more actively invasive or threatening, though it is not explicitly coercive, such as solicitation of sexual favors, repeated invitations to go out, or unwanted touching of a sexual nature, and conduct that is quite openly coercive, such as explicit or implicit threats of reprisal if a student does not engage in the desired sexual conduct with the instructor. (Both of these forms of conduct may be taken to violate clause 1 or 2 of the EOC Guidelines.) Finally, it has been taken to include actual sexual assault.

Definitions that are closely modeled on the EOC Guidelines or that characterize a similarly broad range of behaviors as sexual harassment are problematic in several respects. Because such definitions lump together many different kinds of behaviors, they blur distinctions that may have moral, psychological, and practical relevance. It is wrong for instructor A to coerce a student into a sexual involvement with the threat of academic reprisal (*quid pro quo*), and it may also be wrong for instructor B to offer academic encouragement to a student in order to have more frequent contact with her and thus more opportunities to initiate a sexual relationship with her. It may be wrong for instructor C to make frequent remarks to female students about how "sexy" they are and wrong for D to use classroom humor that relies on jokes and examples that are demeaning to women. However, though the actions of all four instructors may be wrong, they are not wrong for the same reasons, and the differences may be more significant than the similarities, both with respect to the moral assessment of the instructors' conduct and the design of plans or policies to remedy it. The blanket characterization of all four as sexual harassment conceals and may mislead.

Instructor A, the *quid pro quo* harasser, knows that what he is doing is wrong, but since he believes that his power and influence will enable him to get away with doing what he wants to do, he proceeds anyway. He is thus someone who "lives by an outlaw code."[16] His actions involve the intentional or reckless infliction of harm, and they bespeak contempt for his students and for the system.

Instructor B, who offers academic encouragement to a student in hopes of getting her to be romantically or sexually interested in him, may also be acting wrongly. Significant damage is done when a student comes to believe that her instructor's academic encouragement was a ploy to enable him to initiate a sexual relationship with her, and whether or not they are correctly characterized as consensual, relationships between instructors and students are not relationships between equals but rather ones in which the instructor's position enables him to exercise power over the student. The risks involved in ostensibly consensual relationships between students and instructors are certainly not equal: if, as is the fate of many romantic relationships, the relationship dissolves, and the parties are no longer comfortable in each other's presence, it is the student who stands to lose access to resources and opportunities that may be vital to her education and career opportunities, not the instructor. Though instructors may be blind to the potentially coercive aspects of the situation, students are not. Surveys indicate that many of the students who are confronted with undeniable evidence of their instructors' romantic interest in them are made very uncomfortable, and some report that they do not feel free to refuse an instructor's attentions. And so one can fault instructor B for assigning too much importance to his own desires and not enough to his student's needs or interests, or for having an excessively limited perception of the risks his conduct may pose to his student. But B does not willfully and deliberately—or, for that matter, perhaps even consciously—manipulate the student. He may be unaware of his ulterior motives, or he may (shortsightedly but not viciously) view his behavior as a permissible attempt to initiate a consensual relationship with another adult. What he does may be wrong, but both the explanation of its wrongness and the necessary measures for dissuading B from repeating his behavior are very different from the explanations and sanctions needed to account for (and deter) A.

Finally, consider instructors C and D. Both C, who frequently comments on female students "sexiness," and D, whose jokes and examples are demeaning to women, may also act wrongly. That is, they should be encouraged to change their behavior and censured if they make no credible effort to do so. But once again, they may not be willfully or even knowingly manipulating their students, and they may be astonished at receiving the intelligence that their conduct is insulting or discriminatory. ("I was only trying to say something nice" or "I was only trying to break the ice in the classroom.")[17]

All four sorts of behavior are (what I will call) sexually inappropriate, and there are good reasons to discourage all of them. But there are differences among the four that bear both on the moral judgment of the alleged harassers' behavior and on the sorts of measures that are appropriate for dealing with them. Blatant and willful exploitation is different from unwitting insensitivity, and insensitivity is different from acute motivational confusion. Though students deserve protection from the unacknowledged prejudices and insensitivities of their instructors, as well as from more straightforwardly manipulative or coercive behavior, it is unfair to lump the willful exploiter and the unwittingly insensitive instructor together in the same moral (or legal) category and to treat their misconduct as deserving of the same sorts of sanctions. It is also practically unwise, for the measures that are likely to be effective and appropriate means for eliminating willful exploitation are different from those that serve to eliminate insensitivity. It is reasonable to hope that instructors C and D can be got to change their behavior by a gentle but persistent blend of education (consciousness raising) and sensitization: neither their good will nor their good intentions must be called in question; rather, it is their perception and their means of expression that are problematic. They need to be shown how their actions misfire. Sensitization and education are also in order for instructor B, but they may need to be more extensive and perhaps to be supplemented by some counseling if his ulterior motivations remain opaque to him. His problem is not that of merely choosing an infelicitous means to a worthy end. Rather, he operates with an insufficiently rich appreciation of the power he possesses and the harm that his actions may cause, or he fails to take a sufficiently sophisticated view of his own motivations. A's conduct obviously requires a more radical and rather different approach.

It is not necessarily incorrect or unreasonable to use one word to refer to a family of behaviors that are wrong for different reasons: *homicide* refers to involuntary manslaughter as well as to first-degree murder, and they are surely wrong for different reasons. But the undifferentiated use of *sexual harassment* is problematic, for *sexual harassment* is not a neutral description in the way that *homicide* is; it is, rather, a description that carries a great deal of moral opprobrium, as well as the threat of potential legal prosecution. And it may seem unfair to visit the full weight of that opprobrium and that threat on a person who insensitively or unwittingly offends his female students. Moreover, since *sexual harasser* is such a strong term of opprobrium, different views about what is wrong with a piece of (putative) harassing behavior and different interpretations of the seriousness of that wrong are likely to issue in different views about whether the behavior is correctly characterized as sexual harassment in the first place. Examination of studies and surveys confirms this suspicion: there is indeed a good deal of disagreement about how *sexual harassment* should be used, and that disagreement tends to follow gender lines. Men tend to take a very different view of (putatively) harassing behaviors; they are inclined to count a narrower range of behavior as constituting sexual harassment than women do. Though men and women agree that instructor A's conduct constitutes sexual harassment, they tend to part company on B's, C's and D's conduct.[18]

To some degree this divergence can be explained as a difference in sensitivity, based on a difference in experience; it is women, not men, who have been long thought inferior and women, not men, who have almost always been the victims of sex discrimination. Thus, it might perhaps be said, men are inclined to adopt a narrower definition of sexual harassment because they do not take a sufficiently far-ranging view of the possible consequences of their acts or because they do not adopt a suitable critical attitude toward their own motivations. Their narrower definitions are thus shortsighted, and the broader definitions (like the one in the EOC Guidelines) that track women's intuitions are better.

But even if this reply is correct as a piece of diagnosis, it provides little justification for ignoring the disagreement over the definition of sexual harassment or for riding roughshod over men's definitional inclinations in favor of adopting the wider definitions that many men would reject. For doing so ignores a university's purpose in attempting to define sexual harassment in the first place and to formulate policies with respect to it.

Clause 3 of the EOC Guidelines appears to allow that an instructor who makes remarks that are offensive to a student, thus causing her work to suffer, may be guilty of sexual harassment even when he is ignorant that his conduct is offensive (and ignorant of its effects on the student). It is the effect on the victim, and not the intention (or motivation) of the alleged harasser, that is sufficient to determine whether the instructor's conduct constitutes sexual harassment.[19] But if men and women see different conduct as constituting sexual harassment, and it is the effects of men's conduct on the women—that is, the women's perceptions—that are to be used as the major determinant, then the resulting sexual harassment policy is one that is likely to seem unconscionable to men, however "unreasonable" women think men's characterizations of sexual harassment are. If university policies define sexual harassment in a way that most men regard as unreasonable, then they unlikely to take that policy very seriously and are likely, perhaps, to see themselves as victims if they are accused of sexual harassment for doing things they do not think are wrong. This attitude would hardly foster respect for a university's sexual harassment code; indeed, it is likely to engender fear and contempt.

Or to put the point another way, insofar as the EOC Guidelines provide an indication of how sexual harassment is *legally* interpreted, even those men who do not think a certain sort of (putatively harassing) conduct is wrongful will see themselves as having some reason to avoid it. Even if they do not believe, either before or after the fact, that the putatively harassing acts were wrong, the fact that they can be held legally liable and punished for committing such acts will give them incentive (even if it does not give them what they regard as good reason) to avoid committing them. But having incentive to avoid breaking a law or violating a policy is not the same as having respect for the law or policy, and it is respect that those who dissent from inclusive definitions like the one contained in the EOC Guidelines are likely to lack. If they think that sex discrimination laws employ an unreasonable definition of sexual harassment, they are likely to regard those laws as arbitrary and unfair. Though I know of no way to prove the point, I think it plausible to suppose that laws that are thought to be arbitrary and unfair by a significant number of educated and highly articulate people—which academics presumably are— are not laws that are likely to survive or to be assiduously enforced for as long as they do survive. If, as seems plausible, universities' purpose in instituting sexual harassment policies is to reduce or eliminate the incidence of sexually inappropriate behavior on campus, then it may be unwise to incorporate a definition as inclusive as that in the EOC Guidelines, for doing so seems likely to defeat that very purpose. (I shall return to this point.)

II. IGNORANCE

It is clear that both the frequency and the seriousness of sexual harassment in the university are widely underestimated (even when sexual harassment is given its narrow interpretation and taken to refer only to such things as *quid pro quo* threats and actual sexual assault). There are a number of reasons why this is so. Personal, institutional, ideological, and societal factors all conspire to deter students from reporting incidents of sexual harassment and from taking concerted action to follow through with the reports of sexual harassment that they do make. If the data on sexual harassment are correct, it is clear that very few of the victims of sexual harassment in the workplace or in the university report it at all.[20] It is worth making clear what in the university context specifically discourages students from reporting sexual harassment.

Students and professors possess unequal power, influence, confidence, experience, and social standing.[21] And this inequality contributes to students' fears of being ridiculed, disbelieved, punished, or thought incompetent if they come forward with reports of sexually inappropriate conduct on the part of their instructors. Fear of the humiliations that befall many of the women who report rape and other forms of sexual assault evidently makes many women wary of reporting sexual offenses, especially when—as is evidently true in cases of sexual harassment—the attacker is someone who is known to the accuser. The student who has been sexually harassed by her professor is in a particularly vulnerable position, especially if she is known to have had an ongoing personal association with him or has previously submitted to his coercion. The stereotype of the professor as brilliant, principled, and passionately dedicated to his work and to the educational growth of his students leads students to doubt that their allegations would be believed. After all, professors are widely regarded as respectable members of the community. Often enough, students lose confidence in their perceptions of their own actions: if they hadn't done something wrong, then why would this respectable citizen behave so bizarrely?[22] "Blame the victim" sensibilities pervade our society, and so it is not too hard to understand why a confused and distressed victim of sexual harassment would shoulder the blame herself, rather than attribute it to the distinguished, respectable, and (formerly) much-admired professor who was (or appeared to be) so generous with his time and concern.

There are also other factors that erode a woman's confidence, and make her fear that the instructor's harassing behavior must somehow be her fault.[23] Late adolescence and early adulthood are vulnerable and psychologically chaotic times. Among the many difficulties that college-age students face is the struggle to come to terms with their sexuality, and it is easy for them to be insecure in the midst of that process, unclear about their own desires and unsure about how to interpret (and deal with) the many conflicting and ambivalent desires that they have. Though both men and women undoubtedly undergo personal upheaval, their behavior does not meet with the same social interpretation or response, nor are men and women supposed to handle their ambivalences the same way. Men are expected to become more confident and hence more persistent in their pursuit of sexual relationships as they mature. The myth endures that women enjoy being the object of persistent male attentions and invitations but like to play "hard to get" and thus refuse invitations they really wish to accept: when a woman says "no," what she really means is "maybe" or "ask me again later." Since, moreover, women are taught to be polite and nonconfrontational, the woman who tries to act "decently" when confronted with an unwelcome sexual invitation/offer/threat may be seen as thereby expressing ambivalence, which, according to the foregoing myth, may be construed as an expression of interest. If the woman actually does feel ambivalent—she wants to refuse the invitation, but she feels some attraction to the man who has issued it—then she may guiltily believe that she "led him on" even when she said no. And so she may regard the instructor's sexually inappropriate behavior as her fault.[24]

Gender roles and social expectations affect perceptions in other ways as well. Traditionally, women have been judged by their appearance, and they have thus been obliged to devote considerable energy to the attempt to look "attractive," for except among the most wealthy, it was a woman's appearance and good (= compliant) manners that were the principal determinant of whether or not she would attract a man and marry, which was essential for her economic security. Though economics have changed, the traditional view continues to exert an influence on people's thinking, and women still feel pressure to dress attractively and act politely. Yet a woman who is attractive is seen as open to, and perhaps as actually inviting, sexual responses from men. This perception, plus the myth that men's sexual self-control is so fragile that it can be overwhelmed by the presence of an attractive woman, contributes to the view that the women who are sexually harassed are those who "asked for it" (by being physically attractive, or attractively dressed).

Surveys make it clear that there is no correlation between a woman's being attractive (or "sexily" dressed) and her being sexually harassed. Sexual harassment, like rape, is primarily an issue of power, not sex. But the myth persists that it is a female student's appearance that is the cause of her instructor's sexually inappropriate behavior toward her. This myth influences female students' perceptions of both their own and their professors' conduct. And if, as she may well suppose, she bears responsibility for the instructor's behaving as he does, she is likely not to think of his conduct as being sexual harassment.[25]

Popular academic fiction has done a lot to perpetuate these myths, and a lot to reinforce unfortunate gender stereotypes. "Co-eds" are portrayed as lusty seducers of respectable male professors, who are often portrayed as hapless victims of those feminine wiles. One can conjecture that most college-age women have read a few of the standard academic novels and that those novels provide some of the background for their interpretation of their professors' conduct.[26]

Believing that her experience of sexual harassment is rare, believing, perhaps, the various myths surrounding the mechanics of male and female attraction, and being influenced by the myth-supporting academic fiction she reads in English courses, the sexually harassed student may believe that the whole thing is her fault. It is not something that she should report but something she should be ashamed of. And so her energies are likely to be spent trying to cope with or "manage" the incident, not reporting it or attempting to bring the sexual harasser to justice.[27]

The asymmetrical power and influence of students and professors not only affect the student's perception of whether or not her claims of sexual harassment would be believed, they also affect her perception of the risks involved in making such a report (even when she does not fear being disbelieved). The professor holds the power of evaluation, and often enough, the student sees him as gatekeeper to her desired career. If she displeases him, then—whether it is through the mechanism of letters of reference or the more informal workings of the "old boy network"—he may, she fears, ruin her career prospects.[28]

The structural organization of the university also serves to deter victims from reporting sexually inappropriate behavior. The myriad of departments, programs, divisions, and colleges may be quite daunting to an undergraduate, who may not understand the relations between them or be able easily to determine who has authority with respect to what.[29] Nor does it help that some of those people to whom a student might turn appear as confused and powerless as the student herself— or altogether uninterested. A student may summon up her courage to report an incident of sexual misconduct to a professor whom she feels she can trust, only to be told to report it to the department chair, whom she may not know at all. If the department chair has not been through this before or if the chair is overworked or less than sympathetic to her plight, then the student may be met with (what she interprets as) annoyance and indifference ("Well, what do you want me to do about it?") or referred to a dean, who may seem to the student a distant, busy, and daunting individual. The organization of the university, with its convoluted procedures and divisions of responsibility, is quotidian to experienced faculty members who understand the hierarchy and the system. But they may be intimidating to someone who does not understand them and who is already traumatized and alienated.

The attitudes of academics toward their colleagues and students and their views about their own intellectual mission and personal responsibilities may also serve to discourage students from reporting sexual harassment. What is perhaps more important, however, is that those attitudes clearly serve to deter faculty members who learn of a colleague's sexually inappropriate behavior from taking action on it. "Educators see themselves as a community of scholars bound together by common interests and goals."[30] They are reluctant to "break ranks," to do things that they perceive as disloyal or damaging to a colleague. In some cases this reluctance may be an expression of a long-standing liberal commitment to tolerance of difference or a manifestation of the desire to uphold academic freedom or respect the autonomy of one's colleagues.[31] In other cases, and less (ostensibly) nobly, it may be thought to stem from academics' desire to be left alone to get on with their own work, protect their own interests, or stay out of academic politics. But whatever the precise blend of factors (what might be called) the ideology of the faculty tends to support the stance of uninvolvement.

Untenured and non-tenure-tract faculty are in an especially precarious position. The accused senior colleague may wield a good deal of power in the university and in his particular academic field. If displeased or moved to seek retaliation, he may do things that place the untenured faculty member's job at risk. Female faculty members— who are statistically more likely to be untenured or not tenure-track and very much in the minority in their profession—may be particularly vulnerable. Both their professional success thus far and their professional future may well depend upon their being perceived as "good colleagues," people who happen to be female in a largely male context and profession and "don't make a fuss about it." Becoming involved with a sexual harassment case may call attention to a female instructor's gender in ways that make her uncomfortable and may place her in double jeopardy, for she may feel that she is being obliged to risk her own credibility, her good relations with her colleagues, and her own professional connections. And oddly enough, though there is no shortage of good motivations for helping a student who reports an incident of sexual misconduct—a desire to help and protect a student who is hurt and frightened and feels she has nowhere else to turn, the desire to uphold the express and tacit values of the institution, the perception of the need to show students that female faculty members can act with strength and integrity—the female instructor who is willing to assist a student who complains of sexual harassment may find her own motives impugned by resentful male colleagues. As an older woman (and therefore, as convention has it, a less-attractive woman) she may be accused of projecting her unfulfilled desires for male sexual attention onto the student, of being a harridan, or a lesbian who wants to get even with men, of being bitter about her own lack of academic success (which she wrongly and wrongfully attributes to being a woman), and so on.[32]

It is clear that both students' reluctance to come forward with complaints of sexual harassment and faculty members' disinclination to get involved when students do come forward contribute to an underestimation of the scope of the problem of sexual harassment in academia. It is not only the frequency with which sexually inappropriate behavior occurs that is underestimated, however, but the extent of the damage it causes as well. The explanation of why this is so is both complex and multifaceted.

Part of the explanation lies in the invisibility of much of the damage in question. It is easy to see the harm in an instructor's following through on a threat to take reprisals against a student who rejects his demands or in an instructor's tendering an unduly (though perhaps not deliberately or even consciously) harsh evaluation of the student who does not respond favorably to his sexual overtures. Those students are the victims of unfair academic evaluations, and both the professor's integrity and the integrity of the institutions's grading practices are severely compromised by such behavior. But other harms—to the individual student, to other students, to the educational institution, and to the society at large—are less obvious.

Many of the students who find themselves the recipients of unwelcome sexual overtures, remarks, or questions deal with the problem by "managing" it, and the most common form of management is avoidance: the student drops the course, ceases to attend the class, withdraws the application to be a lab assistant, quits coming to office hours, changes her major, or, in the most extreme cases, drops out of school altogether.[33] Though these avoidance tactics may effectively remove the opportunity for an instructor to engage in harassing behavior, they do so at a cost. The student who thinks she can avoid being sexually harassed by simply avoiding the professor in question may thereby be deprived of valuable academic and professional opportunities, and the pool of motivated and intelligent aspirants to the relevant profession is thus reduced. Though, on such a scenario, both the damage to the individual and the loss to society are real, they are largely undetectable. If the number of women in the profession is already low, then the temptation may be to suppose, for example, that "women just aren't interested in engineering" or that "most women just aren't able to do the sort of abstract thinking required for graduate-level physics," adding the insult of misdiagnosis to the injury of sexual harassment. Women who were in fact driven out of the profession by being robbed of the opportunity to pursue their studies in peace are deemed uninterested or incapable. And viewing these women as uninterested or incapable obviously has implications for how other female aspirants to such careers are likely to be viewed, and to view themselves.

Nor does the damage stop there. When a student is given grounds for wondering whether her instructor's academic interest and encouragement were motivated by his sexual interest in her, she may well come to doubt the legitimacy of her previous accomplishments: perhaps her success thus far has owed more to sexual attributes that instructors found attractive than to her own hard work and ability. A good, serious, hardworking student may thus lose the sort of self-confidence that anyone needs to succeed in a competitive field, and that women especially need if they are to succeed in traditionally male professions that remain statistically (if not ideologically) male dominated. If, in addition, other students and instructors attribute the harassed student's academic success to sexual involvement with, or manipulation of, her instructors, then relationships with her peers and her other instructors (and with her own students, if she is a teaching assistant) may well be harmed, and suspicion may be cast on the success of other women. More subtly, both students and instructors may be drawn into a familiar form of overgeneralization and thus may come to harbor the suspicion that women's successes in the academic and professional fields in which they are a significant minority owe more to the women's skills at sexually manipulating those in power than to their hard work and ability. Generalized resentment of women or the unspoken background belief that women do not play fair or cannot "pull their own weight" may result, and this consequence may silently lead instructors to interact differently with male and female students and to approach them with different expectations. Given the insidious working of socialization, neither the students nor the instructors may be aware of the existence of such differential treatment; yet it may well be prejudicial and, ultimately, extremely detrimental. Again, both the existence of the harm and its causation are difficult to pin down in such cases and difficult to distinguish from the apparently statistically supported view that "women just aren't good at (or interested in) physics."

It should be clear from this discussion that sexual harassment (or, more broadly, sexually inappropriate behavior) can cause significant damage to the individuals who are its direct victims, to other women, and to the society at large. But it is hard to make the estimation of that damage more precise, for attempts to arrive at a more precise measure of the damage are complicated by the many other factors that make academic and professional success more difficult for women. It is not likely, after all, that a woman's first or only experience of sex discrimination will occur in a college lecture hall or in a professor's office, and it is plausible to suppose that a woman's prior experiences will influence how much damage will be done to her by an instructor's sexual harassment or other sexually inappropriate behavior. Prior experiences may both magnify the harm that is done to her by sexual harassment and, at the same time, diminish the possibility of perceiving that behavior as the cause of the harm. If women have routinely been victims of sex discrimination or societal sexist attitudes, then how can one say that it is the experience of sexual harassment in the university that is the cause of a woman's subsequent distress or the explanation of her decision to enter a "traditionally female" job or profession?[34]

Reflection on this problem suggests a connection between the two factors I have been examining: widespread ignorance about the extent of sexually inappropriate behavior in the university and the seriousness of the damage it may cause, and the difficulties involved in attempting to come up with a widely acceptable definition of sexual harassment. In a society that many people would characterize as pervaded by sexist attitudes (if not actual sex discrimination) and in one in which there is disagreement about what constitutes (objectionable) sexism and what is merely a response to differences between men and women, it may be difficult, if not impossible, to reach a consensus about what constitutes sexual harassment. Any university policy that hopes to do any good must take note of this fact.

III. POLICY CONSIDERATIONS

Reflection on the two factors I have discussed in sections I and II—difficulties in defining sexual harassment and ignorance of the frequency of on-campus sexual harassment and the seriousness of its effects—should enable us to form some views about how a university's sexual harassment policies should be formulated. More broadly, it should enable us to make some plausible conjectures about what measures are reasonable and likely to be most effective in decreasing the incidence of sexually inappropriate conduct on campus.

I wish to make two suggestions. First, it is a mistake for a university to employ a definition like the one in the EOC Guidelines as its only definition of sexual harassment. Second, universities would do well to shift their primary focus from the sexual harassment component of their policy to the broader range of sexual misconduct that I have been loosely referring to as sexually inappropriate behavior. If a university's purpose in promulgating its policy is to decrease the incidence of the whole range of sexually inappropriate behavior (and not just the more blatant forms of sex discrimination that can easily be classified as sexual harassment), then its energies would be better spent on formulating policies that emphasize education and sensitization of the faculty than on the more legalistic enterprise of defining sexual harassment and detailing the sanctions that should follow upon its commission. These two suggestions are closely connected.

There are a number of reasons why it is a mistake for a university sexual harassment policy to employ the EOC definition of sexual harassment (or one that is similarly inclusive). First, as we have seen, the characterization of a piece of conduct as sexual harassment is inescapably controversial. Though there is little dispute about the more blatant *quid pro quo* cases, agreement quickly dissolves as one moves to those cases in which malign intentions or motivations cannot be easily imputed to an alleged harasser. And a significant portion of the disagreement follows gender lines: men and women evidently have rather different ideas about what sorts of conduct constitute sexual harassment, and about what sexual harassment is.

Not all of the disagreement is necessarily sharp or intractable. Some can be attributed to the continued existence of the evils that sexual harassment policies are supposed to help remedy—that is, sex discrimination or sexist attitudes both in society at large and in the academy. Some can be attributed to the difference in men's and women's experiences and corresponding sensitivities, a difference that may be mirrored in greater male ignorance of the damage that can be caused by (putatively) harassing behavior and in greater reluctance to view the consequences of such behavior as constituting harm. As women come to play a more active and effective role in the university and society at large, it seems reasonable to hope (and not unreasonable to expect) that these things will change and that some of the disagreement will dissolve. But it is important to recognize that not all of the disagreement about what constitutes sexual harassment stems from ignorance and insensitivity. Some is a reflection of other, more ideological and subjective matters. In particular, some of the disagreement about what constitutes sexual harassment is likely to arise from (or reflect) people's more basic and personal disagreements about the meaning (and nature) of being female and the differences between the sexes. And these disagreements are, in turn, connected with disagreements about the nature (and value) of the family, as well as views about what constitutes "proper" relations between the sexes. Barring a convincing demonstration of the rightness of one conception of these things (or the wrongness of all others)—an unlikely, if not impossible, eventuality—there is bound to be continuing disagreement about what constitutes sexual harassment.[35]

Second, if a definition as broad as the one in the EOC Guidelines is taken as the basis for a university policy concerning sexually inappropriate behavior, the policy may be far less effective in eliminating that behavior than an alternative would be. Because the EOC definition of sexual harassment lumps together behaviors that are wrong for very different reasons, it provides a poor foundation for a university policy. A policy that is appropriate for dealing with one form of sexually inappropriate behavior—for example, *quid pro quo* harassment— may not be well suited to other forms of sexually inappropriate behavior, particularly if the behaviors are wrong for different reasons or if some are less clearly (or more controversially) characterized as cases of sexual harassment.

For example, a policy that aims to deal with *quid pro quo* harassment and actual sexual assault must be addressed to individuals who choose to live by an outlaw code. It must seek to deter individuals who know that they are doing wrong but think that they are powerful enough to get away with it. That policy must thus emphasize technical definitional details, complaint procedures, and sanctions: if someone's conduct has features a, b, and c, then its perpetrator is subject to such and such disciplinary procedures.

But the sort of policy that is most appropriate to deter (and punish) the *quid pro quo* harasser is not likely to be the one best suited to put an end to other forms of sexually inappropriate behavior—for example, the use of sexist language and examples and less-than-straightforward attempts to initiate relationships with students. The instructor who offends by the use of sexist examples and the instructor who attempts to initiate a sexual relationship with one of his graduate students without giving thought to the risks and dangers that may await her are insensitive, ignorant, or deficient in their appreciation of others' interests: they are not wilful wrongdoers. Since these perpetrators of sexually inappropriate behavior do not necessarily lack good will or possess the knowledge that what they are doing is wrong, the focus on sanctions is misplaced. The threat of sanction does no good where one does not know that he is doing wrong, and it seems objectionable (and unfair) to apply sanctions when the person who behaved wrongly actually had the will and the intention to do right, unless and until he has had the opportunity to learn why his conduct is objectionable. The sort of policy that is likely to be most effective for dealing with them is thus one that emphasizes education, sensitization, and other more informal methods of response and prevention.

Policies that are designed for dealing with the inadvertent offender need not pay so much attention to definitional details either. If blame and punishment are less the object than behavioral change, then even the instructor who is convinced that his behavior was not wrong (that is, convinced that it was not sexual harassment, that legally proscribed form of sex discrimination, or even morally wrong) can concede that it would be a better thing for his students if he were to change the way he acts. For there are good reasons to cultivate sensitivity to students' feelings and desires whether or not one deems those feelings and desires reasonable.

Careless or insensitive sexually inappropriate behavior is far more frequent on college campuses than blatantly and willfully manipulative behavior.[36] Though every institution's policy should have provisions for dealing harshly with the blatant sexual harassers who persist in living by their outlaw code, it is not those provisions that should dominate a university policy or determine its character.[37] If it is the prevention of all forms of sexually inappropriate behavior that is the university's primary goal—as it should be—then that code does not have to be oriented toward sanctions or the precise allocation of blame. Though it is necessary to present a precise definition of what constitutes blatant sexual harassment (sexual harassment narrowly construed, which includes sexual assault and quid pro quo offers or threats), it is not necessary to present a precise definition of the broader category of sexually inappropriate behavior that is not sexual harassment. Where behavioral change, rather than blame and punishment, is the primary goal, legalistic concerns are less pressing.

Universities tend to adopt definitions of sexual harassment that rely heavily on the EOC Guidelines, for these (or the interpretation of them) constitute the law of the land. But if my line of argument is correct, then a definition like the one in the EOC Guidelines is problematic even when it is narrowly confined to the legal arena: many of the same things that make it unsuitable as the foundation for university policies also impugn its suitability as the foundation for sex discrimination law—that is, it lumps together too many different sorts of (prima facie wrongful) conduct, and it ignores the large ideological component in characterizations of sexual harassment. It thus misinterprets both the nature of disagreements about how sexual harassment should be characterized and the associated fact that many of the alleged perpetrators of sexual harassment might legitimately take issue with the characterization of themselves as sexual harassers, even when they are made aware of the effects of their actions and agree that those effects may be detrimental to the students involved. (Someone can agree that his actions had bad effects without thereby agreeing with their characterization as sexual harassment or thinking that it is legitimate to punish him for committing them.) Sex discrimination laws that are based on the EOC Guidelines are therefore likely to seem unconscionable to a significant number of those who may stand accused of sexual harassment. Whether this consideration is seen as bearing on the justice of laws that rely on the Guidelines, it obviously has a bearing on their efficacy and prospective longevity.

But even if these considerations are not thought to provide persuasive grounds for doubting the fitness of the EOC Guidelines as a basis for sex discrimination laws, they remain powerful objections to taking those Guidelines as the basis for university policies. Though it is necessary for the university to concern itself with avoiding legal liability for the actions of an instructor who is legally guilty of sexual harassment (according to the EOC definition), there is not sufficient justification for treating the legal definition as the (sole, main) foundation of its policies. Lest we forget, universities are institutions of higher learning, and sometimes the learning needs to ascend from the faculty members' classrooms to their own offices and studies. Enlightenment about what it is that is wrong with sexually inappropriate behavior and help in avoiding its commission, rather than intimidation by the threat of sanctions for conduct that the perpetrator may not see as wrong, are more properly concerns for the university. It is education, after all, that is its mission.

NOTES

Acknowledgment: I wish to thank Susan Hobson-Panico, Thomas A. Stermitz, and S. Mickie Grover for their helpful discussion of some of the issues addressed in this essay.

1. Claire Saffran, "What Men Do to Women on the Job," *Redbook* (November 1976), pp. 149, 217–23; see p. 217: "In fact, nearly 9 out of 10 report that they have experienced one or more forms of unwanted attentions on the job. This can be visual (leering and ogling) or verbal (sexual remarks and teasing). It can escalate to pinching, grabbing and touching, to subtle hints and pressures, to overt requests for dates and sexual favors—with the implied threat that it will go against the woman if she refuses."

2. See, e.g., Karen Lindsay, "Sexual Harassment on the Job and How to Stop it," *Ms.* (November 1977), pp. 47–48, 50–51, 74–75, 78; Margaret Mead, "A Proposal: We Need Taboos on Sex at Work," *Redbook* (April 1978), pp. 31, 33, 38; Caryl Rivers, "Sexual Harassment: The Executive's Alternative to Rape," *Mother Jones* (June 1978), pp. 21–24, 28; Claire Saffran, "Sexual Harassment: The View From the Top," *Redbook* (March 1981), pp. 45–51. See also Constance Backhouse and Leah Cohen, *Sexual Harassment on the Job* (Englewood Cliffs, N.J.: Prentice-Hall, 1981), originally published in 1978 as *The Secret Oppression;* and Catherine A. MacKinnon, *Sexual Harassment of Working Women* (New Haven: Yale University Press, 1979).

Popular discussions of sexual harassment in academia include Adrienne Munich, "Seduction in Academe," *Psychology Today* (February 1978), pp. 82–84, 108; Anne Nelson, "Sexual Harassment at Yale," *Nation,* January 14, 1978, pp. 7–10; Lorenzo Middleton, "Sexual Harassment by Professors: An 'Increasingly Visible' Problem," *Chronicle of Higher Education,* September 15, 1980, pp. 1, 4–5; Noel Epstein, "When Professors Swap Good Grades for Sex," *Washington Post,* September 6, 1981, pp. C1, C4; Anne Field, "Harassment on Campus: Sex in a Tenured Position?" *Ms.* (September 1981), pp. 68, 70, 73, 100–102; Suzanne Perry, "Sexual Harassment on the Campuses: Deciding Where to Draw the Line," *Chronicle of Higher Education,* March 23, 1983, pp. 21–22.

3. In *Barnes* v. *Castle,* 561 F2d 983 (D.C. Cir. 1977), which held that sexual harassment is actionable as sex-based discrimination under Title VII and also extended some liability to an employer for the discriminatory acts of its supervisors.

4. *Alexander* v. *Yale University,* 549 F. Supp. 1 (D. Conn 1977), established sexual harassment as sex discrimination under Title IX.

5. *Meritor Savings Bank FSB* v. *Vinson,* 1206 S. Ct. 2399 (1986).

6. Thus both Title VII and Title IX apply when a student is sexually harassed by an instructor. Under Title IX, a student may have a cause of action against the individual instructor who sexually harassed her, and under Title VII, a cause of action against the university that employed that instructor. For relevant discussion, see Annette Gibbs and Robin B. Balthorpe, "Sexual Harassment in the Workplace and Its Ramifications for Academia," *Journal of College Student Personnel* 23 (1982), 158–62.

7. See, for example, "Statement on Professional Ethics," adopted in 1966 (pp. 133–34 of the *AAUP Policy Documents and Reports,* Washington, D.C.:

AAUP, 1984), which condemns "any exploitation for [a teacher's] private advantage" (p. 133); "A Statement of the Association's Council: Freedom and Responsibility," (pp. 135–36), adopted in 1970, which declares that "students are entitled to an atmosphere conductive to learning and to even-handed treatment in all aspects of the teacher-student relationship" (p. 135); and "Sexual Harassment: Suggested Policy and Procedures for Handling Complaints," (pp. 98–100), adopted in 1984, which states, "It is the policy of this institution that no member of the academic community may sexually harass another" (p. 99).

8. See, e.g., Eliza G. C. Collins and Timothy B. Blodgett, "Sexual Harassment . . . Some See It . . . Some Won't," *Harvard Business Review* 59 (1981), 76–95; Phyllis L. Crocker, "An Analysis of University Definitions of Sexual Harassment," *Signs* 8 (1983), 696–707; John Hughes and Larry May, "Sexual Harassment," *Social Theory and Practice* 6 (1980), 249–80; Catherine A. MacKinnon, "Sexual Harassment: Its First Decade in Court," in her *Feminism Unmodified* (Cambridge: Harvard University Press, 1987), pp. 103–16, 251–56; Rosemary Tong, "Sexual Harassment," in her *Women, Sex, and the Law* (Totowa, N.J.: Rowman and Littlefield, 1983).

9. There is some disagreement as to whether it is sex discrimination, but there can be no serious doubt that it is wrongful discrimination. Whether he follows through on the threat and whether or not she submits to it are irrelevant. See, e.g., Crocker, "Analysis of University Definitions," p. 704: "Once a student is propositioned, all her future interactions with, and evaluations by, the professor are tainted and suspect, whether a promise or threat was ever made or carried out."

10. See Phyllis L. Crocker, "Annotated Bibliography on Sexual Harassment in Education," *Women's Rights Law Reporter* 7 (1982), 91–106. And see *Symposium on Sexual Harassment* in *Thought & Action* 5 (1989): 17–52, especially the essay by Anne Traux, "Sexual Harassment in Higher Education: What We've Learned," pp. 25–38, for an overview of surveys and results. Though a good deal of the sexual harassment on campus involves faculty members and administrators as victims, and some involves students as harassers, considerations of space and focus require that I confine this essay to the discussion of sexual harassment that involves students as victims and instructors as harassers. Discussion will also be confined to cases in which it is male instructors who are the harassers and female students who are the victims. As many commentators have observed, the cases in which a female instructor harasses a male student or a male instructor harasses a male student are few and far between. According to Traux, p. 25: "Nationally, about 95 percent of all sexual harassment reports involve men harassing females." See also Gibbs and Balthorpe, "Sexual Harassment in the Workplace"; MacKinnon, "Sexual Harassment: Its First Decade"; Tong, "Sexual Harassment"; Donna J. Benson and Gregg E. Thomson, "Sexual Harassment on a University Campus: The Confluence of Authority Relations, Sexual Interest, and Gender Stratification," *Social Problems* 29 (1982), 236–51; Bernice Lott, Mary Ellen Reilly, and Dale R. Howard, "Sexual Assault and Harassment: A Campus Community Case Study," *Signs* 8 (1982), 296–319.

11. Because—as we shall see—there is so much disagreement about what sorts of conduct constitute actual sexual harassment, and because *sexual harass-*

ment is a legal term that is used to describe certain forms of legally proscribed sex discrimination, I prefer to use the broader (and vaguer) terms *sexually inappropriate behavior* and *sexual misconduct* whenever context and expression permit. If, as I shall argue, there are different kinds of sexually inappropriate behavior that may be wrong but are not (for various reasons) happily classified with the sorts of wrongful behavior that constitute blatant sexual harassment, then it may be misleading to use *sexual harassment* as omnivorously as many commentators—and the Equal Opportunity Commission—have done.

12. It is, of course, possible for a female professor to harass a male student or for a professor of one sex to harass a student of the same sex. But it is clear that the vast majority of harassers are men, and the vast majority of victims are women, and surveys suggest that the incidence of sexual harassment of male students by female instructors is indeed very small. It is of course possible for a female instructor to make a *quid pro quo* offer/threat to a male student. But the fact that women are a minority, both in the upper echelons of the teaching and administrative staff and in most departments, together with the familiar facts about gender expectations and status, suggests that such harassment will be rare. And subtler forms of sexually inappropriate behavior, which the perpetrator does not perceive as unwelcome or coercive, will probably be even rarer.

Involvements between older, established men and young women are accepted as normal, while those between older, established women and young, unestablished men clearly are not. Women who are involved in relationships with young, less-established men are generally the object of criticism, not admiration or even tolerance. In addition, since the determination of a woman's social status is held to depend heavily on the status of the male she is associated with, the attractions of such a relationship are likely not to be great: whereas a female student may gain status by involvement with a male professor, a female professor forfeits status by involvement with a male student. If, as most commentators point out, sexual harassment is primarily an issue of power, not sex, there is considerably less incentive for a female faculty member to seek involvement with a male student, and considerably more disincentive. Finally, one can reasonably suppose that because women have long been in the minority in academia and have long been subject to various forms of sex discrimination and disparagement, they are likely to be more sensitive to the risks and problems that even well-intentioned relationships between persons of unequal power create. Whether or not it is accurate to say that gender is itself a form of hierarchy in a society that has been and continues to be so male-dominated (see MacKinnon, "Sexual Harassment: Its First Decade"), there are good reasons to recognize that, as things now stand, the problem of sexual harassment is almost always one of men harassing women. Though, in the abstract, the issue of sexual harassment—the exploitative use of power—is sex-neutral, if not sex-blind, in circumstances in which it is men who (by and large) possess the power, it is women who will (by and large) be the victims.

That both males and females can be the victims of sexually inappropriate behavior has sometimes—mistakenly—been thought to undercut the claim that sexual harassment is a form of sex discrimination. But the existence of cases in which a male student is victimized by a female instructor does nothing to undercut such a claim, for the effects of being so victimized may be different for men and women, and the background of long-standing and ongoing discrimination against women makes it plausible to suppose that the effects would indeed be different. People suppose that because wrongs are committed both in the case in which a male professor harasses a female student and in the case in which a female professor harasses a male student, they must be the *same* wrong. But this is not obviously a correct assumption. In both cases there is a wrongful abuse of power and authority, but in one of the cases in which there is a wrongful abuse of power and authority, there is also—because of the long-standing and ongoing discrimination against women—another wrong, namely, that of sex discrimination.

Nor does the existence of cases of single-sex harassment undercut the claim that sexual harassment is sex discrimination, unless one regards the obvious and widespread discrimination against homosexuals as some form of discrimination other than sex discrimination or construes sex discrimination so narrowly that conventional gender identity is seen as defining one's sex. Neither of these assumptions is plausible.

There are, indeed, reasons for being uneasy at the characterizion of sexual harassment as a form of sex discrimination. In some cases of sexually inappropriate behavior (which the Equal Opportunity Commission Guidelines would classify as sexual harassment), it is primarily an instructor's obvious disrespect, rather than the sexual cast of that disrespect, that seems more perspicuously identified as the thing that makes his actions wrong.

But the best reasons for uneasiness are probably the pragmatic ones. Recent Supreme Court decisions have significantly weakened the scope of protections against racial discrimination (from Title VII and elsewhere); there is reason to suspect that sex discrimination protections will fare no better. They may even fare worse, for there is good reason to insist that there are no important ineliminable differences between persons of different races, but there are obviously differences between the sexes.

13. One has only to look at advertising or television sitcoms, or —as Billie Wright Dziech and Linda Weiner point out in *The Lecherous Professor* (Boston: Beacon Press, 1984)—watch teenagers interact in a shopping mall to be reminded how powerful and pervasive gender expectations are. See Benson and Thomson, "Sexual Harassment on a University Campus"; MacKinnon, *Sexual Harassment of Working Women*; MacKinnon, "Sexual Harassment: Its First Decade."

14. Codified as 29 CFR 1604, issued November 24, 1965, and last amended by 45 FR 74676, effective November 10, 1980.

15. It may also be a problematically exclusive definition, since, in specifying only *unwelcome* sexual advances as constituting sexual harassment, it may exclude cases that some people might wish to classify as sexual harassment. At the very least, the specification that the sexual advances in question must be unwelcome is curious and difficult to interpret. When there is great disparity in the power and prestige of the individuals involved, as there is in most, if not all, cases of (putative) instructor-student harassment, it may be hard to determine whether or not the sexual overtures were unwelcome, for the student may have been afraid or incapable of giving that indication. It does not help to do what the Court did in *Meritor* when it said, "The fact that sex-

related conduct was 'voluntary,' in the sense that the complainant was not forced to participate against her will, is not a defense to a sexual harassment suit brought under Title VII. The gravemen [sic] of any sexual harassment claims is that the alleged sexual advances were 'unwelcome.' . . . The correct inquiry is whether respondent by her conduct indicated that the alleged sexual advances were unwelcome, not whether her actual participation in sexual intercourse was voluntary." Quoted in Doric Little and John A. Thompson, "Campus Politics, the Law, and Sexual Relationships," in *Symposium on Sexual Harassment*, p. 18.

But who decides what conduct indicates that the sexual advances were unwelcome? Moreover, as Crocker points out "the inclusion of the qualifying words 'unwelcome,' 'unwanted,' and 'inappropriate' suggests that there are 'appropriate' sexual advances, or 'wanted' sexual advances that do not constitute harassment and will not be acted on by university officials," "Analysis of University Definitions," p. 703). Yet one might plausibly hold that any sexual advance an instructor makes is potentially sexual harassment, for he cannot know that it is unwelcome until it is made, and perhaps not even then. Moreover, since the effects of a broken, ostensibly consensual relationship between professor and student can have all the ill effects that initially unwelcome sexual advances have, as well as others, confining sexual harassment complaints to unwelcome sexual advances seems unduly restrictive.

16. Dziech and Weiner, *The Lecherous Professor*, p. 146.

17. Some of the difficulty stems from what might be characterized as generational factors. Older instructors, who for years called female students "girls" or "young ladies" and cultivated a courtly image by complimenting women on their appearance, may be unaware of the problems with continuing to do so. If, moreover, they spent most of their careers dealing only with male colleagues or supervising only male graduate students, then they may be genuinely uncomfortable in the presence of female students and colleagues and unclear about how to interact with them, for they are used to interacting with women socially, not intellectually. Though female students may find the behavior of these older professors both offensive and discriminatory, it is clear that it stems from different sources and calls for different remedies from those needed in cases of blatant *quid pro quo* harassment.

18. Different commentators seem to interpret this "gender gap" differently. According to Collins and Blodgett, "Most people agree on what harassment is. But men and women disagree on how often it occurs" ("Sexual Harassment . . . ," p. 78). In *Intent vs. Impact: How to Effectively Manage Sexual Harassment Investigations* (Washington, D.C.: Bureau of National Affairs, n.d.), Stephen F. Anderson maintains that "men and women usually perceive sexual harassment differently, i.e., what behavior is sexual harassment, when friendly behavior crosses the line and becomes sexual harassment, and how much sexual harassment actually occurs" (p. 8). I believe that considerable insight is shed on the issue by Catherine MacKinnon's observation that a man defines such things as rape and sexual assault as things he thinks *he* doesn't do. See MacKinnon, "Sexual Harassment: Its First Decade," p. 105.

19. Anderson maintains that (*Intent vs. Impact*), according to the definition of sexual harassment in the EOC Guidelines and the laws that are based on it, it is the impact of someone's behavior, not his intent, that determines

whether or not his actions constitute sexual harassment. For reasons that are discussed in the text, I think this definition is not satisfactory: impact is not a fair or reasonable measure of wrongdoing.

20. According to Truax, "Sexual Harassment in Higher Education," p. 26, "Of those harassed, not more than one in 10 actually report the harassment."

21. And as many would point out, women and men are not peers in these areas either.

22. To some degree, what medical ethicists have called "the fallacy of the generalization of expertise" is at work here. People who are thought to be successful or expert in one area are frequently—and unreasonably—thought to be successful or expert in others. Thus some people wrongly suppose that physicians are knowledgeable in matters of medical ethics (simply) because they are knowledgeable in medical matters, and others suppose that the good scholar of history (e.g.) must also be a good and decent person.

23. See Robert Shrank, "Two Women, Three Men on a Raft," *Harvard Business Review* 55 (1977), 100–108, for an interesting discussion of how men may unreflectively work to undermine women's self-confidence.

24. Or she may think that she should "be complimented, not incensed, if confronted with male sexual interest" (see Benson and Thomson, "Sexual Harassment on a Campus," p. 237) and thus feel that she has no right to complain.

25. One of the women interviewed by Collins and Blodgett ("Sexual Harassment . . . ," p. 93) said: "A lot of women hesitate to report sexual harassment because women: (1) don't think they'll be believed; (2) will be punished by smaller raises or cruddy jobs [the analogue in the university context: will be punished by lower grades or undeservedly harsh evaluations]; (3) will be ostracized by male and female employees [students and other instructors]; (4) will be accused of inviting the advance; (5) have guilt feelings that perhaps it was invited subconsciously; (6) fear publicity; (7) are unsure exactly what is harassment and what is just interaction of people."

26. Some of the novels that come to mind here are Joyce Carol Oates, *Them;* John Barth, *The End of the Road;* and Bernard Malamud, *Dubin's Lives.* See Dziech and Weiner, *The Lecherous Professor,* pp. 62–63, 68, 118.

27. See especially Benson and Thomson, "Sexual Harassment on Campus"; and Dziech and Weiner, *The Lecherous Professor,* chap. 4. Also relevant is Judith Berman Brandenburg, "Sexual Harassment in the University: Guidelines for Establishing a Grievance Procedure," *Signs* 8 (1982), 321–36. See Mary P. Rowe, "Dealing with Sexual Harassment," *Harvard Business Review* 59 (1981), 42–47, for a detailed set of proposed procedures for harassed employees that places more emphasis on "management" of sexual harassment in the workplace than on prevention or redress.

28. A quotation from Dziech and Weiner, *The Lecherous Professor,* p. 83, drives this point home. One pre-med student said: It's easy for someone else to say that I should do something about Dr. ____, but how can I? He was the first person at ____ to take my work seriously. At least I think it's my work that made him notice me. He's the one who's pushing for me to get into med school. If I refuse him, then I ruin my whole life."

29. Material in this and the succeeding paragraph benefited from the discussion in chap. 2 of Dziech and Weiner, *The Lecherous Professor.*

30. Ibid., p. 49.

31. I do not mean to suggest that respect for academic freedom or one's colleagues' autonomy requires (or even permits) a faculty member who learns of an incident of sexual harassment to ignore the student who reports it or otherwise discourage her from pressing her complaint. Neither academic freedom nor professional autonomy is absolute, and it is difficult to see what intellectually respectable academic purpose is served by the tolerance of sexual harassment. Of course, a faculty member who believes that some respectable academic purpose *is* served by tolerating a colleague's sexually inappropriate behavior should be given the opportunity to explain his or her views. But such an opportunity can arise only if students are listened to and encouraged, not dissuaded from bringing their sexual harassment complaints forward in the first place.

32. See Dziech and Weiner, *The Lecherous Professor*, chap. 6.

33. See note 27.

34. The old adage that "defendants must take plaintiffs as they find them" is of some help here, but not much.

35. There is thus an obvious parallel with the abortion dispute, which—though few recognize it—turns less on people's metaphysical views about the status of the fetus than on their views about sexuality, sex differences, and the meaning of children, marriage, and the family. See Nancy Davis, "Philosophers and the Abortion Debate: Coming to Terms with the Criticism," working paper available through the Center for Values and Social Policy at the University of Colorado.

36. See Benson and Thomson, "Sexual Harassment on a Campus"; and Crocker, "Analysis of University Definitions," p. 699.

37. Interestingly, very seldom is *quid pro quo* harassment an isolated incident. *Quid pro quo* harassers tend to be repeat harassers, and there is reason to suspect that a great deal of the *quid pro quo* harassment that goes on in an institution is done by a relatively small number of harassers. It is also interesting to note the high proportion of harassment directed at minority women. See, e.g., Benson and Thomson, "Sexual Harassment on a Campus"; and Dziech and Weiner, *The Lecherous Professor*, chap. 5.

10

BEYOND *IN LOCO PARENTIS?*
Parietal Rules and Moral Maturity

David A. Hoekema

> The Housing and Residence Life program of the University
> . . . is designed to be an integral part of students' educational
> experience. Its primary focus is student development in a colle-
> giate educational environment. . . . While Housing and Resi-
> dence Life staff members assist students in this developmental
> process, they do not assume the role of parents. With the advent
> of right-to-privacy legislation, the 'in loco parentis' concept has
> faded from college campuses.
> —*Residence Halls Handbook, 1988–89,*
> of a state university

There is a certain sort of privacy that consists not in being
actually screened from others' view but simply in the practice of not
looking. Privacy of this limited sort is familiar in public restrooms,
locker rooms, and hospitals.

When I was a college student, this kind of privacy—and no other—
prevailed within a hundred-yard circle of the entrance to the women's
residence halls between 10:45 and 11:00 P.M. on weekdays, 12:45 and
1:00 A.M. on weekends. Dozens of couples could be espied bidding
fond farewells on the steps, along the porch railing, and among the
low bushes about the entrance. The attentions mutually bestowed
ranged from hasty kisses to entanglements whose complexity was
limited only by the necessity of being fully and more or less plausibly
clothed for the quick dash inside just before the doors were locked.
Or so it seemed. No one paid attention to what others were doing,
since the aversion of eyes was the only privacy available.

The scene I describe will strike most contemporary college students as an exotic vignette from a far distant time and place. The distance is not in fact very great: it was just twenty years ago, at a middle-sized church-related college, that I dated a woman who lived in a residence hall and became thoroughly familiar with the many restrictions under which she lived. Along with knowledge of the parietal restrictions, of course, went knowledge of how to evade them from time to time—of doors sometimes propped open after hours, of resident advisers who might be corruptible, even, for the more daring, of overnight leaves ostensibly to visit a nearby aunt.

The restrictions on the domestic and amorous life of college students were numerous, and infractions were dealt with sternly: disciplinary hearings and anxious correspondence between deans and parents usually ensued. For the college still purported to stand *in loco parentis*. Parietal rules gave concrete expression to parents' demand that the college be no less firm and directive a parent than they.

Today, at the same college, all restrictions on student hours have been eliminated. Women's residence halls are still locked during the night for safety, but residents carry keys. Still, at this institution, visitation hours for men in women's residence halls and for women in men's residence halls remain very limited. Visits are permitted only on weekend afternoons and evenings, and only with the door ajar.

Limited visitation hours now seem a relic of the dark ages to many students at state universities. Even separate men's and women's residence halls are disappearing, along with the often discriminatory rules that governed them. Nearly every campus offers coeducational accommodations, with men and women on alternating floors or in alternating rooms. On many campuses complicated roommate swaps are arranged informally, permitting students to take up housekeeping with boy friends or girl friends. In coeducational residence halls restrictions on visitation are nearly impossible to enforce, and both students and university administrators seem relieved to see them go.

There was an anachronistic quality about the controversy that erupted recently not only on campuses but on television talk shows over a proposal at Boston University to limit outside guests in residence halls to weekend evenings, to require roommate approval for any overnight guests, and categorically to prohibit overnight guests of the opposite sex.[1] Student demonstrations and editorials berated the university administration for this "insulting and offensive" policy, and a poll conducted by the student newspaper found 95 percent of students opposed to the restrictions, 4 percent in favor, and 1 percent indifferent. (So much for the alleged indifference and apathy of contemporary college students.)

The controversy at Boston University had at least as much to do with academic and cultural politics as with morality, but the same issues have surfaced on many other campuses, and several have recently tightened visiting rules.[2] Moreover, they are issues that face faculty and administrators on every campus, even if many have by now abandoned any attempt to control students' social or sexual behavior. The parietal rules of my university are more or less typical of those at state institutions. In each residence hall, a vote on whether to establish restricted visitation hours will be conducted if such a vote is requested by 15 percent of the residents, and a simple majority will determine any visiting hour regulations. Some residence halls, including those designated as coeducational, are exempt from such restrictions. The residence hall handbook offers no further guidance on distinguishing proper from improper conduct except the statements that "the student is responsible for the conduct of his or her guest" and that "individual room visitation may not infringe upon the rights of the roommate(s)."

Policy guidelines add that residents may have overnight guests of the same sex for no more than three consecutive days and that "the University does not condone members of the opposite sex staying overnight in a residence hall." The latter statement is puzzling in a number of ways, including its odd syntax (is it possible to "condone" a person?) and its suggestion that the entire female or male student population—we can't tell which—is sleeping in the residence halls over the university's principled protest. Perhaps it is unfair to deconstruct college policy statements, or even to read them carefully, when the substance is evident: the university desires all students to know that fornication in the residence hall is, in its considered opinion, a bad thing. Yet the complete control of each residence hall over visiting policies makes this vague prohibition completely unenforceable.

Actual patterns of behavior, students have told me, are governed by informal codes rather then by formally enacted policies, and individual residence halls tend to maintain their predominant character from year to year. A few, including those that house students in the honors program, are generally quiet enough for study, while others are famous for their raucous parties. Those who do not conform face social pressures that are usually sufficient to induce them either to change their behavior or to request a transfer. Thus the quiet residence halls remain relatively free from boisterous drinkers, the party halls free from the irritating habits of serious students. On some campuses these patterns are codified into official regulations: certain residence halls are designated as "quiet," with restrictions on visitors and alcohol, and entering students are invited to state their preference.

However the details of residential life are dealt with, it is noteworthy that university policies now say as little as possible about the very aspects of personal conduct that were once the object of such close scrutiny. Student deans of an earlier generation avoided mention of delicate topics such as sexual relations, venereal disease, and pregnancy not only from a sense of decorum but also because the institutional disapproval of unseemly conduct did not need to be openly stated. Today's student handbooks avoid many of the same topics, but for a quite different reason, namely, an institutional desire to respect privacy and to avoid presuming to make moral judgments on students' behalf. Visitation rules are accorded a few paragraphs in my university's handbook, compared to the policy on "extension cords in residence halls," which covers three columns, encompassing a statement of purpose and fourteen numbered subsections.

One might argue that a responsible parent is no less concerned with proper use of extension cords than with personal and sexual conduct. Perhaps statistical evidence would even show that more students suffer lasting injury from use of substandard extension cords (see section III.J.2.c.: use minimum sixteen gauge, minimum rating thirteen amperes) than from casual sex. But the hands-off policy of the handbook that expresses disapproval of cohabitation but leaves visiting restrictions to majority vote of each residential building is a far cry indeed from the traditional stance of the institution as surrogate parent.

What is the moral significance of this shift? My purpose in this discussion is neither to survey prevailing practices nor to decry the immorality and youth of the young. I write neither as a social scientist nor as a moralist but as a philosopher and teacher. My purpose is to direct attention to the peculiar moral challenges that confront students in an institution that has relinquished its standing *in loco parentis*. If the college or university will not or cannot any longer act as substitute parent, must the contemporary college student find another surrogate? Or is there still a place for the *alma mater in loco parentis*?

The question is worth asking from a philosophical standpoint, not merely for purposes of better college governance. Situations such as that of the college student offer important insights into the nature and structure of ethical decision making itself. Recent ethical theory has been preoccupied with the place of individual autonomy in moral agency. In the modern tradition articulated most forcefully by Kant, morality itself can be defined as a special sort of moral independence from others. To act morally, in Kant's theory, is to be one's own moral lawgiver. Individual self-determination remains the ideal of moral conduct for many who follow in the Kantian tradition, and it is central to what some have called "rights-based" moral theories.[3]

This tradition has been challenged by a contrary tradition that emphasizes the communitarian basis of morality. Numerous recent writers, variously rooted in feminist theory, classical American pragmatism, and Continental social theory, have charged that the modernist vision is a distortion of morality and human agency. Critics argue that moral action consists not of autonomous exercise of individual choice but of choices made in essential relationship to and dependence upon a community.[4]

I cannot here attempt to resolve the dispute between apologists for autonomy and defenders of communitarian morality, but I offer the example of the college student as an ideal test case. The modern American adolescent is perhaps the most perfect exemplification in evolutionary history of the pervasive influence, for good or ill, of a highly particular community. Modes of dress, styles of hair, forms of familiar address, and linguistic patterns are disseminated across campuses nationwide virtually instantaneously, with the inevitable and not unintended effect of baffling and excluding adults as well as young people outside a distinct subcommunity. Yet the years of adolescence and early adulthood are also fundamental to the formation of individual responsibility. Students must make crucial choices concerning future careers and interpersonal relationships, and they must make these choices genuinely their own. Colleges are therefore entirely warranted in ceding a large measure of autonomy to students. College students are at the same time creatures of the community in which they find themselves and products of an emerging capacity for autonomy and self-creation.

The retreat of colleges from the parental stance is at least partly a result of the realization that most college students have reached a point in their moral development when indoctrination and authoritarianism are likely to be ineffective and counterproductive. Rigid parietal rules that cannot be consistently enforced will simply be ignored, and to proclaim them anyway is mere hypocrisy. Hypocrisy has its uses—civilization would not last a day without it, after all—but the eighteen- and nineteen-year-olds who populate our campuses know too much

of the world and its ways either to follow a rigid code of conduct on
the directive of a dean or, like many of their parents and grandparents
when they attended the same colleges, to uphold a narrow moral ideal
publicly while keeping transgressions well concealed.

In any case, the aim of the college insofar as it continues to act *in
loco parentis* should be not to induce moral behavior but rather *to foster
moral maturity*. What defines moral behavior is a matter of endless and
possibly irresolvable controversy. A college is foolish to pretend that
it can articulate a single and univocal moral code that will command
equal respect from students who adhere to Mormonism, orthodox
Judaism, Pentecostalism, and liberal humanist principles, to say nothing of children reared on Rawlsian or act-utilitarian principles. Yet it
is possible to agree all the same on the underlying need of all adults
for *the capacity to make and carry through moral decisions*.

The kind of maturity at issue has little to do with a passage through
successive alleged stages of moral thinking and theorizing, as in the
psychological theories advanced by Jean Piaget and Lawrence Kohl-
berg. I am concerned instead with a more general ability to make a
moral decision in the way that we expect of adults, whatever the
character of the particular morality that is applied. While it would be
beyond the scope of this discussion to attempt a full account of what
such maturity entails, I can suggest three conditions that seem to me
necessary to its exercise.[5]

First, one must make a moral choice with one's eyes open, aware
of a range of other decisions one might make instead. An uninformed
choice is not a fully responsible choice when the lack of information
is a result of one's failure to reflect on one's choice. A mature moral
decision is an informed decision.

Second, moral maturity entails giving appropriate weight to the
ethical views of others without letting them function as a substitute
for one's own considered judgement. It is equally a sign of immaturity
to rely on others to make one's moral decisions as to set aside the
advice and example of others entirely. A mature individual knows
that moral choices must be one's own but that others are often in a
position either to challenge or to corroborate one's judgements.

Third, to make a mature moral decision one must be cognizant of
the likely consequences of one's action and prepared to stand by one's
decision even if the results are not as one hopes. Immaturity may take
the form of acting impulsively and without regard to consequences or
of shirking the responsibility for the consequences of one's acts. Mor-

ally mature individuals may disagree about the best choice, but each will be prepared to make a choice and stand by it.

Nourishment of the capacity for mature moral decision making ought to be a central priority in assessing college programs and policies, and the effect of such policies on students' capacity to make fully responsible decisions should be a primary concern of college faculties and administrators. Colleges ought to act *in loco parentis* in this limited sense: they should strive to create an environment in which students' capacity for moral action is both acknowledged and augmented. Autocratic control over personal decisions demands too little of students and is, in any case, in most circumstances doomed to failure. But withdrawal from the moral ground—the stance that seems too frequently to characterize the university today—demands too much from students and gives them too little assistance in developing the capacity to exercise their freedom.

To what extent are students free to order their own lives, and to what extent are they bound by institutional regulations? External constraints are now few. Colleges insist, with varying degrees of seriousness, on adherence to state and local law, particularly concerning alcohol and drug use. They enjoin respect for others' rights and responsible behavior, but the implications of these vague injunctions are seldom spelled out clearly. Other external constraints play a varying role. The parents, older siblings, and classmates of some students all enforce the standards of the home community; for other students, college makes possible a radical departure from old rules and ways.

Student behavior is shaped more decisively by peer standards and pressures than by college policies. The communities and subcommunities that flourish among students often place a high value on conformity, on loyalty to friends, and also on risk taking and defiance of authority. As the force of parietal rules has diminished, the influence of social expectations has grown correspondingly stronger.

The removal of external constraints has encouraged the emergence of new forms of interaction and problem solving, and the results have been constructive in many ways. A recent study of the students at a large state university, conducted by a social anthropologist, noted that coeducational residence halls have brought about not only greater equality but also healthier relationships between men and women students, fostering daily interaction in a wide range of nonacademic activities.[6] The passing of the panty raid is no loss for American culture.

Yet there is a crucial difference between an environment that fosters student independence and maturity and an environment in which rules are abolished. Unfortunately, as colleges have abandoned the attempt to function *in loco parentis*, they have too often washed their hands of all responsibility for students' moral development. The result is the absurd and ultimately demoralizing situation in which many students find themselves.

It may have been unhealthy and unwise to attempt to deny eighteen-year-olds every opportunity for privacy and freedom in exploring their sexuality, as colleges once did. Branding all physical intimacy sinful may simply make necking appear the equivalent of intercourse. But is it healthier for students to spend the years of self-discovery in an environment in which cohabitation is the norm, and those who resist the pressure are made to feel abnormal—and forced to sleep in the hall? Is it really an improvement on the semipublic necking around dormitories at closing time to place students in a situation where they must pretend to be asleep when a roommate's boy friend slips in to share her bed several nights each week? Universities are probably wise to advocate "responsible drinking" among those legally of age rather than to issue blanket prohibitions they cannot and will not enforce. But when the average student at a state university, according to a recent study, spends an average of twelve hours each week at drinking parties, "responsible drinking" is a sham. I wish I were making these examples up, but unfortunately they are not fictional.[7]

Institutions may adopt one of three essential strategies with respect to parietal rules. In the first place—and this must not be forgotten in generalizing about "today's campuses"—there remain a substantial number of institutions where highly restrictive parietal rules are still promulgated and enforced. Among them are many of the more conservative church-related colleges, yeshivas and Jewish institutions still closely tied to a religious community, and small colleges whose students come mostly from the local community. In such a context the old rules may still apply—if not in strict observance, at least in the maintenance of a plausible pretence that they are observed.

But this stance is increasingly difficult even for socially conservative institutions to maintain. Students know of the much looser rules that govern other institutions and press for loosening of the actual as well as the nominal limits on behavior. Continuing to promulgate a highly restrictive standard—dress and deportment codes, prohibition of all alcohol use, condemnation of nonmarital sexual relations of every kind—can degenerate into hypocrisy, and strict rules may in the end instill the capacity to dissemble rather than the capacity to make independent moral decisions. Such a restrictive stance, in any case, is simply not possible for the administrators of a diverse state institution, or even for many church-related or religiously grounded colleges. Both student and faculty views are too diverse in such institutions to allow it.

Most public institutions and many private ones have embraced a second stance: the hands-off policy of withdrawing from any attempt to control behavior except as necessary to satisfy legal requirements and maintain a reasonable degree of social order. Parietal rules, on this model, emphasize mutual respect and responsibility, the duties and obligations of members of an educational community, and similar generalities, while avoiding so far as possible the translation of these grand principles into concrete rules.

The motive for this withdrawal from the field of moral guidance is evident. Members of the university community hold fundamentally opposed convictions about personal morality. In the absence of a core of shared values sufficient to sustain the more restrictive model, concrete rules about behavior are difficult to maintain. Equally important as a motivation is the desire to afford students the freedom to develop their own capacity to make moral decisions.

But the hands-off policy achieves an appearance of moral responsibility and respect for individual autonomy that, in the end, merely masks the unwillingness of an institution to take its own responsibilities seriously enough. When a college withdraws from the moral playing field altogether, its students may still learn to make moral decisions, but the college will not have provided the help that it should.

Is there a middle way between these two extremes of control and permissiveness? In the remainder of this essay I will make the case for that possibility, for a campus environment that does not attempt to dictate a single standard of moral conduct, yet provides a helpful rather than a merely neutral environment for the formation of moral character. My suggestions will of necessity be sketchy and programmatic. They are offered in the hope that there is a place for the college as a player—but not coach, referee, and rule maker—in the field of moral development. I will argue, in short, that colleges should still serve to a limited degree *in loco parentis* but that their model of the parent's role must be more modest than the one predominant in an earlier generation.

If this third option is not available, if the only choices are authoritarianism and permissiveness, then there is little hope that the college years will consistently advance students' moral development. In that case there may be little to allay either the greatest fear of the political right—fear of a moral vacuum and uncritical relativism—or the nightmare of the political left—fear of indoctrination and rampant hypocrisy. Both are likely to flourish, if not on the same campus.

In seeking to mark out a constructive role for the college *in loco parentis*, it is useful to explore how different categories of behavior are dealt with by college regulatory and disciplinary structures. So far I have cited examples primarily from the realm of personal and sexual relationships. These are inevitably the focus of most discussions of the college's quasi-parietal responsibilities, since there is no other realm in which, to employ Plato's image, the leadership of the intellect and the disorderly power of the appetites clash so violently, especially during the period when young people are learning to replace parental control with self-control. But we can learn more about the potentially constructive role of the campus environment by considering other areas of behavior, especially if we can identify areas in which institutions do succeed in fostering moral maturity.

The handling of alcohol abuse is in many ways a close parallel to that of sexual behavior. Here, too, personal pleasures and social pressures regularly clash with academic demands and the rights of others. But I fear that this is an area that scarcely any campus, from the most permissive to the most restrictive, can cite with any degree of satisfaction. On every campus that I know of—the four where I have taught and dozens more about which I have learned from others—the promulgation and enforcement of the campus alcohol policy are rife with hypocrisy, inconsistency, and self-deception. State universities commonly include in their policy books a solemn declaration that only students over the legal drinking age are permitted to use alcoholic beverages in the privacy of their rooms and that the sharing of such beverages with underage students is strictly forbidden. But none of these institutions segregates students by age in residence halls, and residence hall staff members do not undertake surprise room searches or raids on parties. Such intrusions would no doubt lead to lawsuits for invasion of privacy—in the unlikely event that the staff members survived long enough to be sued.[8] Under these circumstances, however, the antialcohol policies of the college handbook are completely unenforceable. Many smaller colleges state much more restrictive policies, and to diminish the likelihood of legal challenges they may require all students to sign a statement on admission that, for example, they will use no alcoholic beverages on campus. But such policies are still effectively unenforceable—or, at most, enforceable only in the case of flagrant violation.

On many campuses, students report, the lack of any real restrictions on alcohol consumption makes the residence halls unendurable in the late evenings for students who insist on spending their time studying. To proclaim a restrictive alcohol policy without a serious attempt to enforce it undermines respect for college policies and does nothing to foster more responsible alcohol use. There is, of course, a long tradition, stretching back to the ancient world, of boisterous alcohol abuse by the young. What has changed in the last generation, it appears, is that such Dionysian revels have been relocated from the off-campus bar, whose proprietor must accept full responsibility for enforcing the legal drinking age, to the residence hall, where no one is in a position to exercise effective control. So alcohol policy is hardly a success story in the university.

A second area is, I think, more promising, though it is not one traditionally included under the topic of parietal rules. This is the issue of academic dishonesty and plagiarism. Nearly every institution has adopted a clear and detailed policy concerning plagiarism. The policy may in some cases have been drawn up with some student involvement, but nowhere does one find a willingness to let 15 percent of the students call for a redefinition of plagiarism, with the definition to be determined by majority vote. For the rules of the game in this area are, at least on the general level, simple and uncontroversial: it is immoral for any student to present another's work as if it were his or her own or to assist another in doing so.

The difficulty in dealing with plagiarism is not in identifying the proper abstract principles but in applying them. I have yet to encounter any student caught in flagrant cheating who defended her- or himself on the ground that her or his own value system makes cheating acceptable. On the contrary, most students defend themselves by arguing that they did not intend to deceive and did not know that the use they made of their sources would be construed as dishonest. (This excuse will not wash for cribbing answers on an exam, of course, but the less blatant manifestations of dishonesty are precisely those that are most difficult to prevent by practical means. Alternate seating and mixing up questions are effective preventives for cheating on multiple-choice exams, but there are no similarly straightforward methods of preventing dishonest term papers.)

Moreover, in about half the cases I have had any personal involvement in, this defense—self-serving as it was—had a good deal of plausibility. If the immorality of cheating is patent, when considered in those bald terms, the proper and improper use of scholarly sources is in practice a subtle and difficult matter of judgement. One student, anxious to avoid plagiarism, will stuff a three-page essay with fifty footnotes; another will blithely and unwittingly lift entire sentences from the textbook. Students need help not so much in understanding the principle that cheating is wrong but in understanding what constitutes fair or dishonest use of their sources. For just this reason, most colleges embellish the principles of the plagiarism policy with an extensive explanation of the difference between proper and deceptive use of sources. Explanation of these policies is also a central element of the required freshman composition course at many institutions.

Colleges do take their responsibility for moral education seriously, in other words, with respect to plagiarism.[9] They recognize that high school graduates may have so little practice at scholarly research and writing that they cannot draw the line between honest work and improper borrowing. The institution must therefore begin by setting out the relevant principles and helping students understand their implications. After that, strict and consistent enforcement of the rules is possible.

The contrast with the handling of sexual misconduct is striking. In matters of personal morality, decisions are commonly left entirely to individual choice until something terrible happens—an undesired pregnancy, for example, or a sexually transmitted disease. At that point the institution makes its staff available to help students cope with—or possibly avoid—the consequences of their behavior. What is typically offered is essentially nondirective counseling: assistance in understanding the choices the student has made, their consequences, and how they relate to the student's personal and career goals. Such counseling is unquestionably needed, as is education in the physical and social aspects of sexuality. Students may have more experience and sophistication in some aspects of interpersonal relations than their parents or teachers will ever have, yet they may lack elementary information about physiology and disease. What is entirely lacking—in contrast with the example of plagiarism—is any clear or consistent model of responsible sexual behavior. The institution has renounced the attempt to provide one, leaving it to individuals to find their own models and learn to emulate them.[10]

Ought the college to articulate any standard of sexual responsibility? There can be no single answer. For a smaller college united by a coherent set of religious and moral ideals, the answer may be yes, if the considerable costs of the hypocrisy that will result are outweighed by the benefits of upholding a particular conception of what life in a community ought to be like. Such an institution should take great care to make its expectations consistent, avoiding discriminatory treatment of men or women, students or faculty, individuals of heterosexual or homosexual orientation. Fairness of procedure when policies are violated is also crucial. But there is nothing inherently anachronistic, let alone immoral, about a collegewide ban on cohabitation by unmarried heterosexual couples.

Some institutions, in other words, need not find a middle way between restrictiveness and permissiveness. They can still treat sexual behavior in the way most institutions treat plagiarism, through a combination of education, counseling, and disciplinary action. Only a minority of professors and students will choose, today, to be members of such a restrictive community. Those who do but then later find the restrictions stultifying and intolerable will need either to press for a widening of the limits or to find a more tolerant community.

It is the community, in the end, that makes this model still viable. A restrictive campus can exist only if its students and faculty value the close community it provides and are willing to accept its limits. And it is also the community, I believe, that makes it possible to mark out a more moderate stance *in loco parentis* that sets broader limits than this without withdrawing from moral responsibility entirely. Through selective encouragement to the communities in which moral growth takes place, colleges can foster the capacity of their students to make moral decisions without attempting to make decisions for them.

At a large or diverse institution there is no single common community, no shared basis of moral and religious values, that could ground a restrictive set of parietal rules. Respect for students' diversity and personal conviction militates against the attempt to control personal and sexual behavior. But students draw their sense of what is morally fitting not from the entire institutional community but from the smaller constituent groups in which they participate. When the college does not set rigid rules regarding visitation and cohabitation—and even when it does—students gain a sense of what is normal behavior, what is irresponsible conduct, and what makes for rewarding personal relationships from the subcommunities in which they carry on their lives.

Fraternities are an obvious, if uninspiring, example. Fraternity life on too many campuses is characterized by drunken debauchery, interrupted periodically by stunts to raise money for crippled children and short breaks to study for midterms. The moral luster of fraternities has been considerably tarnished in recent years, and a number of universities have either abolished them or placed them under tight control. For better or worse, they hold considerable power to shape their members' sense of moral responsibility. Similarly, at the opposite end of the spectrum, conservative religious organizations such as Campus Crusade for Christ unite students of a strongly evangelical persuasion, and their meetings and activities are no less important in validating and reinforcing participants' adherence to a strict moral code than in preserving and deepening their religious commitments.

Many other communities—political clubs, radio and newspaper staffs, musical and dramatic ensembles, varsity and intramural athletic teams—also provide the ethical models and expectations that the larger campus does not and cannot provide. Their effect, I suspect, is greater the larger the campus and the farther the student from home. More than either the campus community as a whole or the college handbook, such groups become the standard by which students assess their own ethical choices and their intellectual and personal development.

The members of the antiapartheid coalition will insist vehemently, and rightly, that they are united by their commitment to a particular moral and political goal and that they respect one another's diverse convictions about personal and social morality. Yet, if the group is one that has come to work closely and effectively together, the example that its members set in their personal lives—whether they live with their boy or girl friends, whether they sell term papers, whether they keep their parties free of excessive drinking—will influence the behavior of other group members profoundly. And the same is true of the Young Republicans Club, the jazz band, the volleyball team, and the regulars at the Hillel Foundation and the Newman Center.

Contemporary concern for the autonomy of students should not lead universities to overlook the crucial and potentially constructive role of voluntary communities within the institution in shaping behavior and promoting moral maturity. Our moral choices are inescapably individual choices, and yet our most important choices are shaped at least as much by those we see around us and by our ability to imagine ourselves living the lives that they lead as by the inherent attractions of moral rules and principles. If a student graduates from college with a strong sense of responsibility to and for others and a well-developed capacity to make ethical decisions and carry through on them, the credit is bound to belong at least as much to the example of the individuals and groups with which that student has spent time as to any study of moral theory.

What, then, characterizes an institution that is unwilling either to impose a single moral code or to abdicate its role in moral formation? The answer cannot be framed in terms of what is allowed and what is forbidden. There may or may not be restricted visiting hours, coeducational residence floors, and the like. Rules on these matters may be symptoms of a helpful or unhelpful atmosphere, but in themselves they accomplish little. What we will find is an atmosphere in which students feel free to turn to faculty members and to the college staff either for information or for personal counsel when facing difficult choices. We will find college personnel who do not pretend that everyone on campus holds the same morality but at the same time clearly state, and exemplify, their own moral commitments. Equally important, the college will lend its assistance in every way possible to the many voluntary organizations on campus in which personal choices are discussed and shaped, whether explicitly or implicitly. The faculty and staff—from the president and the academic dean to the newly hired instructor and the assistant dean of students—will be regular members of the audience at student-organized political rallies, plays, concerts, and discussions. The college will provide financial and logistical support to groups that demonstrate a commitment and an ability to provide the personal and moral anchoring that students need. Conversely, it will withhold support from groups that encourage irresponsibility and immature or disruptive behavior.

Granted, such distinctions among campus groups are difficult to apply and liable to distorted interpretation; but that is an insufficient reason to abandon them, rather than to undertake to apply them fairly and consistently. Fraternities on many campuses have proven themselves unable to escape their own traditions of irresponsibility or their racist and sexist practices. When that is the case, an institution that is serious about the moral maturity of its students will cut them off from all official ties, administrative and financial. On the other hand, if religious and political student organizations show themselves able to encourage moral formation, they will be rewarded with funds and, equally important, with the visible presence of those who in student eyes symbolize the institution.

The administrators and faculty of such an institution will schedule many special events, both as part of regular courses of study and outside them, that direct the attention of the various communities on campus to the moral choices students face. These might include credit or noncredit minicourses on changing gender roles at home and in the workplace, informational sessions on AIDS and its prevention, guest speakers invited to address ethical issues, even concerts and art exhibits reflecting the complexity and the urgency of the choices students must make.

I offer these suggestions not as a blueprint but as a challenge. The administration and faculty of an institution serious about its limited role *in loco parentis*, its role in fostering moral maturity, can doubtless find other methods more effective than those I have suggested. The life of subcommunities on campus can be enriched and strengthened in countless ways, and the particular means employed must be appropriate to a specific student population and to concrete social circumstances. The only way to learn what measures contribute to students' moral development is to try several, observe their effects, study student and staff responses, and then throw out those that don't work and improve those that do.

Imagine the response if an institution told its entering students, "We have no required courses, no distribution requirements, no majors, and no graduation requirements. However, if 15 percent of you vote to establish any such requirements, we will submit the matter to a majority vote." Such an absurdity would be seen as an abdication of responsibility to the tradition and the students of the college, a pretense that students are wiser and more experienced than the faculty members from whom they hope to learn. But that is, in effect, what many universities now tell their students in the realm of personal behavior. We have no standards of our own, their policies say, and we would not presume to set standards for you: tell us what you want the rules to be. You must learn what morality means, on your own. You are grown-ups, and we can't tell you how. We will watch.

The analogy is imperfect, of course: there is an intellectual authority vested in the faculty that no one on a diverse campus can claim in the moral realm. But in abandoning moralistic oversight, institutions may have overlooked their responsibility to provide an atmosphere conducive to moral maturity. Students deserve and demand a measure of privacy, but they also deserve an environment that helps them to become capable of making and carrying through fundamental personal decisions. When the university responds to moral diversity and disagreement merely by looking in the other direction, it fails in its genuine, if limited, responsibility *in loco parentis*.

Merely to restore restrictive behavioral rules on campus would be no solution at all for the problems I have discussed. Both the campus and the student have changed profoundly since the day when student deans walked the halls during visiting hours and peered around half-closed doors to prevent hanky-panky, and nostalgia will not reverse these changes. The shrubbery around the residence hall entrance is hardly the ideal environment for learning moral maturity, anyway. But neither is the environment on most campuses today. We can change it, and if we care about our students and about the future of society, we must. For colleges and universities owe students an environment in which, by whatever means possible, they are aided in becoming the independent and morally mature individuals that they are learning to be.

NOTES

1. See Connie Leslie, "The Party's over at BU: Dorms Are for Sleeping," *Newsweek*, September 26, 1988, p. 70.

2. See Jill Rachlin, "Rewriting the Code of Conduct on Campus: *In Loco Parentis* Strikes Again," *U.S. News and World Report*, January 9, 1989, p. 56; "Villanova: New-Style Dorm Has Men, Women, and Visiting Rules," *New York Times*, March 27, 1989, p. B5; "South Carolina University to Halt Visitation in Dorms," *New York Times*, April 19, 1989, p. B8.

3. Among recent defenders are John Rawls, *A Theory of Justice* (Cambridge: Harvard University Press, 1971); Ronald Dworkin, *Taking Rights Seriously* (Cambridge: Harvard University Press, 1976); and Dworkin, *Law's Empire* (Cambridge: Harvard University Press, 1986); Bruce Ackerman, *Social Justice in the Liberal State* (New Haven: Yale University Press, 1980).

4. Representative, if diverse, examples can be found in Michael Sandel, *Liberalism and the Limits of Justice* (New Haven: Yale University Press, 1982); Carol Gilligan, *In a Different Voice* (Cambridge: Harvard University Press, 1982); Aladsdair MacIntyre, *After Virtue* (Notre Dame, Ind.: University of Notre Dame Press, 1981); MacIntyre, *Whose Justice? Whose Rationality?* (Notre Dame, Ind.: University of Notre Dame Press, 1987).

5. These conditions are similar in several particulars to the defining conditions put forward by Kurt Baier in *The Moral Point of View: A Rational Basis for Ethics* (Ithaca, N.Y.: Cornell University Press, 1958), although Baier's concern is with the definition of moral reasons and motives, not with questions of maturity.

6. Michael Moffatt, *Coming of Age in New Jersey: College and American Culture* (New Brunswick, N.J.: Rutgers University Press, 1989), excerpted in *Chronicle of Higher Education*, June 7, 1989, pp. A31–32. The book is described, and the author interviewed, in a feature article, "Anthropologist Examines Sex Life on the Raritan," *New York Times*, April 10, 1989, p. B6.

7. The examples of behavior come from student journals and discussions

in a course on moral problems and decision making; the figure on drinking parties is from Moffatt, *Coming of Age*, excerpted in *Chronicle of Higher Education*, June 7, 1989, p. A31.

8. The success of suits over invasion of privacy would crucially depend on the nature of the institution and the terms of the residence hall agreement signed by students. The constitutional ban on unreasonable search and seizure would bar both college officials and police from making surprise searches of the houses of students who live off campus and whose relationship to the institution is limited to registering in a degree program. But a student in a residence hall who has signed a contract granting the institution the right to enter his or her room at any time—not an uncommon provision of such contracts—has waived some, but by no means all, of the rights of off-campus residents. All the same, as a practical matter, students at nearly every institution regard their rooms as their private domains, and any program of surprise searches would be seen as intolerably intrusive.

9. A parallel example not mentioned in the text may also provide a positive model at a substantial number of colleges: the handling of the use of illicit drugs. Every university condemns and prohibits the use of illicit drugs; yet they are present on every campus. The same problems that bedevil alcohol policies make enforcement of the prohibition extremely difficult. The crucial difference is that the official prohibition is categorical, not conditional on a student's age. Thus, even though no university administrator can hope to eradicate drug abuse entirely, it is possible to deal firmly and consistently with those instances that do come to light. Many campuses, including those on which I have taught, seem to me to do so. What is usually missing, by contrast with the plagiarism example, is an effective means of educating students concerning the temptations and the risks of drug use.

10. I leave out here two very important areas in which institutions today do attempt to set and, so far as possible, to enforce clear and consistent standards: forced sexual intimacy, which includes not only violent sexual assault but also "date rape," and sexual harassment of students and junior faculty members. These are important issues on every campus, but they have to do less with personal and sexual morality, the traditional purview of parietal rules, than with the morality of coercion and the abuse of physical or academic power. Forced intercourse is wrong not primarily because it is intercourse but because it is forced.

11

BUSINESS-UNIVERSITY PARTNERSHIPS

Norman E. Bowie

One of the more significant developments in higher education in the 1980s is the growth of partnerships between education and industry. Most of these are research partnerships in the natural sciences, especially in biology. However, partnerships are found in the business education field and in other areas. Examples of such partnerships include a $52 million research fund at Washington University established by Monsanto Company and used by Monsanto and university scientists to develop pharmaceutical drugs and a $60 million fund to support FIDIA–Georgetown Institute, devoted to basic brain research and established by the Italian company FIDIA.[1] In addition, industry-university partnerships are in place at such widely diverse places as Carnegie-Mellon, Stanford, Purdue, Rensselaer, Georgia Tech, Brigham Young, University of Michigan, University of Illinois, University of Tennessee, Auburn University, University of Cincinnati, and Ohio State University.[2]

Although business-university partnerships represent a small percentage of the research efforts of American industry,[3] the percentage is expected to grow. Business leaders and university administrators view such partnerships as a good thing, and those business and university officials who have had actual experience with them are especially enthusiastic.

The advantages to each partner are fairly obvious, although the magnitude of the advantage is not. American business has been widely criticized for investing so little in research and development, especially basic research. American business has been unfavorably compared to business in foreign countries like Japan and West Germany in this respect. Partnerships with universities give business access to research facilities, but far more important, I believe, such partnerships give business access to research professors. Frequently the physical equipment required in such projects is not currently available on campus and has to be purchased by the business partner. Often the business partner cannot even make use of a campus building; a new structure is needed, and frequently the business partner pays for it as well. In theory a building might be used for a number of different projects with different business partners and by spreading the costs, some savings might be effected. Generally, however, business firms do not enter into these partnerships because they provide opportunities to save on capital expenditures.

The access to human capital is far more important. After all, there are many highly skilled researchers who enjoy the life-style associated with universities. These researchers would prefer university employment to a position in an industrial lab. However, the research projects of many university scientists are of great interest to industry. To see why, consider that Howard A. Schneiderman, senior vice-president and chief scientist for corporate research at Monsanto claims that the company decision to purchase G. D. Searle was based in large part on discoveries made by Monsanto's university partners at Washington University. "Through the program we made enough discoveries to justify buying Searle."[4]

Corporate decisions like Monsanto's should put to rest the view that ivory-towered professors aren't doing research that is of benefit to American industry. If further evidence is needed, consider that at an international conference on computer design, about half the nearly one hundred fifty presentations were based on university projects.[5] University research in artificial intelligence, superconductivity, computer architectures and testing, neuroscience, computer-integrated systems, robotics, composite materials, microelectronics, and biotechnology is of great interest to corporations, nor is this list meant to be exhaustive. To be competitive in the international arena, many industry leaders recognize they need access to that research and to secure patent rights and/or licensing agreements to the products of that research.

We should also realize that the executives of foreign businesses are well aware of the potential commercial value of American university research. The growing number of foreign nationals in our science and engineering programs has been widely reported. An anecdote may make the point more vividly than the statistics. Cornell University was considering an affiliation program that would bring affiliate members to Cornell for organized conferences and consulting privileges.

Before embarking on the program, Cornell did a survey to see if there were representatives from industry involved in biotechnology research at Cornell. Provost Robert Barker discovered that there were five—all from Japan.

> And they had been sent by Japanese corporations. They were not junior scientists here for a little trimming up before they started their industrial jobs; most of them had been with their corporations for more than a few years. Two of them had quite responsible positions in their companies but they were at Cornell spending two years to find out what was going on in genetic engineering, in one of the best laboratories in the country.[6]

As important as the research projects of individual professors are, American business should have an interest in the individual researcher per se. These are highly creative people who, if confronted with industrial research problems, may provide a solution. American industry doesn't exhaust the advantages of a research partnership when it comes to the laboratory to see what projects currently being explored have commercial application. It can bring on its own initiative, problems, and projects, in the hope that a university researcher will take an interest. Also a university laboratory is an excellent hunting ground for potential employees. Even if persuading senior professors to give up the advantages of the university is a formidable task, selling graduate students—many of whom have had quite enough of the university environment—on a position in industry is likely to be successful. Jack Sparks, chairman of the board and chief executive officer at Whirlpool puts the point succinctly. "We gain access to outstandingly creative people—both faculty and students. And we get to hire some of them, notably, top-quality students with experience in one or more areas of technology in which we already have interests."[7]

A potential advantage to industry is less well recognized, and as a result there are relatively few partnerships designed to benefit from it. As Robert Barker points out, there are tremendous advantages to industry in just knowing what is going on. Before you can build a partnership around a project or team of creative people, you need to know what kind of research is being done already. Barker points out that there are over forty thousand principal investigators doing research in the universities and that the public literature is "often miles behind the front line of what's happening in the universities."[8] Although Barker has several suggestions for solving the knowledge problem, one is of special relevance to the discussion here. He suggests that companies establish affiliate programs with research-oriented universities that have comprehensive programs in fields of interest to the company. As Barker says,

> If the university is any good and is willing to work with you, it is going to be able to keep you in touch with essentially everything that is going on in the fields of interest, both on site and at other research universities. The only way in which a university scientist can survive is to be in touch with what the competition is doing.[9]

In sum, the corporation receives three distinct advantages from business-university partnerships: access to information, access to potential commercial products, and access to creative, intelligent faculty and students. Since these advantages are achieved simultaneously in any partnership, they can rather quickly be of great assistance to any company in its struggle with competitors.

These partnerships also bring many advantages to the participating universities. The most obvious advantage is money and lots of it. The business partner often provides total support for a number of graduate students and postdoctoral fellows. Scientific equipment has become incredibly expensive; to have someone else purchase it for the university is a great benefit. This funding may be even more important as government funding fails to keep pace with increased needs. In addition, corporations may be less free in open-ended giving to universities. Substituting these partnerships for open-ended giving provides a way for chief executive officers to tell stockholders that there is a return on the money provided to universities.

Although the financial benefit is significant, it is certainly not the only advantage the university receives from university-business partnerships. By adding to the state of knowledge, these partnerships assist universities in one of their primary missions. Some research partnerships combine university faculty and business personnel on the same projects. That interaction enables the university faculty to get a new perspective. Also business research is not organized around disciplines; it is task oriented. Partnerships that break down disciplinary barriers are likely to contribute to an increase in the store of knowledge.

Since business is task oriented, it is likely to speed up the pace of research. University researchers are often accused to being oblivious to deadlines. This criticism is often silly, especially in the sciences, where there is great pressure to get your research results published before your competitors. Nonetheless, business-university research partnerships will put time pressures on some who might otherwise be more relaxed in their research.

Finally, these partnerships will result in more applied research and hence will provide products of interest to the general public more quickly. Everyone will not view increases in applied research as an advantage. However, in state-supported universities, there is a strong public-interest component in the universities overall mission. Land-grant universities have traditionally provided practical advice to farmers based on applied research in colleges of agriculture. Taxpayers may well argue that their support of public universities justifies and perhaps even obligates universities to engage in applied research. University-business partnerships thus become a means for meeting a university's responsibility to the public interest.

In sum, these partnerships are advantageous to the university because they are an important source of funding, they add to the store of knowledge, and by encouraging applied research, they help the university serve the public interest.

Despite the advantages to both parties, these partnership agreements have been strongly criticized. The best criticisms begin with an articulation of the mission of the university and then try to show how such partnerships are inconsistent with that mission.

During the 1960s the mission of the university was a controversial item of discussion. Although the debate is less intense today, it continues nonetheless. But there are areas of agreement among the contending parties. With respect to students, universities are to produce well-rounded, integrated, socially responsible individuals. A philosopher might say that the task of the university is to produce a Kantian person—a rational, autonomous, moral agent who can take his or her place in a moral community.

If the purpose of a university education is to produce well-rounded, integrated, socially responsible individuals, at the very least activities that the university undertakes should not be inconsistent with this mission, and ideally all activities should support the central mission. Before judging business-university research partnerships by this standard, we need to have some idea as to what skills and attitudes the educational community believes can be taught so as to produce the desired result. It is commonly held that a university education should develop the skill of critical, independent thinking and should create a sensitivity to new ideas and an imaginative sympathy with the experience of others.[10]

If independent thinking and a sensitivity to new ideas represent the skills and attitudes a university should instill in its students, what should the university atmosphere be like? On this point too, there is considerable consensus. At a university the search for truth is impartial and unbiased. Competing theories are entitled to a hearing. The university is sometimes called "the marketplace of ideas." An idea is to be accepted or rejected on evidence rather than on the power or prestige of the speaker. Ideas are not to be withheld from the marketplace but are brought forth to be scrutinized by colleagues in the search for truth.

Although I have focused on the student, my overall account of the mission of the university is consistent with the view that sees the university as a trustee for the body of human knowledge. One contemporary analyst has described the trustee mission as follows:

> The function of the university in contemporary society is twofold. On the one hand, the university concerns itself with existing knowledge, preserving it and transmitting it to each new generation. On the other hand, it seeks to increase the body of human knowledge. . . . In the performance of this function, the university has three tasks: (1) to teach, (2) to provide a forum for critical analysis and debate, and (3) to conduct research.[11]

Are university-business research partnerships at cross-purposes with, neutral, or supportive of the mission to produce Kantian persons and to serve as trustee for the body of human knowledge? Some have argued that such partnerships are at cross-purposes with the university's central mission.

Let us begin with some of the specific criticisms. One of the more common is that such partnerships require that the research be kept confidential. The business partner allegedly tries to impose the same rules at the university level that apply in the corporate context, that is, the researcher needs the permission of the business sponsor before the research can be published. Such a requirement would be in clear violation of the university's central mission. It would permit a corporate sponsor to withhold research from the marketplace of ideas; it would prevent the university from adding to the store of knowledge.

There is a relatively simple solution to this problem. No university should agree to a partnership that allows the business sponsor to prevent or delay publication. The first of ten guidelines developed by Robert D. Varrin and Diane S. Kukich for industry-sponsored research is: retain publication rights.[12]

Although I strongly support this guideline, some flexibility on the university's part is required. There are some important ways in which industry-sponsored research is different from standard university research. First, there are difficulties with proprietary information (trade secrets). Some university-business research partnerships involve projects that require that the business partner give university researchers access to trade secrets. As a practical matter the business partner would not agree to the relationship unless trade secrets could be protected. But the business partner would have moral arguments for the protection of trade secrets as well. Among the arguments are the following: (1) the corporation has a property right in the formula, pattern, device, or compilation of information protected as a trade secret; (2) trade secrets are necessary to protect American industry from foreign competitors; (3) trade secrets are necessary if American firms are to undertake heavy expenditures for basic research.

Although these arguments have been contested, let us assume that they justify trade secrets *in the normal business context*. An additional argument is needed to permit honoring trade secrets in the university context. The university should turn a deaf ear to arguments 1 and 2. The university commitment to the basic value of serving as a trustee for the body of knowledge takes priority over the right of a corporation to its intellectual property. On similar grounds, the university should not surrender its central values to help business solve its problems with foreign competitors. However, the third argument does apply to the university setting. The gist of the argument is that trade secrets are necessary if basic research is to be undertaken. In the absence of trade secrets, other firms would be able to ride free on the basic research of others. Hence firms would be unwilling to undertake basic research. Since increasing research is a core task of the university and since these business-university partnerships are designed to enhance the ability of the university to engage in research, the anti-free-rider argument would apply in the university context as well. Corporations do have a legitimate right to insist that their proprietary information be protected.

How is that right to be squared with the guideline that universities should retain publication rights? In discussing this problem, Varrin and Kukich contend the university should agree to keep confidential any proprietary information it acquires to conduct the research and that the business partner should have the right to review manuscripts before publication. Varrin and Kukich insist, however, that the right to review should not amount to a veto power and that "if opinions differ as to whether or not the company's rights have been violated,

202 | NORMAN E. BOWIE

the two parties must attempt to reconcile these differences, with the ultimate decision being left to the university."[13]

But what about new research findings that, if published, could be used by competitors of the business sponsor? For those findings that result in inventions, the appropriate means of protection is to secure patents. If the results aren't patentable, then the university's commitment to expanding the store of knowledge should take priority.

The use of patents brings problems of its own. Publication must be held up in order to allow time for the patent application to be filed. Varrin and Kukich recommend an agreement to delay publication for up to six months and to keep theses sequestered for up to one year.[14] That recommendation could also be justified by the anti-free-rider argument that justified honoring trade secrets in the university context.

A more important issue concerns the ownership of patents. That issue was first addressed at the Pajaro Dunes, California, conference in 1982. The conference was organized by the presidents of five universities: Stanford, Harvard, California Institute of Technology, Massachusetts Institute of Technology, and the University of California. Faculty members and business persons with institutional connections to one of these institutions were among the attendees. Although a statement was issued, no consensus on the ownership of patents was reached.[15] Most major university-industry contracts presently in force provide exclusive rights to the industry sponsor of the research. At a news conference following the conference, Derek Bok, president of Harvard University, is quoted as saying, "Some people feel that exclusive licensing is a perfectly reasonable quid pro quo for providing a significant amount of money for research, without which the research and discovery would never take place at all."[16]

Varrin and Kukich disagree. They maintain that the university partner should retain ownership of all patents. To support their position Varrin and Kukich argue that on occasion a corporate sponsor might not want an invention brought to the marketplace because it would compete with some other more profitable product. In a twist on this argument, Judith Hill points out that agreements with some sponsors might put pressure on a university to refuse partnerships with other corporate sponsors. She cites a report in July 1981 *Harper's* that the Massachusetts Institute of Technology turned down an unsolicited $100,000 grant for gasohol research after already having received two $500,000 grants from Exxon and Ford.[17] Methanol as a substitute for gasoline would have a negative financial impact on both Exxon and Ford.

Although business partners usually want to bring the inventions that result from research to the market, the situations I have described present a powerful argument for having patent rights under the university's control. If a university collaborated with a business sponsor in withholding an invention from the market, the university would be in violation of its central mission to add to the body of knowledge. Similarly a university cannot refuse to conduct research on the grounds that that research may yield an invention that would compete with the product of another university sponsor.

A university policy giving the university ownership of the patents need not deprive corporations of their opportunity to make a financial return. Since the research was jointly sponsored, some sharing of the financial gains among the individual researchers, the university, and the corporate sponsor seems prima facie just. However, if the corporate sponsor put up large amounts of money at considerable risk, it might be fair to let all the financial gain revert to the corporate sponsor. The Georgetown agreement with FIDIA gives FIDIA-Georgetown Institute the right of first refusal. Georgetown University is next in line. If the corporate sponsor of the institute wants the patent, "it must pay a fair market price, to be determined on the basis of either bids from other organizations or by an arbitrator. Sixty percent of the patent royalties would go to the institute and 40 percent to Georgetown."[18] Such an agreement is clearly consistent with the educational mission as we have described it.

Let me briefly take stock of the position I am defending with regard to the publication of research results. Since one of the central missions of the university is to add to the store of knowledge and to bring new knowledge to the community of scholars as quickly as possible, the university should maintain both publication rights and the ownership of all patents. Since the protection of trade secrets and the patenting of inventions can be justified on the grounds that such devices enhance basic research, rather than hinder it, prohibitions against the release of proprietary information received by the university partner in pursuing the research are justified. So are brief publication delays of up to six months so that the business partner might apply for a patent to protect an invention. New information of a nonpatentable nature discovered in the course of the research should be published according to standard academic procedures.

Another standard criticism of university-business partnerships is that they inevitably involve the university and its faculty in conflict of interest. The Pajaro Dunes conference considered two types of conflict of interest. Should a university take an equity position in a company in which one of its faculty members is a major stockholder or officer? The conferees indicated the university should not. Should a university allow faculty members to be affiliated with a biotechnology firm? The conferees left the resolution of that issue to individual institutions.[19]

Varrin and Kukich focused on two other conflict-of-interest problems and issued guidelines prohibiting them. First, they indicated that faculty should not be permitted to consult with sponsors in the sponsored research area. The potential conflict here is that a faculty member might release information from the *jointly* sponsored research that enables the sponsor to obtain a patent (take advantage of a business opportunity) that really belongs at least partially to the university.[20]

Second, Varrin and Kukich argue that a faculty entrepreneur's company should not be permitted to sponsor his or her research on campus. Here the potential conflict of interest seems to be in the faculty entrepreneur's ability to be objective since the entrepreneur has responsibilities both to the educational institution and the venture firm. Varrin and Kukich don't flesh this issue out much further, but they give an example that might help us understand what concerns them. They point out that when an educational institution accepts a research grant, it accepts the responsibility for seeing that the work is done correctly and on time. If the researcher is also the sponsor, he or she becomes both judge and jury. "He or she is hardly in an appropriate position to decide, for example, whether or not a late completion report is acceptable."[21]

This rationale is used to defend a corollary: faculty entrepreneurs should never be allowed to lease or use space in their university departments for private business. Another extension of the guideline is that a researcher's graduate student should not be employed by the researcher's company. The rationale here is that if a graduate student is employed by the researcher's company, the graduate student's choice of a thesis topic might be compromised.

Before these decisions and guidelines can be assessed some conceptual analysis of the term "conflict of interest" is required. Despite frequent use, there is no standard definition. *Webster's New Collegiate Dictionary* doesn't do too badly: "A conflict of interest is a conflict between the private interest and the official responsibilities of a person in a position of trust."[22] After examining the American Bar Association Code of Professional Responsibility, Michael Davis proposes the following generalized definition of a conflict of interest: "A person has a conflict of interest if (a) he is in a relationship with another requiring him to exercise judgment in that other's service and (b) he has an interest tending to interfere with the proper exercise of that judgment."[23]

It might be tempting simply to apply these two definitions to the situations under discussion; however, before doing so, it is important to note that under these definitions conflicts of interest are commonplace and often unavoidable. Faculty members are in a relationship with students that requires an exercise of judgment, and faculty research—to say nothing of consulting—represents an interest tending to interfere with the proper exercise of that judgment. Given the routine occurrence of potential conflict of interest, is institutional policy or general guidelines—a kind of code of ethics for the university-business research partnerships—the way to go? An examination of conflicts of interest in business might be helpful.

An appropriate starting point is with the typical chief executive officer in a publicly held corporation. He or she is a fiduciary agent of the stockholders and is in a position of trust. He or she must make complex business judgments and frequently (almost always) has a personal interest in a given outcome. Our unfortunate CEO is almost always in a conflict of interest. Interestingly, this unhappy situation has been recognized by a federal judge.

In *Johnson* v. *Trueblood*, a federal court used partially moral premises to reject the argument that self-interest on the part of management in a decision affecting stockholders necessarily invalidates the management's action.

> It is frequently said that directors are fiduciaries. Although this statement is true in some senses, it is also obvious that if directors were held to the same standard as ordinary fiduciaries the corporation could not conduct business. For example, an ordinary fiduciary may not have the slightest conflict of interest in any transaction he undertakes on behalf of the trust. Yet by the very nature of corporate life a director has a certain amount of self-interest in everything he does. The very fact that the director wants to enhance corporate profits is in part attributable to his desire to keep shareholders satisfied so that they will not oust him. The business judgment rule seeks to alleviate this problem by

validating certain situations that otherwise would involve a conflict of interest for the ordinary fiduciary. The rule achieves this purpose by postulating that if actions are arguably taken for the benefit of the corporation, then the directors are presumed to have been exercising their sound business judgment rather than responding to any personal motivations.[24]

The court implicitly recognizes the existence of potential conflicts of interest in a board of directors meeting. However, so long as behavior can be defended on sound business grounds, that behavior is legitimate.

Perhaps we need a similar rule in conflict-of-interest cases arising from university-business partnerships. Before I address that issue, it is important to see that conflicts of interest are already fairly common in higher education, especially at the research universities. In a book highly critical of the practices of the Harvard Business School, *The Empire Builders*, J. Paul Mark cites many cases in which he believes the Harvard Business School is involved in a conflict of interest. He reports that Michael Porter conducted a case discussion in class of the United States Football League's suit against the National Football League during which he asked his students what advice he should give Pete Rozelle, commissioner of the NFL. Mark alleges that Porter didn't tell his students that he had a consultancy arrangement with the NFL.[25] Mark also contends that the famous Harvard case method was chosen less on its pedagogical merits than because it enhanced faculty opportunities for consulting and research.[26]

In my review of Mark's book, I indicated that such incidents, if correctly reported, were only magnified examples of conflicts commonplace in academic life.[27] The Porter incident presents a new twist on an old problem. Senior professors constantly use graduate research assistants. When an article bearing the name of the research professor appears, the research assistants are given little if any credit. As for Mark's allegations about the case method, many teachers could be accused of slanting the course content or the readings of a course for a better fit with their own research interests. Students often charge that faculty members are more interested in their consultantships than they are in them.

Some of the conflict of interest can be eliminated by institutional policy. A number of universities, including my own, have a policy limiting consulting to, typically, "one day a week in a six-day week." Public disclosure is often enough to make a conflict of interest disappear. Michael Porter could have eliminated his conflict of interest by simply informing students that he was a consultant for the NFL. If a client knows that his or her chosen agent has either personal interests or conflicting obligations to others, and yet the client agrees to hire the agent anyway, the conflict of interest no longer presents a moral problem. All parties agreed that Richard L. Cook should be appointed to the highest environmental post in the commonwealth of Virginia, despite the fact that Cook was an employee of the Dupont Company, which had been accused of mercury contamination in Virginia and had settled out of court for $1.8 million. Moreover, Cook intended to return to Dupont at the expiration of his term of office. Suffice it to say that Cook was known as a man of great integrity.[28] If faculty members behave with great integrity, the existence of potential conflicts of interest is justifiably less worrisome.

Do university-business partnerships produce any conflicts of interest that are different in logical type from those typically found in academic life? I think not. Allowing faculty members to be affiliated with biotech firms presents the same kind of difficulty as allowing members of the business school faculty to sit on corporate boards. Some institutions may not trust their professors to give sufficient time to their university responsibilities; these institutions will forbid or constrain such affiliation. Others will trust their faculty not to cross the line. This trust should be based on hard evidence, however. I am not convinced that it is always warranted.

I am also less concerned than Varrin and Kukich with a researcher who hires a graduate student for the researcher's company. Either a graduate student has chosen a thesis topic or not. If not, the student might feel forced to choose the researcher as thesis supervisor and the researcher's interests as topic. However, few faculty members have any desire to solicit more responsibilities, and those who are so inclined can just as easily abuse their power relationship with teaching assistants, for example. Most students presumably select their thesis supervisor because there is a match of interests. That their choice happens to be someone who has a company is relatively insignificant. Let's face it, most graduate students try to figure out what their thesis supervisor wants, and then they do it. This is certainly a problem but it is a problem endemic to graduate education.

Neither am I especially concerned about a university owning an equity share in a faculty member's company. Most faculty members in that position would already be tenured full professors—and probably distinguished ones at that. For those who aren't, the normal faculty review process should serve as a sufficient safeguard. Besides, what can a faculty entrepreneur who is not promoted do to retaliate? If the university owns a piece of the company, it owns it. Disgruntled faculty members will hardly scuttle their own companies out of pique at an adverse tenure decision.

Finally, I can't see any definitive reason for Varrin and Kukich's guideline against permitting a faculty entrepreneur's company from sponsoring his or her research on campus. Varrin and Kukich are worried about objectivity. There is the problem of having the faculty member devote too much time to his research and too little time to his other university duties. But every faculty member involved in research and consulting has that problem. Medical school faculty members who operate a private practice in their university teaching hospital predate business-university partnerships. I am not dismissing the problem, but I am saying it is not a new problem.

Varrin and Kukich seem more concerned that the researcher would be judge and jury. But will any harm be done in this case? Suppose the person misses a deadline, and it hurts his firm. Why should the university care? In such cases the university simply doesn't have the responsibility to see that the research is completed correctly and in time. No aspect of the university's mission is violated if it isn't. On the other hand, if the research was being counted toward a university goal—promotion and tenure, for example—I have no doubt that faculty committees will feel free to penalize the researcher-entrepreneur. There will be many who would penalize our entrepreneur for doing applied research at all, even if it were done correctly and on time.

Business-university partnerships do create conflicts of interest but they are similar in type to conflicts of interest that have existed on campus for a couple of generations at least. Insufficient attention has been paid to faculty conflicts of interest; perhaps the addition of those presented by university-business partnerships will focus attention here. However, the specific situations discussed in the literature thus far are really extensions of already existing problems. So long as the behavior of faculty members can be defended on sound academic grounds, we should assume it is legitimate. I do think an academic-judgment rule similar to the business-judgment rule should be operative.

Business-opportunity partnerships do create a problem that is more correctly called a clash of competing interests than a conflict of interest. The core values of the academy and the core values of business are in conflict. As E. E. David, Jr. put it,

Industry is output-oriented; industrial managers aspire to efficient production of goods and services. To the industrialist, paying for research implies ownership of the results, which are used to establish proprietary competitive advantage if at all possible . . . .

On the other hand, university faculty and administrators consider themselves as communities of scholars. The primary research aim is the creation of knowledge, for it is educational values that are seen as most important. There is also a tendency to be averse to commercialization, which is seen by some academicians and public interest groups as exploitation of the public.[29]

Some might argue that university-business partnerships introduce an alien culture into the university.[30] As a result, we can expect universities to be run more like businesses and less like traditional educational institutions. Most academics, including this one, believe that would represent a very bad turn of events.

Nonetheless, the alien-culture concern must be put in perspective. First, we should recognize that the alien culture has already arrived and that university-business partnerships have had little to do with it. Whereas private firms compete for profits, universities compete for funds and prestige. Faculty members, especially in the sciences and engineering, are expected to get grants. University fund raisers are seeking record amounts of money, and fund raising has become a fine art. Universities are competing for nationally known faculty by offering salaries well into six figures as well as by purchasing large amounts of expensive scientific equipment, guaranteeing graduate fellows, and providing secretarial services and travel funds. At the research institutions, teaching stands in a distant second place to research. Many academic "stars" make reduced teaching loads part of their negotiating package. As Whirlpool executive Jack Sparks said,

> Universities have been accused of running years behind schedule, of not recognizing the time pressure of business. This impression comes from another era. Most universities today are *business*-managed . . . many are devotees of strategic planning as is industry . . . and many have tight time disciplines.[31]

This state of affairs has been caused by a public that is more inclined to business values than to academic values. The two major sources of funds besides tuition are tax dollars and corporate support. Since the taxpayers share the values of business, it is not surprising that the public has demanded that the university be run more like a business.

Moreover, as more and more students go to college out of necessity to stay competitive, the vocational role of higher education has become increasingly important. In the words of Fred Hirsch, higher education has become a defensive good—a good purchased not for its intrinsic value but because it is necessary to hold one's edge in the competition for well-paying jobs.[32] Our students who pay tuition are similarly motivated by business values. Those who support our institutions of higher learning—students, taxpayers, and businesspeople—are all either fairly ignorant of or hostile to traditional academic values. However, if there is one of those three groups that is more sympathetic to traditional academic values, I believe it would be the businesspeople. After all, many of them were educated in universities with the traditional academic values, and business has a long history of financial support to private institutions. In any case, it would be naïve to think that a prohibition against university-business research partnerships would do much to stem the flow of business values into the university setting.

But will the expansion of such partnerships accelerate this unwelcome trend or bring about any special problems? One of the special problems discussed in the literature is the possibility that business-university partnerships will skew research toward applied research and away from basic research. Judith Hill argues as follows:

One problem derives from attractiveness of nonbasic research. It is so much easier for the university to get financial support for such projects than for basic research, and the rewards for the people engaged in conducting nonbasic research are so much greater, in financial terms and in terms of creating opportunities for a future career in industry, that when the university has established a precedent of performing nonbasic research it will be tempted to expend more and more of its resources on nonbasic research, and less and less on basic research. The administrators responsible for locating funds for research will focus their energies on industrial sources. The faculty responsible for conducting research will exert pressure to be assigned to industrial projects. Unless the university succeeds in drawing and maintaining an arbitrary line concerning the extent to which it will take on nonbasic research—and there will be every inducement to step over this line, wherever it is drawn—its basic-research program may suffer seriously from neglect.[33]

Martin Kenney picks up on Hill's argument. He maintains that as faculty members succeed in obtaining wealth through applied research, the applied-research professor will serve as the role model. "Will the message to young scientists be to shun basic research and only do commercially applicable research? If so, should it not be expected that further generations of technological innovations will be slowed as increasing numbers of scientists remain in their university chairs and yet devote their energies to commercial activities?"[34]

If these arguments are correct, they present a strong challenge to the permissibility of university-business research projects. After all, training students to be critical and open to new ideas and adding to the store of knowledge through basic research constitute the mission of the university. Activities that undercut that central mission should be abandoned or curtailed. On that point Kenney, Hill, and I are in agreement.

However, I am not so pessimistic about the future of basic research under these partnerships. First, applied research carries with it an intellectual stigma. In the sciences, social sciences, and humanities, basic research is definitely considered superior to applied research. Applied researchers may lose in prestige what they gain in dollars. Second, business may be becoming more appreciative of basic research, recognizing that without strong basic research, the applied research will begin to diminish. Third and most important, the distinction between basic and applied research may be a bogus one, as the line between ethical theory and applied ethics is becoming less clear all the time. In commenting on Judith Hill's article, microbiologist Leon Campbell contends that no sharp line exists in the sciences either.[35] Moreover, many faculty members take exception to the Kenney-Hill analysis. Some academics have found that their own scientific research is better as a result of these partnerships. University of Washington medical school professor Philip Needleman indicated his work on peptides would not have gone as fast if it hadn't been for business collaboration.[36]

There is also a theoretical reason for thinking that business-university research partnerships will enhance basic research rather than hinder it. The strict departmental organization of the university inhibits interdisciplinary research; the resulting narrow specialization has been widely criticized both within the academy and without. Business is much more task oriented; a business will assemble the team it needs to get the job done. The first question a businessperson asks about an applicant is whether the person has the skills needed to help get the job done. A more team-oriented approach to basic research might result in better basic research as well as more basic research.

Kenney and Hill have raised valid concerns, and universities that have university-business partnerships must monitor the overall basic research output, both from the university as a whole and from the partnerships. If the partnerships seem to be hurting basic research, then they would have to be constrained. However, I don't see any reason why business-university partnerships must undermine basic research, and I can see some reasons why such partnerships might enhance it.

My fears are broader yet. I think such partnerships will have unfortunate distributional side effects, both within universities and among universities. Business-university research partnerships will be focused on the sciences and engineering. Humanities partnerships are not likely to appear soon. As a result the rich will get richer and the poor poorer. There is already a growing concern in many universities about the salary differentials between faculty in the fine arts, humanities, and social sciences and those in computer science, engineering, and business. Salaries of natural scientists would be helped by university-business research partnerships but scholars in the other traditional areas will fall behind. I have similar concerns about all the money that is flowing to business faculty. Ironically, in all the research I have done on this topic, the only writer who seems to share my concern was Whirlpool executive Jack Sparks:

> What if industry investments concentrate on the hard sciences to the extent that the soft sciences and humanities keep losing interest and sponsors? . . . What if we race only for technical information, for knowledge, at the possible expense of wisdom? As a businessman with educator interests, I am witness—perhaps a participant—in developments of technology and business sciences. I marvel at the new fields of study and resultant services and products. Yet I decry any de-emphasis on history, philosophy, ethics, religion, linguistics, literature, the arts in all forms.[37]

If business support of higher education shifts from general contributions to primarily scientific research partnerships, the nonscientific disciplines will surely suffer.

I am also concerned about distributional effects among institutions. The primary beneficiaries of these business-university partnerships will be the major scientific research universities. Again we will have a case of the rich getting richer. We are in danger of creating two classes of educational institutions. On the one hand, we will have major research universities which have the latest in expensive, high-tech scientific equipment. The students of these institutions will not only have access to the best professors but to the best jobs in industry and commerce as well. On the other hand, we will have all the other institutions of higher education—the traditionally marginal ones, but also all the state institutions except for the "flagship" campus and all the formerly elite small liberal arts colleges. The scientific education of students at these schools will be considerably impoverished, especially in terms of access to state-of-the-art equipment and other scientific resources. These institutions will be forced to take shortcuts that will leave students less well rounded and less able to compete in the scientific age. There has always been a "pecking order" among institutions, but there has been a wide continuum from elite institutions to marginal ones. If too much money gravitates to the scientific research universities, the continuum will disappear and a gulf will develop. Many formerly excellent liberal arts colleges and smaller universities will end up on the wrong side of the gulf.

What can be done? First, an early objection to business-university partnerships was that the corporation and a university administrator signed an agreement that was inconsistent with university values. The "solution" to that problem was to insist that such agreements not be secret and that the partnership contract be reviewed by faculty. I would add the proviso that some of those faculty reviewers be from traditional academic disciplines other than science. Since these professors have less to gain, they might be more alert to the dangers to traditional academic values.

Second, a mechanism should be established so that the humanities, fine arts, and perhaps the social sciences, will receive economic benefits from these partnerships. Perhaps a percentage of the overhead could be directed to those disciplines. Perhaps a percentage of the royalties from any patent. Perhaps each business partner could make an unrestricted donation to support those programs. I am sure there are many other creative possibilities. The specific mechanism is less important than that some mechanism be in place. Representatives of these disciplines should not have to fight or beg for a share of the resources these partnerships bring the universities. A mechanism that will automatically provide a share will prevent that state of affairs.

214 | NORMAN E. BOWIE

Such a mechanism would also provide a means for business partners to say that the other disciplines not represented in the partnership have value as well.

Third, the university must be more aggressive in asserting the worth of its values outside the university context. First, teaching is one of the traditional professions. Over the past fifty years there has been much debate as to the appropriate definition of a profession. However, possession of a systematic body of knowledge that is passed on through formal training and an altruistic spirit are essential elements of any characterization of a profession. Professionals aren't *simply* in it for the money. The chief function of a professional is to use specialized knowledge to protect ignorant clients from exploitation, not to maximize income. Many professionals seem to have forgotten this important point. Now that it is possible to make six-figure incomes in academic life, some wonder if professors haven't been "corrupted" by money. Critics fear that business-industry partnerships will only exacerbate the growing preoccupation of the university with money.

Since I don't believe we will be able to kick the money changers out of the temple, our best chance is to convert them. In his paper, Martin Kenney takes the traditional Milton Friedman approach regarding the purpose of business. "The primary and overriding duty for an industrial concern is to make profit."[38] However, that view has been discredited by business ethicists. Few chief executive officers believe it either—a fact that has not gone unnoticed by a number of corporate raiders. Management training in many quarters is emphasizing that business can do well by doing good—a view not inconsistent with the attitude of a professional or of Plato. Harvard Business School has as its motto, "To make business a profession." If business is to play a greater role in campus life, it is incumbent upon faculty members to ensure that business partners behave as professionals and not as mere profit makers.

Beyond the role of helping business become a profession, we need to convince businesspeople of the legitimacy of the traditional academic values and to point out how the adoption of those values will improve the practice of business. The first such value is cooperation. Businesspeople must learn the virtues of cooperation as well as competition. Academics do compete—one individual against another, and one institution against the other—but this competition should always be constrained by a cooperative spirit among colleagues in a discipline. Competition often seems to be overemphasized in the business context, so much so that units within a business, for example, labor and management, compete to the greater detriment of the firm.

The second value is community. Academic research, particularly in science, is often conducted by teams. There is also an appreciation of the efforts of other scientists. Each generation knows it builds on the work of past generations. This recognition of a debt owed to the past, in conjunction with the team approach, helps cut the excessive sense of isolated individualism sometimes found in successful corporate persons. Academic life, although hierarchical, is less hierarchical than in the traditional business. Where hierarchies exist in academic life they more closely represent a meritocracy than they do in business.[39]

The third value is respect for government. Academics have a long tradition of partnerships with government. So do Japanese business persons. For too long American business has seen the government as the enemy of business. American business executives must learn to work cooperatively with government. Perhaps the academic arena could provide an appropriate forum.

Lastly, the university has more to offer business than research partnerships. We can help business appreciate the value of the well-educated person. Well-rounded individuals who are creative and critical thinkers make good managers. As the earlier quotation from Whirlpool executive Sparks shows, the humanities and fine arts are important and have much to offer.

It is easy to criticize these final comments as hopelessly naïve and idealistic. However, what is so realistic about railing against a business mentality that is already here? Rather than circle the wagons (a shopworn business metaphor) or retreat to the ivory tower (a shopworn academic metaphor), let us creatively engage businesses, confident in traditional academic values including the value of open-mindedness. If the academic community approaches business-university research partnerships in this spirit, we might avert the dangers—which are real—and affect the practice of business in ways we academics would consider better.

NOTES

1. Emily T. Smith, "Monsanto's College Alliance Is Getting High Marks," *Business Week*, May 12, 1986, pp. 33–34. Deborah M. Barnes, "New University-Industry Pact Signed," *Science*, December 13, 1985, pp. 1255–56.

2. Jack D. Sparks, "The Creative Connection: University-Industry Relations," *Research Management*, 22 (November—December 1985), 19.

3. B. J. Spalding, "Technology by Teamwork," *Chemical Week*, March 11, 1987, pp. 14–15.

4. Smith, "Monsanto's College Alliance," p. 33.

5. Martin Gold, "Industry and Academe Should Band Together to Capitalize on Lab Work," *Electronic Design*, September 19, 1985, p. 27.

6. Robert Barker, "Bringing Science into Industry from Universities," *Research Management* 22 (November–December 1985), 23.

7. Sparks, "The Creative Connection." p. 20.

8. Barker, "Bringing Science into Industry," p. 24.

9. Ibid.

10. See, for example, Sidney Hook, *Education for Modern Man* (New York: Humanities Press, 1973).

11. Judith M. Hill, "The University and Industrial Research: Selling Out?" *Business and Professional Ethics Journal* 2 (Summer 1983), 28.

12. Robert D. Varrin and Diane S. Kukich, "Guidelines for Industry-Sponsored Research at Universities," *Science*, January 25, 1985, p. 385.

13. Ibid.

14. Ibid.

15. Barbara J. Culliton, "Pajaro Dunes: The Search for Consensus," *Science*, April 9, 1982, p. 156.

16. Ibid.

17. Hill, "The University and Industrial Research," p. 34.

18. Barnes, "New University-Industry Pact Signed," p. 1256.

19. Culliton, "Pajaro Dunes," pp. 156–57.

20. Varrin and Kukich, "Guidelines for Industry-Sponsored Research," p. 387.

21. Ibid.

22. *Webster's New Collegiate Dictionary* (1979), p. 235.

23. Michael Davis, "Conflict of Interest," *Business and Professional Ethics Journal* 1 (Summer 1982), 21.

24. *Johnson v. Trueblood*, 629 F2d 387 3rd Cir (1980) at 292.

25. J. Paul Mark, *The Empire Builders* (New York: William Morrow, 1987), pp. 9–13.

26. Ibid., pp. 19–28, 77–79, 266.

27. Norman E. Bowie, review of J. Paul Mark, *The Empire Builders*, in *Academe* May–June 1988, pp. 84–85.

28. See Sandra Sugawara, "Virginia's New Point Man on Ecology," *Washington Post*, December 5, 1974, pp. B1, B9.

29. E. E. David, Jr., "Striking a Bargain between Company and Campus," *Environment* 24 (July–August 1982), 43.

30. Two professors particularly concerned about this issue are Martin Kenney, "The Ethical Dilemmas of University-Industry Collaborations," *Journal of Business Ethics* 6 (1987), 127–35; and Sheldon Krimsky, "The University: Marketing Theories, Not Toothpaste," *Environment* 24 (July–August 1982), 46.

31. Sparks, "The Creative Connection," p. 20.

32. Fred Hirsch, *Social Limits to Growth* (Cambridge: Harvard University Press, 1976), pp. 41–51.

33. Hill, "The University and Industrial Research," p. 33.

34. Kenney, "The Ethical Dilemmas," p. 134.

35. L. Leon Campbell, "Commentary," *Business and Professional Ethics Journal* 2 (Summer 1983), 39.

36. See Smith, "Monsanto's College Alliance," p. 34.

37. Sparks, "The Creative Connection," p. 21

38. Kenney, "The Ethical Dilemmas," p. 129.

39. See, for example, Robert Jackall, *Moral Mazes* (New York: Oxford University Press, 1988).

12

DIVERSITY WITHIN UNIVERSITY FACULTIES

Alan H. Goldman

As a new generation of women and minority group members turns college age and enters the job market, a generation with far fewer victims of discrimination in lower schools than previous generations, one hears less call for affirmative action in university appointments for reasons of compensatory justice and more call for diversity per se among faculties. Diversity in itself is held to be desirable apart from considerations of compensation. In this discussion I shall evaluate this appeal, distinguishing different forms or senses of diversity, different contexts in which the appeal is made, and different justifying arguments.

I

That diversity within college and university populations is of value is not a new idea. It has firm precedent in the practice of many universities of seeking geographic, and more recently racial, gender, and ethnic, diversity among the student population. In the 1978 Supreme Court decision in the Bakke case, Justice Lewis Powell, who was the swing vote for the majority, recognized the quest for a diverse student body as meeting the test for a compelling state interest.[1] The familiar argument that he cited claims that students from different backgrounds bring different experiences and outlooks to the educational context. These distinct points of view allegedly enrich the educational experience of all students and better equip them to deal later with the heterogeneous world outside the university. Insofar as students are collective or cooperative truth seekers, there may lurk in the background premises of this argument as well the Millian assumption that truth in any area of inquiry best emerges from the clash of differing opinions and viewpoints, that all points of view relevant to a dispute should be represented, and that persons from different backgrounds are more likely to represent all those viewpoints in classes and discussions.

Assuming for the sake of the argument the soundness of the position regarding the value of diversity among student populations, there remains the serious question of how much this value ought to count when measured against more straightforward academic qualifications. Questions of both fairness and utility are often begged in the quest for geographical and other sorts of diversity among students, although these questions are made somewhat less pressing to the extent that more orthodox criteria prove unpredictive of performance at the college level. My question here regards the extent to which the argument can be extended from students to faculty. How is the case for diversity among faculty members similar to, stronger, or weaker than the case for student diversity?

II

Certain forms of diversity within particular academic departments of a university seem rather uncontroversially to be considered valuable. If there are different recognized areas within a field, such as ethics, epistemology, and logic within philosophy, then there seems to be good reason to seek specialists in all the major areas. At a minimum, the major areas of the field should be covered in undergraduate curricula, where students generally choose majors without regard for particular specialties within fields. This sort of consideration does not enter the quest for diversity among students, although some universities might seek to diversify their predeclared majors. In this particular respect, then, the case for faculty diversity appears stronger than the case for students. But the important point here is that we are talking about diversity among academic areas, and so there is no suggestion yet of an argument for appointing faculty according to nonacademic criteria. And once more, even the value of this sort of diversity must be weighed against the value of appointing the best person available in the broader field. Many departments, my own included, have opted to pursue the best candidate available, regardless of specialty, at least once the major areas of the subject can be adequately covered in undergraduate courses.

Somewhat more controversial is the value of seeking not only specialists in different content areas of a subject but specialists who

employ differing and opposed methodologies, such as phenomenolo-
gists or hermeneuticists as well as analytic philosophers. One might
wonder why analytic philosophers, who view their methods alone as
proper for confronting and teaching philosophical problems, if they
constitute the majority within a department, would seek to appoint
those whose methods they deem inoptimal at best. How can we
advocate teaching falsehoods (by our own lights) or teaching according
to methods that we consider pedagogically wrong? Similar questions
arise more generally in epistemology and ethics. Why should those
who think they have knowledge ever seek out or even take the time
to consider contrary evidence? Why should those who hold certain
moral views that they consider important tolerate others with opposing views and practices that they consider morally wrong? Both of
these broader questions are relevant to the question of why a majority
within a college department would seek to appoint those with opposing views and methodologies. The latter is a puzzle about a particular
case of individuals who may presume to know their own views to be
correct and yet tolerate and even seriously consider the opposing
views of potential colleagues.

Mill suggested answers to the broader epistemological and moral
questions in arguing for free expression.[2] The first answer appeals to
fallibility. Whether our views concern empirical, moral, political, or
educational matters, most of the time we must admit the possibility
of error, which entails the possibility that some opposing views are
correct. Refusing to consider or tolerate opposing views eliminates the
possibility of correcting one's own. Second, Mill argued that correct
views are better understood and appreciated when confronted with
opposition. Views that remain unchallenged over long periods risk
becoming dull dogmas, the reasons supporting them obscured by
layers of blind habit. Third, and perhaps following from Mill's first two
contentions, is the assumption, already mentioned and also explicitly
endorsed by him, that the best way to the truth is through the clash
of opposing viewpoints in a free marketplace of ideas. Open criticism
has both a cleansing and invigorating effect on received opinions. We
might add in the case of moral and political views that living peaceably
in a heterogeneous and pluralistic society requires tolerating beliefs
and practices with which one disagrees. If our society is not morally
monolithic, then at least some individuals and groups within it must
for the sake of peace tolerate some practices that in their eyes constitute
wrongdoing.

These arguments seem to apply as well to toleration, and even encouragement, of opposing teaching or disciplinary methodologies, which serve the communication of presumed (but fallible) knowledge and values. Of course, in all the areas mentioned there are limits to the application of Mill's arguments. In the case of (nonmoral) knowledge, there are degrees of certainty or confidence that suggest whether it would be worthwhile to seek or consider contrary evidence. No one should be interested now in evaluating the evidence that the earth is flat or the center of the universe. In ethics (and religion), we tolerate some opposing views and practices but forbid behavior that violates our fundamental moral rules, whether those engaged in that behavior perceive it as wrong, morally indifferent, or even ethically or religiously required.

We can immediately note similar limits to the encouragement or toleration of diverse beliefs, specialties, and methodologies among faculties at universities. No sane academician would recommend positions in astrology alongside astronomy, or alchemy alongside chemistry. Equally, few in this country would advocate known Nazis or Fascists as political science or political philosophy instructors. The latter limitations need not be construed as direct constraints on free speech. In appointing faculty members we do not simply tolerate the opinions they will communicate but subsidize or support those opinions, or at least their communication. We can refuse to subsidize certain forms of speech without prohibiting or constraining them.

On the question of prohibiting or tolerating free expression, Mill, of course, supported the arguments for toleration by appeal to the deeper principle of utility. Indeed, since it is generally worse to be silenced oneself than to be prevented from silencing others (whether one's views are correct or incorrect), a principle of tolerating speech or expression can be justified by appeal to utility or to a contractual model of society or to a principle of respect for persons (and their fundamental interests). The utilitarian justification, if applied to particular episodes, runs into trouble, as is typical, when large majorities are offended, and so the argument requires moving to rules or contracts that must be obeyed in individual cases.

Justifying not merely toleration but subsidization of different and diverse forms of expression, as with faculty appointments, requires appeal not to underlying moral principles but to the epistemic principle of fallibility. It is only to the extent that we cannot be certain of our knowledge claims or methodologies that we would seek to appoint faculty members with generally opposing views. The moral principles mentioned in the previous paragraph operate largely independently of the truth of the views or expressions whose toleration they support (although Mill tried to link truth to utility more closely in his arguments). By contrast, we subsidize or support diverse or opposing views only to the extent that we admit that they might be true or lead to the truth. If the epistemic considerations were not uppermost here, then we would be obligated to provide academic positions for astrologers or card readers.

While the difference between subsidy and toleration of diverse views (the former being most relevant to the question of academic diversity in a faculty) is reflected in this difference in the underlying principles that justify supporting or allowing diversity, the line between the two must be drawn finely in academia, as in the news media. The news media facilitate the broadcast or communication of views, which function goes beyond toleration but may fall short of support. (Media executives need not agree with or support the views they broadcast.) This broadcast function therefore blurs the distinction between toleration and support as applied in practice. In academia the line is made less distinct as well, for example, by the difference between appointing and retaining faculty members. Mainline advocates of freedom of expression in a university would probably tolerate the expression of Fascist views by a professor already on the faculty (to the extent of not seeking the professor's dismissal), but would not seek to appoint someone who had expressed such views prior to applying for an appointment. Thus, retaining members of the faculty also seems to fall between toleration and support of their views.

Continuing the example of philosophy departments, presumably hermeneutics, theology, and phenomenology have more to recommend them as methodologies than do astrology or numerology, although the atheist analytic philosopher may believe that theology and phenomenology are no less riddled with error and nonsense. We cannot base academic support on the degree to which various disciplines or methodologies reflect the public's beliefs, since, on the one hand, many legitimate disciplines, such as particle physics, are known to very few in the general public, and on the other hand, many (including some in high places) appear to believe in such obvious frauds as astrology. There seems to be no recourse but to allow experts, namely, those presently on faculties within currently recognized academic disciplines, to judge their own degrees of fallibility regarding methodologies within their fields and to aim at just the degree of diversity or balance within departments that they believe will best serve the goals of teaching and research. Narrow paradigms may dominate within particular fields throughout certain periods of time, but there is also a strong impetus toward novelty or progress in fields that seek truth or creative expression. This impetus within existing academic structures is evidenced by shifts in dominant paradigms and by the many new fields that have separated themselves from broader disciplines established earlier.

III

When we turn from the value of diverse representation within faculties by different areas of academic subjects to the call for other sorts of diversity, the issues become cloudier. One might try to extend directly the arguments in favor of diversity within student bodies. If class discussions benefit from the input of opposing points of view and diverse experiences and if this diversity in points of view and experience is more likely to occur among students with different geographic, social, and ethnic backgrounds, then shouldn't a similar diversity within the faculty enable students to form more informed views about particular and general, value and value-neutral matters? If, as I have been assuming for the sake of argument, the truth at least in controversial matters is more likely to emerge from the clash of opposing views, and if faculty, like students, from diverse backgrounds are more likely to hold opposing views and to base them on different experiences, then we might expect social, ethnic, and gender diversity within the faculty to be of similar value to them and to their students.

Problems for this argument arise first from disanalogies between students and faculty members beyond those pointed out earlier. In the case of students, there is probably no more direct way to aim at diversity of opinion than through aiming to admit those from diverse social and geographic backgrounds. Students' opinions on controversial issues concerning academic subjects and values may not be well formed or stable at the time of applying to college, so that direct attempts to gauge them will often fail. We can assume, however, that diverse backgrounds will have a diversifying effect on opinions on various subjects. Applicants for faculty positions, by contrast, normally have well-formed views on matters within their disciplines, so that departments and administrators can aim more directly and reliably at diversity of opinion or methodology if such differences are deemed desirable. Thus, if the goal is input from faculty members of differing opinions and points of view to academic debates that seek the truth, then seeking less-than-direct means to reach it seems unjustified or at least inoptimal. The case for faculty diversity differs from that for student diversity in this respect. The criteria for academic appointments remain academic, given just the goal of diversity of opinion.

It might be replied that views on certain subject matters are directly determined by the race or sex of their advocates, or that these views are based on experiences available in our society only to those of a particular race or gender. Some feminist philosophers have suggested such claims in regard to ethics and epistemology, and similar claims could be advanced in the areas of black or women's studies programs. If these claims were true, then, at least in these areas, aiming at faculty diversity in regard to race or gender would be aiming more or less directly at diversity of opinion or ability to teach different academic subjects. But the "more or less" is still significant here. If there is a subject, feminist epistemology, that ought to be taught (I cannot assess the writings in this area here), then the direct aim would be to appoint someone who could teach it well, presumably but not necessarily a woman. Ability to teach other subject areas would be correlated less directly with gender or race, and the aim, so far as this argument goes, would be to appoint the best professors for these subjects. This argument still cannot establish a goal of diversity among faculty in nonacademic respects.

A second disanalogy between the cases for student and faculty diversity in nonacademic respects concerns the desirability of having students spend their formative years in an environment approximating a microcosm of the "real world" in which they will have to function after graduation. I am, first of all, not certain of the truth of the premise here. Most colleges and universities aim to accept a student body that is intellectually privileged and well trained at the secondary level. In this respect they aim precisely to avoid a microcosm of the broader social environment. No one advocates a fair sampling of the smart and the dumb for entering freshman classes, and yet such a mix is a prominent and significant feature of the world in which students will later have to function. Even if the aim to mirror the broader social environment is sound within the constraint of accepting only academically capable students, the parallel case for diversity within a faculty seems weaker. The university is to approximate the world outside for its students, not its faculty, and the microcosm for students is constituted by other students, not by faculty. Professors are rarely perceived as typical members of the social environment, and in any case, students socialize mainly or only with other students.

IV

It has been claimed that professors should be representative of the broader society for a different reason, namely, to serve as role models for students from minority backgrounds. The role-model argument has been widely assessed in prior discussions of affirmative action, and I shall be brief here. Its main problem is the assumption of empirically untested and, to me at least, counterintuitive psychological premises. While younger children may well be motivated initially in certain career directions by their admiration for certain adults in roles prominent to them, it seems doubtful that this source of motivation would be primary for college-age students. Those enrolled in college or university courses have closer and more accurate access to the demands and rewards of various professions and careers, and they can base career decisions on more rational grounds than admiration for particular individuals. Minority professors constitute role models only for the role of professor in any case, and I am not sure why universities should be in the business of encouraging by nonrational means academic as opposed to other careers. Even if being a role model is one function that a professor may serve, should that function have any weight in appointment decisions if it is in conflict with the primary criterion of ability to extend and transmit the body of knowledge in an academic field? In part, the answer to that question may depend on the degree of scarcity of role models in various prestigious positions for members of particular minorities. At the present time models abound in the news media and elsewhere. A related question also arises in response: How effective will an academic role model be if perceived as academically less qualified than others?

It appears that appeal to neither diversity of opinion on academic matters nor to the need for role models can justify nonacademic criteria for faculty appointments. Yet a third related reason might be offered in favor of faculty diversity in respect to race, gender, or ethnicity. It might be claimed that while professors need not mirror the broader community in ethnic and gender diversity in order to serve as role models, they nevertheless ought to mirror the minority ratios within the student body (which in turn ought to mirror the broader society for reasons already given). It is unfair, it could be argued, for black students to have all white professors or for female students to have almost all male teachers. I do not deny that all-white all-male faculties would be evidence of unjust appointment practices. Our question here, however, is whether diversity in these areas is of value in itself or instrumentally valuable for promoting other desirable goals. In regard to fairness, the question now is whether white male faculties would be unfair to students who are not white males. The claim would seemingly have to rest on the premise that students learn better or are graded more leniently by members of their own race and sex. The premise is once more empirically questionable, although some studies have suggested the influence of biases in grading. More important, the acceptance of the conclusion would seem to require quotas that would work against minority candidates for faculty positions once the faculty matched the student ratio in a particular category.

V

It has been argued, finally, along these lines that professors ought to mirror not the racial and gender makeup of the student body, but their political, economic, religious, and moral views or, more precisely, those of their parents and the alumni of the school in question. One of the first calls to appoint faculty on grounds other than academic qualifications was issued not by supporters of liberal affirmative action programs, but by William Buckley in *God and Man at Yale*.[3] There, Buckley laments the presence of so many atheists and socialists on the faculty at Yale, an institution with predominantly religious and politically conservative trustees, alumni, and parents of students. Buckley bases his argument largely on a principle of consumer or investor choice, a principle that is at least suitably neutral in itself between the conservative values he endorses and the liberal values he condemns. His is a call not for diversity within the faculty but rather for uniformity, although he would have been satisfied with a more diverse Yale faculty than the one he perceived. But his argument is relevant to our discussion here because it supports nonacademic criteria for faculty appointments and because criticism of it brings out weaknesses in more recent calls for diversity.

Buckley points out that criteria for faculty appointments can never be value-neutral. First of all, academic values must obviously be seen as relevant. Trivially, each department seeks to add only professors that it considers good within the disciplinary field. Second, I have admitted in agreement with Buckley that faculties at American universities would undoubtedly seek to avoid appointing known Nazis, for example. But the avoidance of such fanatics does not imply the general relevance of political views to faculty appointment decisions. It remains consistent to base such decisions on academic criteria except in extreme cases, perhaps when views on other matters call into question a candidate's ability to make sound judgments within the academic field.

What should I say of Buckley's principle of consumer or investor sovereignty? That a group of private individuals has the right to appoint a group of teachers to teach their children, and to appoint them on whatever nondiscriminatory, nonacademic grounds they choose, seems plausible. This minimal claim may be seen to underlie Buckley's call to the alumni, trustees, and parents of Yale to require that only professors who reflect their values be appointed. But this is far from an accurate organizational picture of Yale University. Yale's endowment reaches back generations, and it receives financial support from many and diverse sources (including government, although not in Buckley's time). The university is not owned by its trustees, parents, or alumni; so the principle of investor sovereignty seems largely inapplicable. A university such as Yale must recognize itself, as others recognize it, as a guardian of academic values for society. Buckley's quaint picture of the private university is less applicable today than it was in 1950 and, needless to say, not applicable at all to state universities.

It remains true, of course, that parents need not pay to send their children to colleges of whose faculties they disapprove. But this liberty seems to exhaust their claim to consumer sovereignty. Faculties must answer to students in the demand to communicate their knowledge clearly and effectively; but they must answer to their disciplines and to the broader society in the demand to extend that knowledge through research. It is a platitude that the research function requires freedom from the tyranny of received views and from political pressures. Recognizing that platitude, and another to the effect that great researchers need not be great teachers, Buckley suggests separating the functions and requiring value conformity only from teachers.[4] But although the second platitude is true as well, his suggestion is once more naïve in neglecting the extent to which good teaching and good research remain closely linked in the typical case of the good professor.

I have argued in this section that trustees, alumni, and parents do not have a right to impose their political and religious values on the faculties of private universities, that principles of investor and consumer sovereignty do not apply here. In regard to students, it is obvious neither that they should want their immature views reinforced rather than challenged by faculty nor that these wants, if they exist, should determine how faculty members are appointed or retained. There does not appear to be any reason beyond this misapplied appeal to consumer sovereignty (and beyond the appeals to fairness and to academic diversity that I considered earlier) why a faculty should mirror the makeup of the student body in regard to political, economic, or religious beliefs and values.

VI

I have pointed to several different dimensions along which faculty diversity might be sought, approved the quest for academic diversity but suggested proper limits to support for those whose beliefs or methodologies oppose received views, and found no reason to seek diversity in itself along other dimensions through the use of nonacademic criteria for appointments. The case for student diversity has been contrasted with arguments for diversity within faculties. One way in which students and faculty are alike, however, and which weakens the call for diversity along specific nonacademic dimensions, is in the almost countless respects in which individuals differ.

Justice Powell, who, as previously noted, endorsed the quest for student diversity as a compelling interest of universities, also pointed out that an exclusive focus on ethnic or racial diversity would hinder the attainment of genuine or overall diversity within the student body.[5] This claim sounds plausible, once we recognize that ethnic differences represent only one among many dimensions along which to measure diversity, but this recognition also raises the question whether we can make sense of the notion of overall diversity. Steven M. Cahn lists the following nonacademic respects in which prospective faculty appointees can differ: age, gender, race, religion, nationality, ethnicity, regional background, economic class, social stratum, military experience, bodily appearance, physical soundness, sexual orientation, marital status, familial relationships, ethical standards, political commitments, cultural values, intellectual interests, avocations, personalities, and life-styles.[6] Even this list, of course, is only partial, including only respects that might be suggested to be relevant to appointments once we allow nonacademic criteria to enter the decision-making process.

In the case of students, the multiplicity of such differences is not so troubling to the case for diversity. The goals there are, first, to ensure the existence within the student body of different points of view on academic or academically relevant matters and, second, to mirror the social environment in which students will later have to function. These goals can be met by varying some of the factors in

Cahn's list that correlate with or determine different social and cultural experiences. And as I argued earlier, they cannot be met more efficiently by aiming directly at academic diversity.

But in the case of faculty, it was argued, academic diversity, insofar as it is desirable, can be achieved directly. This possibility raises questions regarding which of the many nonacademic kinds of diversity should also be made goals of faculty appointment, and why. I have concentrated on gender and race (along with a diversion to Buckley's discussion of political and moral values), but these factors seem relevant only in the context of arguments for compensation for past injustice or in favor of quotas (hard or soft) as a means of achieving equal opportunity. Diversity ceases to be of value in itself or as a means to achieve academic goals.

I have discussed questions of compensation for discrimination at length elsewhere and will not repeat those arguments here.[7] It suffices to say that a goal of diversity per se and within present faculties bears no obvious relation to compensating real past victims of injustice. A connection between diversity along race and gender lines and equal opportunity for members of groups that historically were targets of discrimination is more plausible. But we must be careful to specify the right connection. It is certainly true, as noted, that lack of diversity within the faculties of whole universities can be taken as evidence of discrimination, overt or otherwise, in appointment practices. Of course, this is defeasible evidence, and as we consider smaller samples—for example, individual department ratios—the other variables that can affect these ratios become more significant. There is also the connection, already considered, between equal opportunity for young members of minority groups and the availability of role models in various prestigious positions. But, as I argued, role models are presently available, as they might not have been earlier, without aiming at diversity per se as a factor to be considered independently in hiring decisions.

We cannot move beyond these connections simply to equate degree of equal opportunity, in this case opportunity of becoming a university professor, with degree of representation of various groups within faculties. If the latter is to be our only or primary measure, then the opportunities of those from groups already well represented in particular areas will be severely limited. One justification for a requirement of equal opportunity, I have argued elsewhere, appeals to considerations of desert: when the relevant obstacles to achieving positions are made equal, then individuals deserve the positions that they achieve (although, as Thomas Nagel has pointed out, just rewards for those positions is another matter).[8] But when race and gender are made in themselves primary criteria for appointment, then desert is ignored and, with it, reasonable conceptions of equal opportunity. (Once more, there may be other, overriding morally relevant considerations, such as compensation.)

Although lack of diversity along these lines is evidence of past injustice, present diversity in itself is not evidence of justice; it depends how that diversity came about. Precisely to the extent that nonacademic diversity is made a goal in itself, its measure becomes, instead, counterevidence to the claim of having attained justified appointment criteria. That goal is not necessary for achieving the more legitimate aim of academic diversity within a faculty, and I have found no other compelling reasons for pursuing it in the present context. Nevertheless, when justified academic criteria are made the basis for appointment decisions, and when legitimate forms of compensation supplement those criteria, then faculties should become more diverse in nonacademic respects. This development should eliminate calls for diversity as a means or end in itself.

NOTES

1. Powell's opinion is reprinted in Kent Greenwalt, *Discrimination and Reverse Discrimination* (New York: Knopf, 1983).

2. John Stuart Mill, *On Liberty* (Chicago: Henry Regnery, 1955), chap. 2.

3. William Buckley, *God and Man at Yale* (Chicago: Henry Regnery, 1951).

4. Ibid., pp. 182–85.

5. Greenwalt, *Discrimination and Reverse Discrimination*, p. 189.

6. Steven M. Cahn, personal correspondence.

7. See Alan Goldman, *Justice and Reverse Discrimination* (Princeton: Princeton University Press, 1979), chap. 3.

8. Thomas Nagel, "Equal Treatment and Compensatory Discrimination," *Philosophy and Public Affairs* 2 (1973), 348–63.

13

ACADEMIC APPOINTMENTS: Why Ignore the Advantage of Being Right?

David Lewis

I

Universities exist for the sake of the advancement of knowledge: its transmission by teaching, its expansion by research. Most of those who make academic decisions on behalf of universities will take the advancement of knowledge as their predominant, ultimate aim.

Of course, some people in universities have different aims in mind. They may think the advancement of knowledge is meaningless, or square, or worthless, or unattainable, or just outweighed by some more urgent aim—the cultivation of entertaining new ideas regardless of truth, perhaps, or the civilizing of the future rulers, or the recruiting of a mighty army to smash the state. But let us imagine an especially lucky university, where nearly everyone pursues the ultimate aim of advancing knowledge and where the few dissenters pursue aims so diverse as to cancel one another out.

As a philosopher, I shall tell a story about the philosophy department of this lucky university. But the story applies more broadly. Not perhaps to the department of frenchified literary theory, where skepticism runs rampant and the pursuit of truth is reckoned passé. Not perhaps to the mathematics department, where they are in confident agreement about what's true and how to tell, and they disagree only about what's fruitful and interesting. But in most departments, as in philosophy, (1) the advancement of knowledge is the agreed aim; but (2) there are prolonged disputes over what's true. Wherever both conditions are met, whether it's a matter of the extinction of dinosaurs or of superstrings or of legal realism, my story may be told.

One big academic decision is the decision whom to appoint to the faculty. In the lucky university we are imagining, this decision will be

231

made by those who are already on the faculty in the discipline in question. When there is a vacancy in the department of philosophy, for instance, the members of that department will decide by vote who shall be offered the appointment. In making this decision, they will all be guided (or they will nearly all be predominantly guided) by the aim of advancing knowledge. They will make the offer to the candidate whose appointment would best serve that aim.

(Let me assume hard times: a buyers' market so bad that the disappointed candidates are unlikely to have an academic career elsewhere. Otherwise I might have to assume that the members of the appointing department aim not at the advancement of knowledge per se, but rather at the advancement of knowledge only insofar as it goes on at their own university.)

Note well that in discussing academic appointments, I am not discussing academic freedom. Nobody's academic freedom is violated if the job he wanted goes to someone else, provided he had no prior claim and provided the decision is made on proper grounds.

II

There are many disputed questions in philosophy—as in most disciplines—and each member of the appointing department will hold some opinions about which philosophical doctrines are true and which are false. The candidates for appointment likewise will hold, and will be known to hold, various opinions. Each member of the department can judge, by his own lights, to what extent any given candidate holds true doctrines, and to what extent he is in error.

Holding true doctrines, and not being in error, would seem *prima facie* to be an important qualification for a job of contributing to the advancement of knowledge by teaching and research. *Knowledge* means, in part, being right. It is redundant to talk of knowing the truth, it is a contradiction in terms to talk of knowing what isn't so. (Such talk cries out for scare-quotes: he "knows" it, that is he *thinks* he knows it.) What is not true cannot be known. Advancement of error cannot be advancement of knowledge.

Unless a teacher conceals his opinions altogether, or presents them in an especially unconvincing fashion (both faults in their own right), his students will to some extent come to share his opinions. But to the extent that the teacher imparts false doctrines, what the students gain cannot be knowledge. To the extent that a researcher is guided by false doctrines, he is liable to arrive at new and different false doctrines, since he will choose them partly to cohere with the doctrines he held before. To that extent, the fruits of his research cannot be new knowledge. So error makes one worse at doing the job of advancing knowledge. Being right is a big advantage.

So when the appointing department assesses the qualifications of the candidates, to choose the one who can contribute best to the advancement of knowledge, it would seem that they ought to give a great deal of weight to the doctrines the candidates hold true and hold false. They ought, *ceteris paribus*, to prefer the candidates who hold true rather than false doctrines. Of course this will be a difficult thing to do collectively, if the members of the department disagree with one another. But, as always, each should do the best he can by his own lights, voting in the way that best serves the advancement of knowledge according to his own opinions.

So, by and large and *ceteris paribus*, we would expect the materialists in the philosophy department to vote for the materialist candidate, the dualists to vote for the dualist, and so forth. Likewise elsewhere: we would expect the transformational grammarians to vote for the transformationalist, the Marxist historians to vote for the Marxist, the biologists who think that all evolution is adaptive to vote for the adaptationist. . . . I say this not out of cynicism. Rather, this seems to be how they *ought* to vote, and unabashedly, if they are sincere in their opinions and serious about doing the best they can, each by his own lights, to serve the advancement of knowledge. We can well understand how countervailing considerations might sometimes be judged to outweigh the advantage of being right, but it would be very strange if the advantage of being right were left out of the balance altogether.

Yet what do we see? I put it to you that an appointing department will typically behave as if the truth or falsehood of the candidate's doctrines are weightless, not a legitimate consideration at all. No speaker will ever argue that a candidate should rank high because he has the advantage of being right on many important questions, or low because he is sunk in all manner of error. No speaker will argue thus, not even if he thinks the great majority of his colleagues will agree with him about what is true and false on the matter in question. Most likely, there will be no mention of whether the candidate's doctrines are true or false. If there is mention, the speaker will make clear by hook or crook that what he says is a mere comment, not an argument for or against the candidate. (The signal might be a joking tone: don't say "false," say "goofy." Or it might be a reminder that one's opinion is only one's own, or it might be the placing of the comment within a speech to the opposite effect: "I hate his views myself, but still . . . .") There will be arguments galore that a candidate has academic virtues that conduce to getting things right or vices that conduce to error: "his work is undisciplined," "what he said was shallow and inane," but it will never be said that the virtues or vices have actually led to truth or error. (I wonder why traits conducive to truth and error should be relevant considerations if truth and error themselves are not?) Maybe someone will be accused of being influenced by the fact that he agrees or disagrees with the candidate's views, and all present will presuppose that this ought not to happen. It will seem for all the world, in short, as if the department were convinced that being right or wrong is an illegitimate consideration; but a consideration that tempts them and that they must guard against. It would be less shocking, I think, to hear a case made that some candidate should be preferred on grounds of race or sex, than to hear a case made that the department should appoint the candidate who holds the true philosophy.

(My evidence? Participation in the deliberations of two philosophy departments, in each case over a period long enough to permit a good deal of turnover of colleagues. But also, hundreds of letters written on behalf of candidates by referees hoping to be persuasive, and presumably guided by their expectations about which considerations a department will deem relevant and proper. To be sure, my experience does not come out of the lucky situation in which all concerned are wholeheartedly devoted to the advancement of knowledge. But it comes from something close enough that I think I may be permitted the extrapolation. Accordingly, I shall no longer bother to distinguish actual universities from the hypothetical lucky one.)

Suppose the question whether being right is an advantage came up in a different connection. Suppose we were considering the history of the advancement of knowledge about a certain subject. Then we would find it perfectly in order to explain the success of some researcher by noting that he had been on the right track, that he was right about a lot of things to begin with and therefore found it easy to get more and more things right afterward. And we would also find it easy to explain his head start, in turn, by the fact that he was the student of a teacher who also was right about a lot of things. In this connection, at least, we would have no trouble believing in the advantage of being right.

Or suppose a squad of detectives have investigated a murder, working independently, and different ones began by suspecting different suspects. If, after the fact, we know that Plum dunnit, then once we know that it was Poirot who suspected Plum from the start, we understand very well why Poirot's investigation progressed by leaps and bounds, while his rivals bogged down and got nowhere. Or if some bystander knows from the start who dunnit (as Plum does, for one) then once he finds out that it is Poirot who has the advantage of being right, he will expect Poirot to forge ahead. In fact, anyone who learns that Poirot alone is right about some aspect of the case (even if he does not know just what Poirot is right about) should expect Poirot to gain an advantage thereby in contributing to the advancement of knowledge.

If, instead of a criminal investigation, it were the history of some branch of science or of philosophy, the same should be true. (Unless it is history done from the standpoint of utter skepticism about the subject, in which case it could not claim to be history of the advancement of knowledge.) We know very well, outside the department meeting at any rate, that being right is one important factor that makes for success in advancing knowledge.

III

There are other factors, of course. We can list the costs of blindly going for the candidate who has the advantage of being right, and the possible benefits of preferring the candidate who is in error but has compensating virtues of ingenuity, rigor, originality, open-mindedness, clarity, curiosity, thoroughness, or just difference from the present members of the department. Up to a point, we can make the list *neutral:* equally acceptable to those on both sides of any of the disputed philosophical questions. First comes—

RISK OF ERROR. *We might try for the candidate who has the advantage of being right, but we might be wrong ourselves and therefore choose the candidate who has the disadvantage of being wrong.*

Yes, we run a risk. But as Mill writes, "If we were never to act on our opinions, because those opinions may be wrong, we should leave all our interests uncared for, and all our duties unperformed. . . . There is no such thing as absolute certainty, but there is assurance sufficient for the purposes of human life. We may, and must, assume our opinion to be true for the guidance of our own conduct."[1]

But is it so, perhaps, that our philosophical opinions are not real opinions? Do we pay them lip service, but always give them credence so close to fifty-fifty that they can play no role in guiding decision? If that were so, and were expected to remain so indefinitely, then it is hard to see how philosophers could be aiming at the advancement of knowledge. For what isn't even believed cannot be known.

But I do think we might be guided by our philosophical opinions, even to the point of betting our lives. Consider our opinions about teletransportation, an imaginary process that works as follows: the scanner here will take apart one's brain and body, while recording the exact state of all one's cells. It will then transmit this information by radio. Traveling at the speed of light, the message will reach the replicator. This will then build, out of new matter, a brain and body exactly like the one that was scanned.[2] Some philosophical positions on personal identity imply that one survives teletransportation (unless it malfunctions). Others imply that teletransportation is certain death. Now imagine that a philosopher is caught on the seventeenth story of a burning building. He has some hope, but no certainty, of the ordinary sort of rescue. Then he is offered escape by teletransportation, provided he accepts the invitation right away.[3] At that point, I think his philosophical opinion may very well guide his decision. If he thinks what I do, he will accept teletransportation even if he reckons his chance of ordinary rescue to be quite high. If he thinks what many of my colleagues do, he will decline the offer even if he reckons his chance of ordinary rescue to be quite low. Either way, he stakes his very life on the truth of his philosophy. And yet if this philosopher does survive, only to find himself in a department meeting the next day, he will probably decline to stake the fortunes of the advancement of knowledge on the very same opinion.

However it may be with philosophy, consider the social scientists. A professor of economics, put in charge of the university budget in desperate times, may dare to stake the university's very survival—and *a fortiori* its contribution to the advancement of knowledge—on the truth of his disputed opinions about the causes of inflation. A professor of government who has been appointed to advise on national security may dare to stake the lives or liberty of millions on the truth of his disputed opinions about foreign affairs. If these same professors are not too busy to vote in their own departments, and if they must decide which candidates have the advantage of being right and which appointments best serve the advancement of knowledge, shall they then find their opinions too uncertain to play any role in guiding decisions?

When we bear in mind the risk of error, and so are less than certain of our own opinions, we might have reason to promote—

DIVISION OF LABOR. *The researcher who is not running with the crowd may do more to advance knowledge, if he does turn out to be right, just because he is not duplicating others' efforts. Even if we think it probable that he will fail because he lacks the advantage of being right, we can expect a more important success from him in case he does succeed. It may be worth backing the long shot in hopes of winning big.*[4]

Consider again that squad of detectives, and suppose you've just taken charge of the investigation. There are several suspects, and at the present stage of the investigation, there's good reason to suspect some more than others. What to do: assign your entire squad to concentrate on the leading suspect? That means giving each detective the maximum chance to benefit from the advantage of being right. But also it probably means diminishing marginal returns: some bits of investigating are apt to get done several times over. Divide your squad equally between the suspects, then, so as to minimize redundant effort? That makes sure that most of their work will go to waste. Compromise, say with five detectives assigned to the leading suspect, two to the runner-up, and one to all the rest? No solution is right a priori. It depends: on whether you're shorthanded, on how far the leading suspect leads the rest, on how good your detectives are at cooperating. . . . There may well be considerations that weigh heavily against the advantage of being right—but not necessarily.

Likewise, *mutatis mutandis*, if you are an only-moderately-convinced materialist choosing between two finalist job candidates. One would be the department's seventh materialist: probably right, you think, but also redundant. The other, would be only its second dualist: probably wrong, you think, but possibly right and not redundant. All things considered, the dualist may well be the better bet. But not necessarily—again, it depends.

Continuing our neutral list, we come to—

CHANGE. *He who is wrong today may be right tomorrow. If he is open to argument and not too proud to change his mind, his present errors may not persist. And he who is right today may afterward go wrong.*

That may happen, sure enough. There are philosophers whose position is in a state of permanent revolution. But it's rare. We would expect to find a strong correlation between positions held now and positions held twenty years later, therefore between having or lacking the advantage of being right now and having or lacking it then.

DIFFERENT QUESTIONS. *Someone who has been wrong about the questions he has so far addressed may yet, if he has the virtues conducive to being right, have the advantage of being right about different questions that he will take up later.*

There are two cases. One is that he may take up entirely unrelated questions and arrive at true views about them. The other is that he may be right about a host of subsidiary questions in the vicinity of the big question he is wrong about. An antirealist may be right about the flaw in the argument that was meant as the grand bombshell against realism; a champion of epiphenomenal qualia may be right about why one materialist theory of mind works better than another.[5] In general, a philosopher may be importantly right about what the menu of positions looks like, he may know all the advantages and drawbacks and moves and countermoves very well, even though he makes the wrong choice from that menu. Likewise an honest physicist might, on balance, favor the wrong explanation of superconductivity; and yet he might be the very one who best points out which problems his preferred hypothesis does not solve. And whenever the evidence is misleading, as sometimes it is, whoever is right about the balance of the evidence will be wrong about the truth of the matter, and vice versa.

DEAD DOGMA. *The advocate of error will challenge those on the side of truth. He will keep them on their toes, compelling them to think of questions hitherto ignored, and causing them to improve their positions even more in order to answer his arguments.*

This may happen or it may not. It depends. Sometimes there is bedrock disagreement, and both sides go their separate ways. Sometimes our only answer to an argument—a fair answer, if unsatisfying—is that since it leads to a false conclusion, it must have some flaw we can't find.

THE SPECIMEN. *The advocate of error may play a role somewhat like the native informant in the linguistics department, or the snake in formaldehyde in the biology department. Error can be better understood, and better rejected, when it is seen close up. Know your enemy.*

Not a respectful attitude toward a prospective colleague!—Still, there's truth to it.

IV

I am not satisfied. Yes, these considerations are cogent. Yes, they carry weight. But they do not, not even all together, carry *enough* weight to do the job. They might sometimes, or even often, outweigh the advantage of being right. But it is not credible that they always and overwhelmingly outweigh the advantage of being right; and that is what they would have to do before they could explain why we treat the advantage of being right as though it were weightless. It remains a mystery why, if someone aims to support the candidate who can contribute most to advancing knowledge, he should not even weigh the holding of true doctrine as one important qualification among others, but rather should dismiss it as an irrelevant or improper consideration.

Indeed, if it's specimens of diverse errors that someone wants, or challengers to dead dogma, or insurance against the risk of his own error, then he should not dismiss being right as irrelevant. Rather he should treat it as, to some extent, a *dis*advantage! This attitude to appointments is not altogether unknown, and not quite as disreputable as trying to pack a department with right-thinking colleagues would be. We hear of "zoo departments" that try to procure one specimen of each main school of thought. (Too bad for the candidate who's so original as to defy classification! And you might think it's a scruffy specimen who'd consent to live in a zoo.) Still, I think the more usual attitude is that the truth of a candidate's position is not a proper consideration one way or the other. Is that because we think the advantage of being right and the advantage of being wrong always cancel exactly?—No; they can't always cancel, because the listed advantages of being wrong will vary greatly depending on the initial composition of the department.

V

Why ignore the advantage of being right? The considerations just listed do not go far enough. But I think there is a better explanation. We ignore the advantage of being right because we comply with a tacit treaty to do so. It is reasonable for all of us to think that this treaty, and therefore our present compliance that sustains it, serves the advancement of knowledge. However we should not all think this for the same neutral reasons.[6]

First, take a simple two-sided case: the materialists versus the dualists. (Assume, what may be none too realistic, that all concerned think the errors of their opponents matter more than the errors of their misguided allies.) In my own opinion as a materialist, the best thing for the advancement of knowledge would be the universal acceptance of the true philosophy: materialism. Or near-universal, anyway; I can see some good in preserving a small dualist minority as insurance against the risk that we're wrong, or as challengers, or as specimens. Worst would be the universal, or near-universal, acceptance of dualist error. Second best would be a mixture, as at present. A treaty requiring us all to ignore the advantage of being right when we make appointments will raise the probability of that second-best outcome and lower the probability both of the best and of the worst. If the dualists are willing, we can have the treaty if we like. We cannot have what we might like better, which is a rule that only dualists shall ignore the advantage of being right (that is, of being what dualists take to be right). If the treaty is on offer, we can take it or leave it.

It may well seem to us materialists, on balance, that taking it is what serves materialism best, and therefore serves knowledge best. For if we decline the treaty, who knows what may happen in the long run? We cannot predict the fortunes of voting. Majorities in our department, and in the profession of philosophy at large, may shift in unpredictable ways. Even if we are on top here and now, some of us may move away, or change their minds, or decide that the advantage of being right is somehow outweighed in some particular case. And besides, we cannot predict the swing votes of those colleagues who suspend judgment between materialism and dualism.

Likewise, *mutatis mutandis*, according to the dualists' opinions. They too may fear the shifting fortunes of voting. So they may think it better for dualism, hence better for knowledge, to join us in making and sustaining the treaty. What they count as the main benefit of a treaty to ignore the advantage of being right is what we count as its main cost: it tends to prevent the triumph of materialism. And what they count as the main cost is what we count as the main benefit. But however much we disagree about which is the cost and which is the benefit, we may yet agree that the benefit exceeds the cost. It is not inevitable that they and we should both think this. (They will not think it if they think the triumph of dualism is just around the corner.) But if both sides do think it, as they reasonably might, that should come as no surprise. And if both sides are found complying with a tacit treaty, that is evidence that (in some inexplicit way) both sides do consider the treaty worthwhile. I suggest that this is exactly what we do find.

In the complex real world, we have not just one disputed question but many, dividing philosophers in crisscrossing ways. Should we therefore expect a big network of crisscrossing little treaties, each one binding the parties to ignore the advantage of being right on a certain specific question? That would be too complicated to be workable. It would be too hard to keep track of which positions are under the protection of which treaty and which are unprotected. Mistakes would be made; and since the treaties are sustained by the expectation of reciprocation, mistakes would tend to unravel the whole network. It would work better to have one big, many-sided treaty to ignore the advantage of being right across the board. True, that would protect schools of thought so weak that others have no need to make a treaty with them.[7] If that is the price we must pay for a workable, stable arrangement that prolongs stalemate, and protects true doctrine from the triumph of its opponents, we may find the price well worth paying. Alas, it stops us from doing all we can to keep error out of the university. But in return it helps stop error from keeping out truth.

I stipulated that at the lucky university, advancement of knowledge was the predominant aim. But if the treaty is sustained by a sense of fair play or by respect for customary propriety, are those not quite different aims? Yes, and maybe those different aims are there, but they are extra. The treaty does not require them. It can be sustained solely by its foreseen benefits for the advancement of knowledge. For we cannot gain its benefits once and for all, and then double-cross our partners. As we know all too well, the work of appointments is never done. There will always be a next time.

If we're serious about aiming for the advancement of knowledge, and if we sincerely believe that the advantage of being right matters to the advancement of knowledge, then why ignore it? Because if we, in the service of truth, decided to stop ignoring it, we know that others, in the service of error, also would stop ignoring it. We have exchanged our forbearance for theirs. If you think that a bad bargain, think well who might come out on top if we gave it up. Are you so sure that knowledge would be the winner?

NOTES

Acknowledgment: This paper is based on a lecture given at Ormond College, Melbourne, in July 1988. I thank the audience on that occasion and also Paul Benacerraf, Steven M. Cahn, Philip Kitcher, T. M. Scanlon, and others, for valuable comments.

Editor's Note: The preferred practice of Temple University Press is to use "he or she" in contexts in which the author uses "he."

1. John Stuart Mill, *On Liberty* (Indianapolis: Bobbs-Merrill, 1959), pp. 23–24. These words are in the mouth of a hypothetical critic, but Mill does not dispute them.

2. Derek Parfit, *Reasons and Persons* (Oxford: Oxford University Press,

242 | DAVID LEWIS

1984), p. 199. I have amended his description so as not to say that the scanned body is destroyed; for just as it may be held that the person survives teletransportation, so too it may be held that the brain and body survive. The same process, except with the scanning done remotely from the receiving end, is better known as "beaming up."

3. Do not grumble about a far-fetched example. The decision problem requires only that the philosopher *thinks* he is offered escape by teletransportation. It is farfetched that teletransportation should be available. It is not farfetched that a philosopher should be bamboozled.

4. See Philip Kitcher, "The Division of Cognitive Labor," *Journal of Philosophy* 87 (1990), 5–22.

5. G. H. Merrill, "The Model-Theoretic Argument against Realism," *Philosophy of Science*, 47 (1980), 69–81; and Frank Jackson, "A Note of Physicalism and Heat," *Australasian Journal of Philosophy* 58 (1980), 26–34.

6. Here I parallel the suggestion I offered in "Mill and Milquetoast," *Australasian Journal of Philosophy* 67 (1989), 152–71, concerning a utilitarian defense of toleration. Put society in place of the university; utility in place of advancement of knowledge; toleration of dangerous opinions in place of ignoring the advantage of being right. A Millian neutral list of the benefits of toleration does carry weight. But too little weight, sometimes, for those who most fear the grave disutility of dangerous opinions. If a utilitarian inquisitor thinks that exposure to heresy conduces to eternal damnation, he will find a Millian defense of toleration lightweight to the point of frivolity. But even he might think that a treaty of toleration serves utility on balance, if he sees it as preventing not only the eradication of heresy but also the possible triumph of heresy. Rather than chance the doubtful fortunes of war, he might think it better, for the cause of salvation and hence for the cause of utility, to give away both the hope of victory and the risk of defeat.

7. Maybe the treaty is limited to "respectable" schools of thought, as opposed to ratbag notions. Is this because a school of thought gains respectability when it gains numbers enough to be a threat, so that bringing it into the treaty is worthwhile protection? I think not. If I am not mistaken, hard-line paraconsistency—the thesis that there are true contradictions—is just now gaining respectability. But not because it has the numbers; the overwhelming majority of philosophers still think it certainly and necessarily false. To gain respectability, all it takes seems to be a handful of coherent and otherwise respectable defenders. Or not quite that, even—rather, defenders who satisfy all standards of coherence save those that are part of the very question at issue (as consistency is at issue when paraconsistency is defended). Graham Priest, author of *In Contradiction* (Dordrecht: Nijhoff, 1987), probably could have made hard-line paraconsistency respectable even if he had been a minority of one.

14

A DEFENSE OF THE NEUTRAL UNIVERSITY

Robert L. Simon

In times of major social controversy, should colleges and universities function as political agents on behalf of particular causes? Although this issue is often forgotten in times of political quiescence, it rises to the surface again during times of political conflict. Protests against the Vietnam War, as well as concern in the 1980s over divestment of university investments in corporations doing business in South Africa, have generated criticism of the view that universities should be politically neutral. Can academic institutions justifiably remain silent in the face of such events as genocide, the waging of unjust wars, systematic and pervasive racial discrimination, political oppression, and world hunger? On the other hand, if a university or college becomes a partisan political agent, can it fulfill other functions, including the academic ones that are its very reason for being? Are there moral reasons, based on academic functions, for the university to refrain from partisan political action?

Questions such as these have at least two important characteristics. First, they are normative in that they concern the principles or norms that *ought* to guide the behavior of institutions of higher learning in the political arena. Their focus is not what the behavior of such institutions is but what it should be. Second, they concern the behavior of colleges and universities as *institutions*, not the behavior of the individuals, such as faculty members and students, who may attend or be employed there.

Consider the claim that colleges and universities as institutions should be politically neutral. Before examining substantive arguments for and against it, it is important to realize that much of the controversy over the neutrality thesis is conceptual rather than moral. That is, what looks like heated moral disagreement over whether universities

should be neutral will often, upon analysis, rest on divergent conceptions of the nature of neutrality itself. If different parties to an argument mean different things by neutrality, they may not be disagreeing
about the same issue in the first place. It is important not to assume
that the meaning of *neutrality* is clear or understood the same by all of
us, in considering the issue with which I will begin: whether it is even
possible for colleges and universities to be neutral.

I. SKEPTICISM AND THE CONCEPT OF NEUTRALITY

Many critics of the ideal of a politically neutral university would deny
that the central issue at stake is whether colleges and universities
should be politically neutral. On their view, since it makes sense to say
universities ought to act a certain way only if they *can* act in that way,
the fundamental issue is whether neutrality is even possible. In the
view of many, it is not. Thus, Robert Paul Wolff argues in an acute
critique of the university from the point of view of radicalism of the
1960s that

> as a prescription for institutional behavior, the doctrine of value
> neutrality suffers from the worst disability which can afflict a norm:
> what it prescribes is not wrong; it is impossible. A large university
> in America simply cannot adopt a value-neutral stance, either ex-
> ternally or internally, no matter how hard it tries.[1]

However, we need to be careful before accepting such a conclusion
too quickly. Perhaps, as John Searle has suggested, skeptics about the
very possibility of neutrality are like certain sorts of epistemological
skeptics who question whether knowledge is possible. The kind of
skeptic Searle has in mind simply defines knowledge in such a way
that it can never be attained.[2] But of course, just because knowledge
in the skeptic's sense is unattainable, it does not follow that knowledge
in some other significant sense is unattainable as well. Similarly, perhaps the skeptic can show that neutrality, conceived in some particular
way, is impossible. It does not follow, however, that neutrality conceived in some other way is necessarily impossible or worthless.

For example, one popular argument is that no university can be
value-neutral, because the principle that the university *ought* to be
value-neutral is itself a normative claim that expresses a value. A
second argument points out that a university by its very nature is
committed to values such as knowledge, truth, and rational discourse.
Such arguments do show that no university can be strictly value-

free. They bring out the salutary point that the commitment to be neutral, like other value commitments, requires a rational defense. However, they undermine the ideal of the politically neutral university only if political neutrality and total value-freedom are equivalent. But as we will see, there are some significant senses of value-neutrality that are not equivalent to total value freedom. Hence, even if the university cannot (and should not) be value free, that is irrelevant to the evaluation of at least some significant versions of the neutrality thesis.

Other skeptics point out that the university's action (or inaction) must have political consequences. Therefore, they conclude that neutrality is impossible, for on their view, even the failure to take a stand on significant issues has causal implications. Therefore, no matter what the university does, it has political consequences. At the very least, the status quo is left unchanged. As Wolff argues in *The Ideal of the University*,

> Omissions are frequently even more significant politically than commissions in American politics, for those in positions of decision usually rule by default rather than by consent. Hence, acquiescence in governmental acts, under the guise of impartiality, actually strengthens the established forces and makes successful opposition all the harder.[3]

The skeptic makes a number of strong points here. Clearly, in at least some contexts, the failure to act can be of moral significance and require moral justification. Thus, if I learn that a killer will attempt to murder you at a particular place and time, and I can warn you at little cost to myself, my failure to do so is morally culpable.

However, from my moral responsibility for acts of omission as well as acts of commission, it does not follow that I automatically fail to be neutral. All that follows is that neutrality requires a defense, not that it is a myth.

This is an important point and is perhaps best illustrated by the constitutional prohibition in the United States against an establishment of religion. This clause requires at least that the government be neutral toward particular religions and is minimally satisfied if the government does nothing to favor one religion over another. Of course, the decision to be neutral in such a way requires a moral defense. It is not necessarily value-free. Nevertheless, the government is neutral toward particular religions.

The skeptic might protest that by not actively favoring a minority religion, the government is covertly preserving the status quo and so is not really neutral after all. But all the situation amounts to is that the government is leaving things as they otherwise would be. It is keeping its nose out of religion. That is just what proponents of governmental neutrality toward religion *mean* by governmental neutrality. So the skeptic's legitimate point that the decision to be neutral requires a moral justification does not establish that neutrality is a myth but only that neutrality itself is hardly uncontroversial or value-free.

Let us consider further the logic of "you are either with us or against us." The argument, when exposed to the light of day, seems to go as follows:

1. Failure to actually support me has the consequence of making my opponents' position better off than it would have been had you supported me.
2. Hence, your failure to support me has the consequence of making my opponents better off.
3. Hence, you have actually supported my opponents.
4. Clearly, you are not neutral but rather are my opponent as well.

One point worth considering is that premise 1 is not more plausible than position 1:

1'. Failure to support my opponents has the consequence of making my position better off than it would have been had you supported them.

By substituting 1' for 1 and then making the same inferences, one can with equal plausibility conclude that you have chosen my side rather than that of my opponents. It is of course true that failure to take a stand deprives one side of an issue of support. But the point is that it does so as well for the other side! That is exactly why it is neutral, not in the sense of being consequence-free but in the sense of being nonpartisan, of not interfering on behalf of any one religion.

The fallacy involved in the assertion that "you are either with me or against me" is that it can be said by *either side* to third parties. The implications are logically devastating. Both sides could regard the third party as an opponent (since if it is not with us it is against us) or, with equal plausibility, as an ally (since it is not for our opponent, it must be with us). Surely, any formula that implies such blatant contradictions must be rejected as logically incoherent.

However, if, in spite of this point, the skeptic still wants to stipulate that the failure to actively support one side aids the other, then it follows trivially (by definition) that *any* decision, including the decision not to make a decision, has political consequences and is not neutral. Let us call an act or policy that has no effect, from either action or inaction, on a political controversy consequentially neutral. Given the skeptic's assumptions, no agent can be consequentially neutral. However, even if we ignore the logical incoherence already pointed out, the skeptic's victory is a hollow one. Even if consequential neutrality is unattainable, many other kinds of neutrality may be quite feasible. Thus, even if the government fails to be consequentially neutral with respect to religion, it can be neutral in some other sense. For example, it can provide no active support for any particular religion over any other, and it may be important that it does not. Similarly, although it is doubtful if a university can avoid performing any act that would have political consequences—a conceptual impossibility once we define failure to aid one side as aiding the other—the university can still avoid becoming a partisan on many issues. It can also avoid acting with political motive or intent.

Accordingly, it is doubtful if the skeptical arguments I have considered show that neutrality is impossible. Moreover, even if they do show that some kinds of neutrality, such as absolute value-freedom or consequential neutrality, are impossible, they leave open whether other significant forms of neutrality are possible. Skeptical arguments do remind us that the decision to be neutral is itself a morally significant one for which the agent may be held morally responsible. Whether or not we ought to be neutral is itself an ethical issue. Be that as it may, the skeptic's premises that universities cannot be value-free, that the stance of neutrality itself is value-laden, and that inaction as well as action has political consequences, do not imply that all kinds of neutrality are conceptually incoherent or logically beyond our grasp.

II. NEUTRALITY AND PROFESSORIAL ETHICS

I recently came across an article on the teaching of ethics in which a philosophy professor declared that his goal as a teacher was to "save students from their parents."[4] I would have agreed with that statement when I started my teaching career, but as my children grew I started to have doubts. Now that my eldest son has just entered college, I'm sure it is false.

Be that as it may, the author's claim raises a number of important general issues. Should a professor in an ethics course attempt to get students to question their own values? Should the professor go further and aim at having the students reject a particular set of traditional norms? May such a professor permissibly aim at having students adopt the specific values deemed most acceptable by the instructor? Is there any sense in which the individual instructor in the college classroom should be neutral with respect to ethical or political values?

Let me begin by considering two admittedly extreme responses to this question. According to the first, which we can call the model of partisanship, the professor should try, using whatever means of persuasion will prove most effective, to get students to adopt the values the instructor thinks are most important.

Clearly, this model will have few if any adherents. It has little if anything to do with education but in effect views the professor as someone whose role it is to indoctrinate students. Students are not treated as persons in their own right but as things to be manipulated by whatever persuasive techniques work best. In effect, the veneer of education is employed to cloak what is really going on, namely, indoctrination of the less powerful by the more powerful. Indeed, using one's status as a professor to impose one's values on students through nonrational means is a form of harassment, ethically on par with sexual harassment, in which a person in a position of power uses it to coerce or to manipulate others.

If there are adherents of the extreme partisan view, they may retort that the alternative is nonexistent, since there really are no rules of rational inquiry that are ideologically neutral. According to this retort, even to adopt ground rules of inquiry is a political act that has covert ideological implications. Now, in a trivial sense, this reply is correct, if only because, as we have seen, rationality is itself a value. Moreover, the decision to adopt rational procedures may have as a consequence that certain political positions receive more support than others, since they appear more reasonable to rational investigators. It does not follow, however, that the rules fail to be neutral in a significant sense; they may have intellectual warrant or standing apart from the political preferences of those who hold them.

Thus, if the model of partisanship is to be defended in public discourse and not just imposed upon us by manipulative techniques or coercion, its adherents themselves must appeal to rules of rational inquiry. If no such rules had any warrant or justification, apart from the political preferences of those who employ them, the whole institution of public rational discourse and critical inquiry would be an illusion. Not only would the university itself be a fraud, but no partisan advocate of any position could show it to be more justified than any other. The very process of justification would be nothing more than a manifestation of the very political commitment to be justified. This is a very high price to be paid for the model of partisanship. Indeed, since the model implies that its advocates can give us no good reason for accepting it, since "good reasons" themselves are a fiction, we cannot both accept the model and conduct a rational inquiry into the nature of neutrality. Accordingly, the model of partisanship, at least in its extreme form, must be rejected by all those committed to the university as a center of rational inquiry and critical discussion.

This point does not necessarily presuppose that totally value-free or uncontroversial principles of inquiry and discussion can be justified. It does imply, rather, that the instructor is committed to employing some standards of inquiry and evaluation that are regarded as at least provisionally warranted, and not simply because their use supports the ideology or partisan value commitments of the user. Such warrant may be broadly pragmatic, and far from value-free, but it must constitute an independent test of the positions the user attempts to justify within inquiry itself. Thus, even the Rawlsian method of reflective equilibrium, which requires us to test our considered judgments of particular cases against our principles so as to promote overall systematic coherence in our moral conceptual scheme, allows the possibility that some of our most cherished beliefs may be undermined by the weight of overall systematic considerations with which they might clash.[5]

Consider now the second model of professorial ethics, which I can call the model of absolute neutrality. According to this model, the professor must be absolutely value-neutral in the classroom. The instructor's job, on this view, is just to present information, not to evaluate it. Where there is controversy in a discipline, different positions are to be explained, but the professor is not to take a stand on which is most plausible. While it might be permissible for the professor to take the position of an advocate of each important viewpoint as it is presented to the student, no special preference or weight is to be given for the viewpoint the professor favors. Thereby, respect is shown for the autonomy of students, since no one attempts to impose a position upon them, and instructors refrain from using their superior knowledge or the prestige of their position to influence students by nonrational means.

While the respect for individual autonomy underlying the model of absolute neutrality is admirable, it is far from clear that the model itself is even coherent. Surely an instructor *must* make at least some value judgments, for example, judgments about what material ought to be included in the course, what controversies are worth exploring, and what arguments are significant enough to explore in depth. Moreover, the instructor's commitment to respecting the autonomy of students is itself a fundamental moral value.

Accordingly, neither the model of neutrality nor that of partisanship is fully acceptable, at least in their extreme forms. Of course, the extreme versions of each model may be modified to escape the sort of objections I have considered. For example, an advocate of neutrality might attempt to distinguish between *professional* value judgments, such as judgments about the relative importance of various issues for the discipline, which cannot be avoided by the instructor, and personal *moral or political* value judgments, which can be avoided. An advocate of partisanship might acknowledge rational constraints on discourse but maintain that instructors should defend their moral and political convictions within the universe of critical discourse demarcated by such criteria of rationality.

Rather than pursue questions raised by various modifications of the different models, the important point for my purpose is that both kinds of modifications limit the *partisanship* of the instructor. Both presuppose that the instructor is a scholar first and a partisan second. More precisely, partisanship is governed by rules of scholarship and critical inquiry. Thus, on the revised model of neutrality, it is acknowledged that value judgments must be made, but they are to be based on the professional judgment of the scholar and presumably can be defended by appeal to commonly accepted professional standards. Similarly, advocates of a modified model of partisanship concede that advocacy must be limited by such canons of critical inquiry as respect for the evidence, rules of logical argumentation, openness to objection, and the like. Students are to be persuaded by rational discourse or not persuaded at all. Manipulation by persuasive but nonrational techniques is prohibited.

There is a sense, then, in which proponents of both models should concede that the professor is to be *neutral*. Proponents of both models should acknowledge that classroom discussion must take place within a framework of rules of critical inquiry. Adherence to those rules is neutral in the sense that adherence by itself does not dictate the substantive position that emerges. On the contrary, substantive positions that prove unsatisfactory within such a framework must either be revised or replaced when a more satisfactory competitor is available.

Let us call this kind of neutrality *critical neutrality* because it requires adherence to rules of critical inquiry that do not by themselves determine which substantive positions will prove most satisfactory within the realm of inquiry they govern. Such rules need not themselves be value-free or neutral in any other sense. They are neutral only in the sense that they constitute a court of appeal independent of the personal preferences of the investigators.

Adherence to critical neutrality does not require neutrality in any of the senses that the skeptic has found incoherent. In particular, it does not require value-freedom. Neither does it require consequential neutrality. On the contrary, adherence to canons of critical neutrality may have profound effects on students and on other professionals working in the discipline. Neither does it require that the teacher avoid advocacy of substantive positions. As long as advocacy is carried out within the critical framework, it may well be educationally desirable, so long as students are sufficiently mature and possess sufficient critical tools to be able to form reasonably independent judgments of their own.

Before turning to this last constraint, consider whether critical neutrality really is possible. If possible, is it desirable? Whether critical neutrality is possible depends upon whether rules of critical inquiry exist for various disciplines independently of internal substantive positions as specified. This is not the place to argue that such rules do exist. However, it certainly is possible that they do. More important, their existence seems to be a presupposition of critical inquiry itself. Indeed, it is hard to see how the skeptic could *rationally* maintain that there are no such rules without implicitly appealing to them in the course of the argument. Thus, at the very least, the burden of proof is on the skeptic why skepticism abut critical neutrality is not itself incoherent, since it undermines the very framework within which justification takes place.

Assuming, then, that critical neutrality is possible, I can ask if it is also desirable. In fact, two sorts of arguments can be given for showing not only that critical neutrality is desirable but that adherence to the framework of critical neutrality is morally required for instructors in higher education.

The first is based on rights or entitlements generated by the autonomy of students and colleagues. As autonomous agents, such individ-

uals are wronged if they are manipulated by the intentional presentation of misinformation or by persuasive use of nonrational emotive
techniques designed to distort inquiry so as promote acceptance of
the instructor's own views. In such a case, the offending instructor is
subject to the same criticism as one who misuses professorial authority
or prestige to secure sexual favors from students. In each case, power
is being wrongly used to manipulate others to one's own advantage,
thereby limiting the other's possibilities for autonomous choice.

Second, violation of critical neutrality is a violation of the canons
of inquiry that govern the central educational function of the college
or university. Respect for critical inquiry can be seen as intrinsically
valuable, for an atmosphere where different points of view can be
freely debated and examined best promotes free and informed choice
by us all. Even if there are extreme cases in which it seems defensible
to violate critical neutrality, general conformity surely is desirable.
Moreover, given the moral weight of the reasons supporting conformity, only countervailing moral considerations of the weightiest kind
could justify overriding the ethics of critical inquiry in specific cases.

We can conclude, then, that individual instructors should be committed neither to the extreme model of neutrality nor to the extreme
model of partisanship. Rather, regardless of their other values or
positions, they should be committed to a general policy of adherence
to the ethics of critical inquiry. Because of the especially significant
values underlying such an ethic, it can be outweighed only when even
more significant considerations count in favor of making an exception.

III. NEUTRALITY AND THE UNIVERSITY

Although the university cannot be value-neutral in the sense of being
totally value-free, my discussion so far suggests that there may be
other senses of neutrality worth considering. In particular, it can be
argued that just as the individual instructor is obligated to respect the
rules and canons of rational inquiry in the classroom, so the university
is morally required to maintain an institutional climate in which such
rules govern discourse and inquiry. If so, it can be argued that the
university as an institution must be neutral in a sense similar to the
way an umpire in baseball must be neutral. Just as the umpire has an
ethical obligation to be a neutral arbiter rather than a partisan of one
team or another, the university also may have an ethical obligation
not to become just another partisan with an interest in defeating
opponents.

Perhaps, then, the kind of neutrality appropriate for colleges and universities may be *institutional critical neutrality*, namely, adherence to the values, rules, and principles of critical inquiry and discussion regardless of which substantive positions are thereby advanced.

Clearly, institutional critical neutrality is not an uncontroversial notion. To begin with, critics may argue that to support rules of rational discourse is itself to take a substantive position in opposition to opponents of rationality or adherents of faith over reason. But since proponents of institutional critical neutrality need not claim that the university can or should be value-neutral, the objection in this form need not bother them. Their point is not that neutrality requires total suspension of values. On the contrary, as we have seen, institutional critical neutrality is itself a value posture that requires an ethical defense. What such neutrality requires is not total value-freedom but rather adherence to and protection of those values and norms that are constituents of critical inquiry and promotion of conditions under which critical inquiry can flourish.

A more troublesome form of the objection is the denial that there is any neutral set of rules or norms constitutive of critical inquiry. Rather, critical inquiry itself is arguably an essentially contested concept, conceived of in different ways by proponents of different ideological positions.[6] Thus, the kind of norms of critical inquiry supported by a Marxist or a pragmatist may differ from those favored by an ethical emotivist, who relies on the epistemology of classical empiricism. Indeed, it is at least arguable that the values we hold influence the kind of norms of critical inquiry we think most warranted. Thus, a pragmatist might maintain that evaluation of scientific theories, and hence of what count as facts, properly takes into account value-laden judgments concerning the overall satisfactoriness of the theory and its rivals.[7] If so, there may be no favored conception of "the canons" of critical inquiry that is value-free.

While these points surely have force, it is far from clear that institutional critical neutrality requires the university to take a stand on such controversial epistemological questions. Rather, the commitment is to an institution within which such controversies can be pursued, where positions are defended by argument rather than force and debate is open to those qualified to participate in it. This commitment does not require the university to decide between, say, Quine and Popper, but only to ensure that the parties to the debate have a fair opportunity to present their arguments.

But aren't proponents of different ideological views all too likely to disagree over what counts as a fair opportunity to participate in debate? When debate is open or closed and what counts as defending a position by reason can be equally controversial. Neutral accounts of such notions, we may be told, are not to be found.

Important disputes can arise over the nature of free inquiry, but they arguably concern borderline cases. Arguably, there is a common core of principles that all constituents of a university community must accept, including the commitment to consider evidence, even evidence against one's own position, on its merits and the rejection of coercion as a means of silencing opposition. Without allegiance to these core elements of rational inquiry, no rational debate seems possible to begin with.

However, even if we ignore the case for core elements of rational inquiry, it doesn't necessarily follow that institutional critical neutrality is undermined. Even if the nature of critical inquiry is itself inherently controversial, it doesn't follow that the values at stake in debate among various conceptions of critical inquiry are political values, let alone the same political values at stake in currently controversial issues. Thus, canons of critical inquiry are still neutral in the sense that the position one takes in epistemological debate need not determine or be determined by one's partisan political stance. For example, parties who disagree on divestment can still agree that different sides should be heard in debate on each side of the issue. Similarly, commitment to divestment does not necessarily imply commitment to acceptance of the legitimacy of specific forms of protest against universities that do not divest. Thus, even if there are no inherently uncontroversial principles of critical inquiry, it still may be the case that for every dispute, there are some higher-order principles of inquiry accepted by all sides.[8]

But doesn't the university itself restrict debate in favor of already established positions.? Aren't proponents of many "eccentric" epistemological positions excluded from the university community? Thus, there are no departments of astrology on campus, nor is creationism often defended, let alone given equal footing with evolutionary biology.

Clearly, not all epistemological positions or world views are represented in the university. But it does not follow that institutional critical neutrality is a fraud. To see why, consider again the constitutional requirement that prohibits the establishment of religion in America. As interpreted by the courts, the establishment clause does not require government hostility toward religion. Rather, it requires the separation of religion from public life and prohibits the active government support of one religion over others.

Now it would be absurd to argue that neutrality has been violated simply because some religions have no adherents. If commitment to particular religions is based on the decisions of the citizens themselves, rather than government intervention, neutrality is preserved. The point of neutrality is not to ensure that every religion has some supporters but rather to ensure that government policy does not officially sanction some religions and suppress others.

A related point can be made about institutional critical neutrality in the university. Just as individual citizens themselves have the right to make their own religious commitments, so scholars have the right (and obligation) to determine what views to explore and defend within their areas of professional competency. If such scholars, as a result of their inquiries, determine that some views are not worth examining, or are different in kind from those that can be examined within critical inquiry, then that decision does not violate the institution's neutrality. Rather, a major purpose served by institutional critical neutrality is to promote an atmosphere in which various hypotheses can be evaluated, whether they are metahypotheses about the rules for critical inquiry or first-order hypotheses within particular disciplines.

It is important to keep in mind here the distinction between limitations on debate *within* a field and limitations on metadebate *about* the limitations within a particular field.[9] Thus, no respectable scientific department would offer courses in astrology, but debate on whether there is a justifiable difference between science and astrology might take place in a course on philosophy of science. Thus, I would suggest that limits on debate within the university, and on views that may be represented, are justified when (1) the limitations are supportable by appeal to the publicly accessible results of critical inquiry; (2) the limitations are proportional in force to the degree of support in their favor; and (3) the limitations are debatable in meta-inquiry about the discipline in question. These conditions allow inquirers to concentrate on areas of examination they consider significant, while containing checks against dogmatism and intolerance.

My discussion suggests that institutional critical neutrality is ultimately grounded on the values of personal autonomy and critical investigation. Such a justification of neutrality can now be examined more closely.

IV. IS THE NEUTRAL UNIVERSITY DESIRABLE?

Perhaps enough has been said to show that common skeptical arguments against the very possibility of a neutral university face serious problems. At the very least, the burden of proof is on the skeptic either to show how the objections can be avoided or to construct new skeptical arguments.

However, to say that neutrality is possible is one thing; to show that it also is morally defensible is another. Perhaps a beginning has been made in that direction by suggesting a connection between institutional critical neutrality and respect for the autonomy of individual members of the university community. The key idea here is that if the university becomes a political agent, individual members of the university community will be in a less favorable position to make decisions on the basis of the very kind of critical inquiry it is the university's first obligation to protect.

Although no knock-down proof of this thesis can be supplied here, perhaps the following considerations are sufficient to create a presumptive case in favor of the importance of institutional critical neutrality. As we will see, the argument for it is multifaceted. A variety of factors each lends some weight to the justification of neutrality. The argument gains force as the weight of the different factors is aggregated.

To begin with, when the university takes a partisan political stand in an area outside the sphere of values bound up with critical inquiry, it at least implicitly lends its authority, prestige, and power to a particular side. The university then becomes vulnerable to conflicts of interest between its duty to maintain the framework of political inquiry and its new political obligations. For example, if the university *qua* takes the position that aid to the Nicaraguan Contras is immoral and should not be supported, what policy implications follow for issuing invitations to speakers who support the Contras, appointing professors who are sympathetic to the Contras, donating funds to groups opposing the Contras, reacting to pro-Contra demonstrations, and the like? While it may be possible for the university to simply take a stand, yet take no other action, it is likely that if the stand is genuine, the very act of taking it may have negative implications for critical inquiry. Indeed, the same argument supporting the taking of a stand is also likely to support more direct and forceful action in favor of political goals as well.

Even if the university is still willing to appoint instructors who dissent from its political stands, to invite speakers representing a diversity of views, and so on, is it as likely that such people will be attracted to an institution where their views have been officially rejected, perhaps even designated as immoral, or at least placed in an initially subordinate position? Even if some are attracted or remain, they have been labeled as dissenters from an official position and must argue under an imposed handicap that arises not from consideration or evaluation of evidence but from a political act by the institution that employs them. Loss of neutrality may result in the emergence of the partisan university, which stands for a set of political and ideological principles and is far too intellectually homogeneous as a result. The diversity so essential for critical inquiry would be absent or, at best, be at serious risk.

Moreover, once the university is identified in the broader society as a (perhaps powerful) political agent, it can expect to be on the receiving as well as the giving end of political battles. The privileges and immunities extended to it because of its nonpartisan character surely are likely to come under fire. Why should opponents of the university's political stance allow it tax exemptions because of its educational status when more and more of its resources and energies are devoted to support of political positions contrary to their own? Why not treat it like any other political opponent instead? Why not try to weaken it? And as still more of the university's resources are devoted to fighting off such attacks, greater conflict with the needs of and support for critical inquiry can be expected.

Most important, in the partisan university would each individual be as free as we would wish to pursue inquiry where it led, to dissent from prevailing views, to follow independent paths? If not, individuals themselves would have less of an opportunity to develop autonomously, and critical inquiry itself would be harmed. All of us would be impoverished in the same way we are impoverished whenever any view becomes orthodox not because of its merits as established in open inquiry but because it has been artificially protected from the challenges such inquiry generates.

But hasn't it already been conceded that at the individual level, the classroom instructor under certain conditions may argue for substantive positions without undermining the autonomy of students? Why doesn't a similar conclusion follow about the taking of substantive political stands by the university itself?

This objection would be decisive if the roles of the individual teacher and the college or university were logically parallel. However, consider whether the two are relevantly different. Classroom instructors are individuals whose primary professional obligation is to engage in inquiry and disseminate the results. The scholar's findings, in other words, should reflect judicious evaluation of evidence, and evaluation that can be criticized in appropriate professional and public forums. The university, however, were it to take overt political stands, is likely to do so not as a result of evaluation of evidence but because of compromise or consensus among its various factions. It follows, then, that the university's taking of a political stance is not a contribution to inquiry in the same way as is the taking of a substantive position by a trained scholar.

More important, the individual does not play the same institutional role as the university with respect to critical inquiry. The latter, but not the former, is the institutional protector of the values essential to critical inquiry. For the very institution designed to umpire the critical process also to become a player within the process raises the problems I have already discussed. Accordingly, it is at best far from clear whether my earlier analysis of the right and obligations of the individual instructor can be applied without modification to the institution as well. To assume the two are parallel is as dangerous as assuming that because individuals may adopt particular religious perspectives, the state may permissibly do so as well.

To summarize, for the university to become a partisan political agent would create inherent conflicts of interest between different kinds of goals. Thus, the prestige and power of the university would be placed on one side of various political debates; yet the university would also have the obligation to encourage independent thinking on these issues and not to load the dice in favor of particular positions in advance of inquiry. Not only would decisions favoring particular sides to political conflicts appear biased, they might actually be biased. The very institution charged with the responsibility of protecting the values of open, rational inquiry becomes committed to a second set of values, which, on occasion, may call for subverting open, rational inquiry or at least diverting substantial attention (and sometimes resources) from it. It would be as if the state were held to be the partisan of particular religious perspective and, at one and the same time, charged with protecting religious freedom and tolerance. Because the potential for conflict of interest is so great and the danger to religious liberty so serious, we require state neutrality toward religion. Is the case for university neutrality any different?

I do not mean to say that universities generally *are* neutral or that they generally *do* uphold the canons of critical inquiry. Rather, violations of neutrality may occur, but their existence does not refute the neutrality thesis. Violations of institutional critical neutrality are grounds for criticism in the same of neutrality, not reasons for rejecting neutrality itself.

My discussion suggests, then, that an important case can be made for institutional critical neutrality. That is, just as state neutrality toward religion is a significant protection for the freedom of individuals to make their own religious choices, so institutional critical neutrality provides similar protection for individuals to make their own choices within critical inquiry. The case parallels that for state neutrality toward religion. If neutrality in one area is justifiable, so too is a similar kind of neutrality in the other.

However, adherence to institutional critical neutrality may have its limits. Critics of neutrality may point to hard cases in which it is far from clear not only that colleges and universities are or have been neutral but also that they *should* be neutral to begin with.

V. HARD CASES FOR THE NEUTRALITY THESIS

One set of hard cases concerns university regulation of student behavior. The claim here is that the university enforces a set of socially approved values, or values deemed desirable by the university itself, which imply the taking of substantive moral positions. Although the passing of *in loco parentis* may have reduced the degree to which institutions of higher learning regulate student social life, some core values often are enforced or supported. While these vary from institution to institution, even the most liberal colleges and universities frequently regulate consumption of alcohol and drugs, assign roommates only of the same gender, and in light of the AIDS epidemic, adopt value-laden policies (either by making condoms available or by urging sexual abstinence) on what might otherwise be appropriate sexual behavior.

Consider first whether policies regulating the use of drugs necessarily violate neutrality. Normally, university regulations in such areas follow legal requirements but they may also sometimes reflect nonneutral values about the nature of the good life. However, at least some form of regulation may also be justifiable without such appeal. In particular, since the university's commitment is to rational inquiry, it can promulgate rules designed to protect rational discourse without violation of the requirement of critical neutrality. Drug abuse can undermine critical inquiry either by harming the health of users, generating addiction (which undermines autonomy), or creating a climate hostile to intellectual endeavor. Accordingly, drug and alcohol regulations need not be inconsistent with neutrality but, at least in some forms, can be justified by appeal to the very values central to the university's intellectual mission.

While this kind of argument does have force, it raises serious questions if pushed too far. Can appeal to the need for an intellectually healthy institutional climate be used to silence disturbing views? For example, can offensive speech be regulated on the grounds that it promotes such disharmony within the community that inquiry itself is threatened? What if the expression of some views is so offensive to minority groups that they feel harassed and even threatened? Should the expression of the offending view points be forbidden on the grounds of preserving the kind of diverse community in which intellectual inquiry is best carried on? Or should free expression carry the day, since, without it, opinions that any sufficiently powerful or vocal group finds offensive will be excluded a priori from rational debate and discussion.

The problem arises because institutional critical neutrality encompasses a cluster of related values that are normally mutually reinforcing but can conflict in unusual circumstances. Thus, critical inquiry requires free and open debate but also requires a diverse community so that issues can be examined from a variety of perspectives. The problem is that in pursuing one of these values, we may sometimes be faced with hard choices about limiting pursuit of the others. Free and open debate, for example, may permit the expression of opinion that some groups find intimidating and may lead to their withdrawal from the university community.[10]

While I doubt if there are any easy formulas for reconciling such conflicts, two general points at least deserve consideration. The first is that the possible conflict of values at issue does not undermine the case for university neutrality, because the conflict is not between neutrality and some other value, such as partisanship, but rather over how neutrality itself is to be understood. In the kind of example I have cited, both open debate and a diverse community are essential for significant critical discussion; the issue is a conflict between two aspects of institutional critical neutrality itself.

Second, while there may be cases in which free speech should be limited in the name of preserving community, it is plausible to think that the burden of proof should be on those who would set limits in particular cases. Surely, when one enters the university, one is in effect consenting to engage in that activity for which the university exists: critical investigation of difficult and significant questions. It is unlikely that many people can seriously engage in such an activity without sometimes encountering views that offend them or that they find threatening. In a sense, the risk of being offended is one we expect members of the university community to bear, just as the risk of being hit by an errant shot is one golfers assume when they enter the golf course. Both are part of the normal context of the activity in question. Therefore, a special case must be made if inquiry is to be silenced on the grounds of potential disruption of the intellectual community. The speech in question must not be merely offensive to some group or individuals. It must amount to a threat or a form of harassment that undermines the rights of the victims to engage in inquiry as full members of the university community.

Keeping these points in mind, consider university regulations that bear on sexual morality. They also raise difficulties for the neutrality thesis, but perhaps they can be handled in ways already suggested. For example, a university might react to the threat of AIDS in different ways. Suppose it were argued that any response will reflect a particular view of sexual morality and so will fail to be neutral. Thus, if the university urges sexual abstinence as the first line of defense, it seems to be reflecting one moral perspective, whereas if it distributes condoms, it seems to be reflecting quite another. Either way, the critic will argue, the university has taken a partisan stand on a controversial moral and political issue.

Remember, however, that neutrality as defended here is not value-free. It is not the refusal to endorse any set of values whatsoever. Rather, institutional critical neutrality encompasses a particular set of values, namely, those necessary for the university to carry out its mission as a center of critical inquiry and discussion. With this proviso in mind, a neutral policy does seem possible. That is, the university should inform students of alternatives, indicating that sexual abstinence clearly will enable one to avoid AIDS but adding that if individuals choose not be sexually abstinent, the use of condoms makes sex considerably safer than would otherwise be the case. Making condoms actually available can be justified along lines similar to those justifying policies on drugs and alcohol: lowering risk to other members of the university community and promoting a climate in which intellectual inquiry can flourish.

By adopting such a policy, the university shows respect for the rationality and autonomy of its students, faculty, and staff. There is no one official position that the institution endorses. Rather, it makes information available and supports individuals in the choices they themselves make.

But isn't this stance itself value-laden, inconsistent with other ethical positions? In particular, doesn't it rest on a particular conception of the good that is widely accepted within what might broadly be called the Western liberal-individualist tradition but that would be rejected from many alternative political and social perspectives? In particular, hasn't the university embraced as a normative ideal the conception of the individual as rational and autonomous? The good life is identified as the life of the rational autonomous individual. While this may be a defensible conception of the good, the critic will argue that it is hardly a neutral one.[11]

This point has considerable force. Indeed, I believe it should be accepted, once its implications are properly understood. That is, although this point has force when directed against a certain conception of neutrality—neutrality as value-freedom—it does not have force against the conception defended in this essay. If the kind of neutrality proper to the university is not value-freedom or even neutrality with respect to the good, then the objection loses force.

My suggestion has been that the kind of neutrality proper to the university is institutional critical neutrality. That is, it is the kind of neutrality presupposed by regard for critical inquiry and rational discussion. Critical inquiry and rational discussion are defensible, in turn, because of their role in the search for truth and in the development of free, autonomous individuals. Moreover, these ultimate values of the university are not merely arbitrary, just one set of culturally bound variables among others. Rather, they are presupposed by *any* attempt to arrive at *justified* or *defensible* answers to problems. For example, anyone who seriously discusses whether the university should be politically neutral attempts to come to an autonomous decision based on truths, or at least justified beliefs. Therefore, the university's mission is presupposed by the very attempt to ask what its mission should be.

Neutrality of the limited kind defended in this essay is far from value-free. In fact, it is founded on values so fundamental that they can reasonably be regarded as presuppositions of any further inquiry, including inquiry into the nature of value itself. Hence, they cannot be lightly disregarded by any civilization worthy of the name.

Accordingly, although all counterexamples cannot be discussed here, we have seen that there are strategies available for dealing with some especially difficult cases. Some of the alleged counterexamples will be seen upon analysis not to involve a conflict between neutrality and an overriding value, but to be between two aspects of neutrality itself. Others assume that neutrality requires value-freedom, ignoring the point that the university may legitimately enforce values central to its function as a guardian of critical inquiry. Still other conflicts may be resolved without violation of neutrality by presenting autonomous individuals with the options available to them and letting them make their own decisions. Finally, as we have seen in an earlier section, some value judgments may be enforced, subject to expressed limitations, if sufficient support is found within critical inquiry itself (for example, astrology may be excluded from the curriculum). Such strategies may not be adequate to deal with all counterexamples, as we will see in the next section. However, they may at least suggest that genuine counterexamples may be far harder to come by than at first might be thought and that sufficient reason exists for the burden of proof in particular cases to be on opponents of neutrality, not supporters.

The university, however is not only a refuge from society in which critical reflection takes place; it is also an actor or agent in that society as well. In our own time, considerable controversy has arisen over the university's attempts to raise the funds needed for its operation. In particular, does neutrality allow the university to use any efficient means necessary to carry out its mission, regardless of the morality of the means involved? For example, should universities invest in companies doing business in oppressive societies? In particular, does a commitment to university neutrality imply that colleges and universities need not even consider the morality of investing in companies that do business in South Africa, thus, according to critics, indirectly supporting the systematic, pervasive, and oppressive racist system that is dominant there?

VI. DIVESTMENT: A COUNTEREXAMPLE TO NEUTRALITY?

Is a neutral policy with respect to university investments even possible? Isn't investing in a business supporting it? Indeed, don't universities fail to be neutral in investing in businesses and corporations, for by so doing, are they not part and parcel of the Western capitalist system?

Some of these questions raise issues discussed earlier. Clearly, there is a sense in which investment precludes a certain kind of neutrality. Investments have consequences, and these consequences might be politically significant. However, they do not preclude neutrality in all significant senses. Thus, my decision to order a certain textbook for my course might have the consequence of supporting a particular publisher and harming a rival publisher of a competing text, but that need not have been my intent. My intent was only to order the best available text, not to favor one publisher over another. Similarly, a university's intent in investing may not be to favor one regime over another, one corporation over another, or one economic system over another. It may simply be to help carry out the mission of the university as effectively as possible.[12]

But isn't this neutrality of intent merely trivial? After all, if our action has terrible consequences, isn't it simple bad faith to say that we intended to be neutral? In any case, isn't it at least possible that the obligation to refrain from doing evil sometimes overrides the obligation to be neutral?

I think the answer is sometimes yes. However, before turning to such exceptional cases, something needs to be said for a general policy of neutrality of intent in making investments. In particular, consider whether universities would be more justified in following a neutral investment policy, aimed at maximizing financial return, over one in which all major investment decisions were made so as to maximize some moral value—for example, good consequences, social justice, or equality.

There are at least four arguments against the second alternative that are worth considering. First, it is often unclear just what investment will promote the moral value in question. Since university officials (as well as faculty) have no special moral insight into what is the truly moral investment and since the university's own educational function is especially worth supporting, priority should be given to maximizing profit—profit that benefits education.

Second, unless the university makes clear in advance just what its moral values are, it will be using contributions of donors, fees obtained from students, and taxpayers' dollars for reasons that were not knowable at the time the funds were provided. Indeed, donors might be morally opposed to some of the uses (either positive investments in a particular enterprise or diversion of funds away from an enterprise) to which money was put. In a sense, the donors would be used as mere means for implementing the moral sensibilities of others. Such a policy would not only tend to have the effect of drastically lowering support for education, it would wrong individuals whose contributions were obtained under false pretenses.

Third, how is the university to decide which investments are the truly moral ones? Who speaks for the university? Surely, it is not just the majority of the faculty who should make such a decision. At best, it is simply unclear in most cases who has the authority to make moral decisions of the kind in question for the institution.

Finally, and most important, the consequent politicization of the university is all too likely to threaten institutional critical neutrality in the ways outlined earlier. If all or even most investment decisions were made in part on moral grounds, the university would have to take official positions on a large number of significant moral and political issues. Taking such positions not only might undermine support for higher education within the larger society; it would create the kinds of conflicts between educational and political values discussed in section II.

However, even if there are good reasons for a *general* policy of neutrality of intent in investment policy, there still may be specific exceptions. In some cases, an injustice may be so gross, so uncontroversial in character that all reasonable people recognize it for what it is. Moreover, it may be that for the university to invest in a way that helps perpetuate the injustice or to illegitimately profit from it, is to commit a great wrong.[13] Whereas its purposes may be noble, the university has no more right than any other agent or institution to actually commit gross injustice or to violate the rights of others. For example, if a university in a large urban setting owns property it rents to tenants, it surely has the same obligation as any other landlord to treat its tenants justly and not to exploit them. That is, although the university arguably may not have an obligation to do good, or even to avoid doing *any* evil, however small, it surely has an obligation not to commit gross injustice; especially not to engage or participate in what a colleague has called a moral catastrophe.[14] Moreover, even if investment decisions made for the purpose of avoiding the commission of serious injustice do involve some unfairness to donors, the donors themselves have no right to contribute to promotion of injustice. In such special cases, moral concerns may override neutrality of intent.

Thus, proponents of divestment seem to me to have a sound case when they argue that the university should not be neutral where a moral catastrophe, such as the present oppression of people of color in South Africa, is concerned. On the other hand, it is far from clear to me that opponents of divestment actually appeal, or need to appeal, to neutrality either. As a matter of fact, most colleges and universities that have not fully divested endorse the Sullivan Principles, which sanction investment in companies doing business in South Africa only if those companies meet specific standards of nondiscriminatory treatment of workers. By accepting the Sullivan Principles, which set moral limits on investment policy, institutions have already ceased to be neutral.

The real debate between proponents and opponents of divestment, it seems to me, is not and should not be over neutrality. Rather, it is whether divestment is required to prevent the university from participating in or illegitimately making a profit from gross, systematic, and blatant injustice and oppression. I suggest that both proponents and opponents of divestment should accept this ground rule. Both should acknowledge that divestment is required if otherwise the university would cause, be an agent of, or profit in a morally illegitimate way from moral catastrophe. This principle is neutral with respect to both positions: an opponent of divestment can accept the principle but oppose divestment by rejecting its application to the actual situation of the university.

In fact, the most sensitive and thoughtful opponents of divestment always have argued that the university would be committing an injustice *by divesting*.[15] According to such a view, divesting would lead to withdrawal of American companies from South Africa, which would in turn place greater control of the South African economy in the hands of white South Africans, the very group most resistant to reform and most likely to mistreat black and colored workers. My point is not that such a highly controversial view is correct, for it clearly is debatable on a variety of grounds, but rather to suggest that the real argument in this area is not over neutrality but over what is the truly moral policy. Opponents of divestment do themselves a disservice when they hide behind the banner of neutrality, which I suggest cannot be stretched so far as to cover the actual committing of or participation in gross and blatant injustice and oppression. On the other hand, proponents of divestment may distort the true issue when they speak as if all their critics care about is profits, as if there were no moral concerns that might lead people to disagree in this area.[16] Moreover, they do a great disservice to the university itself when they jump from the premise that neutrality does not shield the university from moral examination of the divestment issue, to the conclusion that neutrality itself is but a sham and illusion.

VII. CONCLUSIONS

What I have tried to show in this essay is that a case can be made for the claim that universities ought to be politically neutral. In order to make this case, however, different conceptions of neutrality need to be distinguished. Not all kinds of neutrality are either possible or defensible. Perhaps enough has been said, however, to show that the skeptical claim that neutrality is impossible rests either on dubious conceptual maneuvers or where successful, rules out only certain conceptions of neutrality but not others.

I have tried to show that one conception, institutional critical neutrality, is both possible and defensible. I have also argued that it supports a general policy of neutrality of intent in investments. Such a policy, as we have seen, need not be absolute or without exception. However, given the arguments in its favor, the burden of proof properly rests on those who want the exception made. Thus, the argument of this essay supports a general policy of neutrality but suggests principles that allow for rare exceptions, of which the case for divestment may well be most prominent.

Much of the case for university neutrality, as we have seen, is *indirect*. The neutral university is as defensible as state neutrality toward religion. Accordingly, if I have pointed to genuine parallels between the two kinds of neutrality, those committed to state neutrality toward religion may find there is more to be said for university neutrality—at least when construed in the limited way suggested here—than they might otherwise have thought.

None of this explication denies that the university fulfills useful social functions and that many of these functions serve the interests of powerful groups in society (although it is also true that much—perhaps most—criticism of existing institutions comes from the university as well).[17] Thus, the consequences of university behavior often have political implications, as does state neutrality towards religion. However, the kind of neutrality defended here is not consequentialist neutrality but institutional critical neutrality, which is morally defensible because of its connection with free inquiry and respect for the autonomy of persons. Moreover, it does not follow because the skills universities impart are socially useful that universities are *conservative*, since those skills may be just as applicable to social criticism (and may even engender it) as to preservation of existing injustice.

In any case, the argument for neutrality should not be confused with a plea for a value-free university. Instead, like state neutrality with respect to religion, for which a parallel case can be made, the kind of neutrality defended here is deeply value-laden. It requires respect for individual autonomy and for the values implicit in critical inquiry. Although such neutrality may sometimes be outweighed by competing moral values, it itself rests on moral considerations of great force. Therefore, it should never be overridden lightly. The burden of proof is properly placed on those who want to violate it. Institutional neutrality, then, is not the all-purpose shield that some proponents have used to preclude even the possibility of the moral critique of institutional policy. On the other hand, neither is it the sham that critics have dismissed as conceptually incoherent. Instead, it is an especially important value that we disregard only at our own peril, and at the peril of the intellectual life itself.

NOTES

Acknowledgment: My work on this paper was supported by a Hamilton College Faculty Fellowship. I am very grateful for this support. I am also grateful for helpful suggestions for revision made by a reviewer for Temple University Press.

I addressed the topic of the neutral university sixteen years ago in a paper titled "The Concept of a Politically Neutral University,"which appeared in *Philosophy and Political Action*, ed. Virginia Held, Kai Nielson, and Charles Parsons (New York: Oxford University Press, 1972), pp. 217–33. Although I still think many of the themes of that article are defensible—and try to develop them more fully and defend them here—I hope this paper remedies what I now see as defects of the earlier one.

1. Robert Paul Wolff, *The Ideal of the University* (Boston: Beacon Press, 1969), p. 70.

2. John Searle, *The Campus War: A Sympathetic Look at the University in Agony* (New York: World, 1971), pp. 199–200.

3. Wolff, *Ideal of the University*, p.71.

4. Richard Mohr, "Teaching as Politics,"*Report from the Center for Philosophy and Public Policy* 6 (Summer 1986), 8.

5. John Rawls, *A Theory of Justice* (Cambridge: Harvard University Press, 1971), pp. 46–53. For appeal to"wide" reflective equilibrium in favor of a more radical form of egalitarianism than Rawls supports, see Kai Nielson, *Equality and Liberty* (Totowa, N.J.: Rowman and Allanheld, 1985), pp. 13–44.

6. Thus, there may be different conceptions of critical inquiry just as there can be different conceptions of justice, equality, or liberty.

7. However, even within pragmatism, "satisfactoriness" need not be construed to include political and moral value judgments. Rather, justification may depend on "systematic virtues", such as coherence and consistency, which need not be at issue in partisan political debates. See, for example, W.

V. Quine and J. S. Ullian, *The Web of Belief* (New York: Random House, 1978), pp. 64–82, for an account of scientific justification in terms of the epistemic (but not necessarily political) virtues of systems of thought.

8. If not, it is unclear whether critical inquiry is even possible as a rational activity. That is, if there are no ground rules that different sides of a debate find acceptable, the debate has no rational resolution. If all or even most issues were like that, it is far from clear that an institution devoted to the pursuit of truth and rational inquiry would even be possible. Universities might still exist, but they would perform other functions, e.g., professional training. Accordingly, the belief that there are general ground rules of critical inquiry available for adjudication of particular disputes within disciplines is a presupposition of the institution of the university, as conceived in this paper.

9. I borrow this point from my earlier paper, "The Concept of a Politically Neutral University," p. 231.

10. Alternatively, some forms of affirmative action may be justified, consistent with institutional critical neutrality, as means of promoting needed diversity within the university.

11. I owe this point to discussions with Patrick Neal and to his paper ,"A Liberal Theory of the Good?"*Canadian Journal of Philosophy* 17. 3 (1987), 567–82.

12. I stated this point in "The Concept of a Politically Neutral University," p. 226, in terms of a distinction between overt and covert neutrality.

13. The question of whether it is wrong to accept profits from injustice is more complex than many parties to the divestment debate may acknowledge. To begin with, a sensitive opponent of divestment would deny that universities that invest in certain corporations doing business in South Africa actually do profit from injustice. For such a person surely would argue that if the corporations treat their employees equally, regardless of race, they are not contributing to injustice but opposing it. Such an argument may be incorrect, but that needs to be shown and not just assumed.

More important, we need to beware of double standards in this area. Just as opponents of divestment are often too quick to hide uncritically behind the banner of neutrality, so too are proponents sometimes too quick to impose on others moral standards that they seem reluctant to apply to themselves. Thus, if it is wrong for the university to profit from injustice in South Africa, is it also equally wrong for individuals? If one's college does not divest, is one morally required to "divest" from it? If a college divests from corporations doing business in South Africa, can it accept gifts from them? If not, can students legitimately accept employment from such companies? What about scholarships, financial aid, or grants offered by such corporations?

Finally, is it wrong or morally prohibited to profit in *any* way from injustice, however small the profit or however indirectly it is obtained? If so, isn't such wrongdoing virtually unavoidable in a complex, interdependent world? If not, we need to be careful about where we draw the line. It is all too easy to do so in what may be a biased way; the university's profits from injustice are grossly immoral, but the individual benefits we ourselves do not choose to for go are simply the necessary by-products of living in a complex society.

Because such issues cannot be addressed here, I accept the principle that the university should not profit from injustice in morally illegitimate ways, leaving open which specific ways of profiting from injustice are morally illegitimate.

For a useful discussion of the double standard, from the point of view of a critic of the divestment movement, see Robert L. Payton, "Tainted Money: The Ethics and Rhetoric of Divestment," *Change* 19 (May–June 1987), 55–60.

14. I owe this way of putting the point to Rick Werner.

15. See, for example, Payton, "Tainted Money," esp. p. 58.

16. Thus, even given total moral agreement about the gross immorality of apartheid in South Africa, the morality of divestment as a *means* for ending apartheid or of divorcing the university from it is a separate issue of significant complexity.

17. For an argument that the university's social functions in our actual society make it an agent of the status quo, see Michael Parenti, *Power and the Powerless* (New York: St. Martin's Press, 1978), pp. 158–63. A proponent of institutional critical neutrality could respond in a variety of ways. For example, if the university's functions compromise institutional critical neutrality, the proponent of neutrality would reject them. Proponents of neutrality also, as we have seen, can consistently reject university commission of serious injustice. On the other hand, it is no more a violation of institutional critical neutrality if schools and colleges reward certain virtues (such as the disposition to complete assignments on time) that are also useful for corporate employees than it is a failure of state neutrality toward religion if some organized religions advocate certain socially useful virtues (such as compassion and altruism).

ABOUT THE AUTHORS

ROBERT AUDI is Professor of Philosophy at the University of Nebraska, Lincoln. He is the author of *Belief, Justification, and Knowledge* (1988) and *Practical Reasoning* (1989). He writes chiefly in the areas of epistemology, philosophy of mind, and ethics. He is a past president of the American Philosophical Association and has directed seminars for visiting philosophers under grants from the National Endowment for the Humanities.

THEODORE M. BENDITT is Professor of Philosophy and dean of the School of Arts and Humanities at the University of Alabama at Birmingham. He has taught at Duke University, the University of Southern California, and the University of Pittsburgh. He is the author of *Law as Rule and Principle* (1978) and *Rights* (1982), and of a number of articles in the areas of legal, moral, social, and political philosophy.

NORMAN E. BOWIE is Professor of Corporate Responsibility at the University of Minnesota. Previously he served as director of the Center for the Study of Values, Professor of Philosophy, and Professor of Business Administration at the University of Delaware. He is the former executive secretary of the American Philosophical Association. His books include *Ethical Issues in Government* (1981), *Business Ethics* (1982), *Making Ethical Decisions* (1985), and *Equal Opportunity* (1988). He is also the coauthor or coeditor of nine other books and a frequent contributor to scholarly journals.

STEVEN M. CAHN is Professor of Philosophy and provost and vice-president for academic affairs at the Graduate School of the City University of New York. Previously he taught at Vassar College, New York University, and the University of Vermont, where he chaired the Department of Philosophy. He is the author of *Fate, Logic, and Time* (1967), *A New Introduction to Philosophy* (1971), *The Eclipse of Excellence* (1973), *Education and the Democratic Ideal* (1979), *Saints and Scamps: Ethics in Academia* (1986), and *Philosophical Explorations: Freedom, God, and Goodness* (1989). He has edited eight other volumes, including *The*

Philosophical Foundations of Education (1970), *Classics of Western Philosophy* (1977), and *Scholars Who Teach: The Art of College Teaching* (1978).

NANCY ("ANN") DAVIS is Associate Professor of Philosophy and an associate of the Center for Values and Social Policy at the University of Colorado at Boulder. She has published papers on various topics in moral philosophy, with emphasis on the connections between moral theory and moral practice.

JUDITH WAGNER DECEW is Assistant Professor of Philosophy and Alice Higgins Faculty Fellow for 1989–1990 at Clark University. Previously she taught at Massachusetts Institute of Technology. She has held research fellowships from the American Council of Learned Societies, the American Association of University Women, Harvard Law School, and the Radcliffe Bunting Institute. She has published papers on applied and theoretical ethics, philosophy of law, and deontic logic.

PAUL D. EISENBERG is Professor of Philosophy at Indiana University, Bloomington. He has held visiting appointments at the University of Illinois, Champaign, and at the University of Massachusetts, Amherst. He has translated Spinoza's *Treatise on the Improvement of the Understanding* and has provided an extended textual commentary on it (1977). In addition to his other articles on Spinoza, he has also written on Plato, Kant, and Nietzsche, among others.

ALAN GEWIRTH is Edward Carson Waller Distinguished Service Professor of Philosophy at the University of Chicago. His books include *Reason and Morality* (1978), *Human Rights: Essays on Justification and Applications* (1982), *Marsilius of Padua and Medieval Political Philosophy* (1951), and *The Defensor Pacis of Marsilius*, which he translated with an introduction and appendices (1956). He is a past president of the American Philosophical Association and of the American Society for Political and Legal Philosophy and is a fellow of the American Academy of Arts and Sciences.

ALAN H. GOLDMAN is Professor of Philosophy and chairman of the Department of Philosophy at the University of Miami. He is author of *Moral Knowledge* (1988), *Empirical Knowledge* (1988), *The Moral Foundations of Professional Ethics* (1980), and *Justice and Reverse Discrimination* (1979) and has contributed to many philosophical journals.

DAVID A. HOEKEMA is Associate Professor of Philosophy at the University of Delaware and executive director of the American Philosophical Association. He taught previously at Saint Olaf College, Calvin College, and Princeton University. He is the author of *Rights and Wrongs: Coercion, Punishment, and the State* (1986) and has contributed articles to philosophical journals on topics in the theory of punishment, the ethics of nuclear deterrence, and the philosophy of art.

DAVID LEWIS is Professor of Philosophy at Princeton University. Previously he taught at the University of California at Los Angeles. His books include *Convention: A Philosophical Study* (1969), *Counterfactuals* (1973), and *On the Plurality of Worlds* (1986). He has written articles dealing with topics in metaphysics and other areas of philosophy.

PETER J. MARKIE is Professor of Philosophy and chairman of the Department of Philosophy at the University of Missouri, Columbia. He is the author of *Descartes's Gambit* (1986) and has contributed articles on ethics, intentionality, and Descartes to various philosophical journals.

ANDREW OLDENQUIST is Professor of Philosophy at the Ohio State University. His books include *Moral Philosophy: Text and Readings* (1978), *Normative Behavior* (1983), *The Non-Suicidal Society* (1986), and (with Richard Garner, coeditor) *Society and the Individual* (1989). He has published many articles on the philosophy of education, social philosophy, political philosophy, and ethics.

ROBERT L. SIMON is Professor of Philosophy at Hamilton College, where he chairs the Philosophy Department. He is the coauthor of *The Individual and the Political Order* (1977) and author of *Sports and Social Values* (1985). He has also written articles on a wide variety of topics in ethical theory and social philosophy and has served as associate editor of *Ethics: An International Journal of Social, Political, and Legal Philosophy*.

RUDOLPH H. WEINGARTNER is Professor of Philosophy at the University of Pittsburgh, where he served as provost and senior vice-president. Previously he taught at Columbia University; at San Francisco State College and Vassar College, chairing the Philosophy Departments at both these institutions; and at Northwestern University, where he served as dean of the College of Arts and Sciences. He is the author of *Experience and Culture: The Philosophy of Georg Simmel* (1962) and *The Unity of the Platonic Dialogue: The Cratylus, the Protagoras, and the Parmenides* (1973). He coedited *Philosophy in the West: A Book of Readings in Ancient and Medieval Philosophy* (1965) and has written articles on the philosophy of history and social philosophy, among other topics.

Morality, responsibility,
and the university